INK ART

INK ART

PAST AS
PRESENT IN
CONTEMPORARY
CHINA

Maxwell K. Hearn

THE METROPOLITAN MUSEUM OF ART, NEW YORK

Distributed by Yale University Press, New Haven and London

This catalogue is published in conjunction with "Ink Art: Past as Present in Contemporary China," on view at The Metropolitan Museum of Art, New York, from December 11, 2013, through April 6, 2014.

This publication is made possible by The Andrew W. Mellon Foundation, the Richard and Geneva Hofheimer Memorial Fund, and Marie-Hélène Weill.

Published by The Metropolitan Museum of Art, New York

Mark Polizzotti, Publisher and Editor in Chief

Gwen Roginsky, Associate Publisher and General Manager of Publications

Peter Antony, Chief Production Manager

Michael Sittenfeld, Managing Editor

Robert Weisberg, Senior Project Manager

Edited by Marcie M. Muscat

Designed by Roy Brooks, Fold Four, Inc.

Production by Christopher Zichello

Bibliography edited by Jean Wagner

Image Acquisitions and Permissions by Ling Hu

Photographs of works in the Metropolitan Museum's collection are by The Photograph Studio, The Metropolitan Museum of Art.

Additional photography credits appear on p. 206.

Typeset in DFHeiGB, TheMix, TheSans, TheSans Mono, and STHeitei

Printed on 135 gsm Tatami White

Separations by Professional Graphics, Inc., Rockford, Illinois

Printed and bound by Conti Tipocolor S.p.A., Florence, Italy

The Metropolitan Museum of Art
1000 Fifth Avenue
New York, New York 10028
metmuseum.org

Distributed by
Yale University Press, New Haven and London
yalebooks.com/art
yalebooks.co.uk

Library of Congress Cataloging-in-Publication Data

"This catalogue is published in conjunction with Ink Art : Past as Present in Contemporary China, on view at The Metropolitan Museum of Art, New York, from December 11, 2013, through April 6, 2014."

Includes bibliographical references and index.

ISBN 978-1-58839-504-7 (the metropolitan museum of art)-- ISBN 978-0-300-19703-7 (yale university press) 1. Art, Chinese--20th century--Themes, motives--Exhibitions. 2. Art, Chinese--21st century--Themes, motives--Exhibitions. 3. Ink painting, Chinese--Influence--Exhibitions. 4. Eclecticism in art--Exhibitions. I. Hearn, Maxwell K. Ink art. II. Wu Hung, 1945- Transcending the East/West dichotomy. III. Metropolitan Museum of Art (New York, N.Y.)

N7345.I55 2013
751.42'51--dc23

2013028906

Note to the Reader

Unless otherwise indicated, dimensions in the captions and exhibition checklist exclude mountings; height precedes width precedes depth.

Chinese names are given in the traditional order, with surname first, with the exception of scholars who are better known for publishing in English. Transliteration of Chinese words follows the Pinyin system of romanization.

With a few noted exceptions, the handscrolls illustrated in this volume are read from right to left in accordance with Chinese tradition.

Translations from the Chinese are by the authors unless otherwise noted.

Cover illustrations: Zhang Huan (b. 1965). *Family Tree*, 2001 (fig. 46, details)

Title page: Yang Yongliang (b. 1980). *View of Tide*, 2008 (fig. 79, detail)

CONTENTS

Ink Art: Past as Present in Contemporary China is published in conjunction with the first exhibition at The Metropolitan Museum of Art devoted solely to the contemporary art of China. A unique feature of this landmark event is how it positions contemporary art from a non-Western culture within an encyclopedic art museum: displayed in the Museum's permanent galleries for Chinese painting and calligraphy, the exhibition examines these works as part of the continuum of Chinese culture, a tradition that extends back for millennia. While these works may also be appreciated from the perspective of global contemporary art, examining them through the lens of China's historical artistic paradigms reveals layers of meaning and cultural significance that might otherwise go unnoticed.

Curated by Maxwell K. Hearn, Douglas Dillon Chairman of the Department of Asian Art, the exhibition treats a particular segment of Chinese art—that which subscribes to an "ink art" aesthetic—created during the past thirty years, a period in which China has emerged as a major economic and political power. Chinese contemporary art has witnessed a similarly astonishing development during this time, with works by Chinese artists becoming a significant presence in international exhibitions and museum collections, and the Chinese art market becoming one of the largest in the world. While China's entry onto the global stage has been heralded in many ways, *Ink Art* seeks to demonstrate that any assessment of its artists and their achievements must also take into account China's rich cultural legacy.

The Metropolitan has a long tradition of exhibiting contemporary art, including works by Chinese artists that were shown here in 1943, when, in support of the war effort, the Museum mounted an exhibition of living Chinese painters. In recent years we have begun to exhibit and add works of contemporary Chinese art to the collection, where they complement meaningfully our holdings of both traditional and global art. We are therefore most grateful to several generous donations and promised gifts that have come in response to the Museum's renewed commitment to this area. My thanks go to Susan L. Beningson, Chung Ching-hsin, Pearl Lam, Frank Kong Siu Ming, Thomas Yaping Ou, Cynthia Hazen Polsky, Shao Fan, and Wang Dongling. The Museum also acknowledges the Friends of Asian Art, whose ongoing support has been instrumental in the acquisition of a number of contemporary artworks, including several published here.

Essential to the realization of this exhibition and publication were the many important loans from a number of institutions, private individuals, and artists, all of whom are enumerated in the accompanying list of lenders. This undertaking was not only greatly enriched by their generosity but simply would not have been possible without it, and I thank them for the vital role they played in its success.

The significance of bringing together this group of artworks was greatly enhanced by an artists' day, symposium, and lecture program, made possible by the generosity of Adrian Cheng. Through his support, we were able to further the dialogue between artists, critics, and scholars, and to share their insights with our public. I also thank The Andrew W. Mellon Foundation, the Richard and Geneva Hofheimer Memorial Fund, and Marie-Hélène Weill for helping make possible this publication.

Finally, I gratefully acknowledge the artists featured in *Ink Art*. They have graciously granted permission for the Museum to exhibit and publish their work, and it is their remarkable creativity that is celebrated here. In the face of many challenges, they exemplify the spirit of Chinese culture and demonstrate that the world's oldest living cultural tradition continues to be one of the most vibrant.

Thomas P. Campbell
Director, The Metropolitan Museum of Art

What constitutes contemporary Chinese ink art? As I set out to define an ancient mode of expression in contemporary terms, I began with works that adhered quite literally to the media (ink and paper), formats (scrolls and albums), and techniques (brushwork) that have long characterized Chinese ink painting. But as my search continued, I encountered works of art that resonate powerfully with ancient traditions while making use of more recently developed and globalized media (oil on canvas, photography, and video, among others) and forms of expression (including abstraction, installation, and performance). This volume is the result. It is not intended as an exhaustive survey of contemporary Chinese art. Rather, it suggests the diverse ways in which Chinese artists have continued to draw inspiration from their cultural heritage, creating works that resonate with, either overtly or implicitly, the principles inherent in the Chinese artistic tradition. As such, the works presented here perpetuate an age-old practice in China by which artists respond to, revive, and transform past models and concepts.

Included in this survey are works in diverse media in which I have identified an underlying aesthetic that is harmonious with fundamental aspects of China's indigenous artistic heritage. Excluded are works that hew closely to the canons of *guohua* (traditional Chinese-style painting) or to *guohua*'s modern engagement with Soviet-style Socialist Realism. Also excluded are those works that by their technique, subject matter, format, and aesthetic references are best understood in the context of Western modernism. Finally, I have limited this study to artists born in mainland China, even though there are artists from Taiwan, Hong Kong, Singapore, and the West whose works would otherwise be very comfortable within the parameters of this book.

As an historian of traditional Chinese art, my perspective is different from those whose principal focus is global contemporary art, including photography, video, installation, and performance. My purpose here is not to negate those perspectives, which are not only valid but also, increasingly, the necessary starting point for evaluating such works within a global context. Rather, it is my assumption that, for Western specialists, interpreting a Chinese work can be like judging a work of literature in translation. Much of the form and narrative content can be understood, but certain words and concepts may not be readily translatable and can only be savored in the original language. Even if a Chinese author were to write in English, it should be possible for someone sensitive to Chinese culture to detect patterns of thought and cultural echoes in his or her writing. In the visual arts, style is a language that carries deep cultural meaning. It is my contention that, while all art can be viewed from multiple vantage points, so long as Chinese ink art remains a vital tradition, an appreciation of that art—including that produced by today's practitioners—can only be deepened and enriched by viewing it in the context of China's unique heritage of image making and critical writing.

Maxwell K. Hearn
Douglas Dillon Chairman, Department of Asian Art,
The Metropolitan Museum of Art

ACKNOWLEDGMENTS

Looking at art in the company of friends is one of the oldest traditions in Chinese culture. Often, guests at such "literary gatherings" would contribute paintings to commemorate the occasion or embellish artworks by adding poetic inscriptions. This project has often brought such interactions to mind, as I have benefited from many shared conversations and exchanges that have not only meaningfully shaped the content and form of this volume but also offered encouragement and friendship.

Jane DeBevoise and her late husband, Paul Calello, were an early inspiration and stalwart advocates for extending the study of China's great artistic traditions down to the present. Through both her writing and her collecting, Jane has been most articulate in demonstrating that the past is present in Chinese art. She has been a steadfast, generous guide and mentor whose involvement in this project has ranged from the selection and presentation of artworks to helping determine its title and content. I have relied on her insights and discernment throughout and am deeply grateful for her wise counsel.

A particular privilege of this project has been the opportunity to get to know Uli Sigg, a visionary Swiss diplomat and businessman who has led the way in the collecting of contemporary Chinese art. His munificent transfer in 2012 of some fifteen hundred works from his collection to the newly formed M+ museum in Hong Kong has returned an important chapter of China's art history to its native soil. Uli has been a generous lender to many exhibitions in the belief that the contemporary art of China has a great deal to offer to the wider art world. I am most grateful to him and to M+ for the major loans they have granted.

The China Art Foundation, led by Pearl Lam, Susan Hayden, and Philip Dodd, provided another formative influence. In 2008 CAF brought together artists, critics, academics, and museum professionals at Ditchley, outside Oxford, to discuss the state of contemporary Chinese art. A second forum was convened in Hangzhou in 2010. These meetings offered a valuable colloquium for artists, critics, academics, and curators from China and the West to discuss recent developments in the field of contemporary Chinese art. Pearl Lam was also instrumental in introducing me to several artists and facilitating a number of important donations to the Museum.

In New York, many good friends have shared their enthusiasm for contemporary art. Marie-Hélène and Guy Weill's passion for both Abstract Expressionism and Chinese painting has been influential and inspiring. Early on Patricia Tang encouraged me to unroll scrolls in her hallway as a prelude to unrolling them at the Met. Akiko Yamazaki and Jerry Yang have generously hosted literary gatherings to encourage dialogue between artists, dealers, collectors, curators, and academics. Christopher Tsai and André Stockamp welcomed a group of friends to their beautiful upstate New York home, designed by Ai Weiwei. Christophe Mao and John Tancock, Richard and Ann Solomon, Christopher Phillips, David Solo, Kit Luce, Sophia and Abel Sheng, Arnold Chang, and Michael Cherney have been similarly welcoming. All have shared viewings and offered insights into the complex terrain of the contemporary art world; their knowledge of and commitment to the field have been inspiring.

A number of scholars—in conversations and in their writings—have guided my thinking in ways to which endnotes alone cannot do justice. Wu Hung, Harrie A. Vanderstappen Distinguished Service Professor in Art History and East Asian Languages and Civilizations at the University of Chicago, who has written extensively on traditional China, has been equally prolific and insightful in his treatment of China's contemporary art. In addition to contributing an important essay to this volume, he was an early and generous adviser to the project. Kuiyi Shen and Julia F. Andrews have been pioneers in the field, and Kuiyi's talk about the Third Chengdu Biennale at a meeting of the Association of Modern Chinese Art sparked the possibility of exploring this topic. I particularly admire the eloquent scholarship of Britta Erickson, Martina Köppel-Yang, and Jerome Silbergeld; the informative published interviews of Jérôme Sans; the groundbreaking exhibitions and essays of Johnson Chang; the substantial exhibitions and catalogues of Alexandra Munroe; and the invaluable resources provided by Asia Art Archive. It is inconceivable to have attempted this study without the important work of these colleagues.

As someone accustomed to studying ancient art, it has been exciting to meet many of the artists included in this volume and to have benefited from firsthand discussions of their work. My thanks to Ai Weiwei, Cai Guo-Qiang, Chen Shaoxiong, Fang Lijun, Fung Mingchip, Gu Wenda, Hong Hao, Huang Yongping, Liu Dan, Qiu Anxiong, Shao Fan, Song Dong, Wang Dongling, Wang Jin, Wang Tiande, Xu Bing, Yang Fudong, Yang Jiechang, Zeng Fanzhi, Zhang Huan, and Zhang Yu for welcoming me to their studios or meeting with me in other venues. They and others have been generous in sharing their homes, workspaces, thoughts, and art, and several have donated works to the Museum or helped arrange for donations from patrons. I would particularly like to express my appreciation in this regard to Susan L. Beningson, Chung Ching-hsin, Pearl Lam, Frank Kong Siu Ming, Thomas Yaping Ou, Cynthia Hazen Polsky, Shao Fan, and Wang Dongling. Through the great generosity of Adrian Cheng, we were able to organize in conjunction with our exhibition a daylong dialogue with artists, a symposium, and a series of lectures, thus bringing artists and scholars together to discuss some of the themes explored in *Ink Art*.

I acknowledge with gratitude the many institutions and individuals named in the accompanying list of lenders whose loans have made possible this publication and the exhibition it accompanies. I feel fortunate to have been given the exciting opportunity to study so many marvelous works of art and to share them with the Museum's international audience.

The privilege of working at the Metropolitan Museum has made all the difference in undertaking a project of this magnitude and scope. An extraordinary staff of professionals has nurtured every facet of this publication and the exhibition that was its genesis. This support begins with the dynamic leadership and innovative thinking of Thomas P. Campbell, who has offered encouragement for the exhibition, for the publication, and for the acquisition of contemporary art by the Department of Asian Art. Associate Director for Exhibitions Jennifer Russell and her office oversaw the logistical challenges of bringing together works from three continents. Allison Bosch, Assistant Registrar, coordinated all loans in close cooperation with the Asian Art Department's Collections Management team, led by Hwai-ling Yeh-Lewis and Alison Clark. Alison also scheduled new photography of many works with Joseph Coscia Jr., Anna-Marie Kellen, and Oi-Cheong Lee of the Museum's Photograph Studio. The exhibition installation was masterfully enhanced by Exhibition Design Manager Daniel Kershaw and Graphic Design Manager Sue Koch.

One great advantage of working in an encyclopedic institution is the benefit of receiving counsel from colleagues with a range of expertise, notably Sheena Wagstaff, Leonard A. Lauder Chairman of Modern and Contemporary Art, and Douglas Eklund, Curator in the Department of Photographs, both of whom offered helpful comments on my manuscript.

I have been particularly fortunate that the entire Department of Asian Art was so supportive while I readied *Ink Art* for publication. Likewise, it was a team effort to mount this complex exhibition in the Asian Art galleries. Judith Smith, Jill Wickenheisser, Jennifer Cuminale, and Sunny Ching Hui Wang kept everything running smoothly with the capable aid of our departmental technicians: Beatrice Pinto, Imtikar Ally, Luis Nuñez, and Lori Carrier. Curator Zhixin Jason Sun has been a wise source of counsel.

Joseph Scheier-Dolberg, Assistant Curator for Chinese Painting, offered many thoughtful comments on this manuscript and worked with me to realize the installation and prepare the labels. Conservators Yuan-li Hou and Kewei Wang checked the condition of every work in the exhibition, mounting or repairing those in need of special care. But I am most indebted to my research assistant, Xin Wang, who worked tirelessly for two years to provide resources, check facts, and liaise with artists and lenders. Having recently earned her master's degree from Columbia University with a thesis on Chinese video art, Xin used her command of the field and her personal acquaintance with a number of the artists to effectively gather research materials and confirm information through firsthand communication.

The extraordinary professionalism of the Museum's Editorial Department has made my role as author a privilege as well as a pleasure. I have been supported and encouraged at every stage by Publisher and Editor in Chief Mark Polizzotti and his able team, led by Associate Publisher and General Manager Gwen Roginsky, Chief Production Manager Peter Antony, and Managing Editor Michael Sittenfeld.

I am particularly indebted to my editor, Marcie Muscat, who not only assessed every word I wrote with good humor and care but also brought concision and clarity to the words that remain. I am enormously grateful for her astute comments, thoughtful suggestions, and editorial refinements. The endnotes and bibliography were meticulously edited by Jean Wagner; Image Acquisitions Manager Jane S. Tai, together with Ling Hu, tracked down all the figures and secured permissions from the artists; Christopher Zichello coordinated the book's production; and Kamilah Foreman and Kathleen Friello provided additional editorial assistance. Once the texts took shape, designer Roy Brooks transformed the manuscript into a beautiful book that is itself a contemporary work of art.

There is not enough ink in China to record my appreciation for my wife, Vera, and our children and their partners—Garrett and Wei and Alex and Justin—who with good cheer and much love have endured the many weekends and late nights that this project has demanded. Vera, in particular, has been a loving and wise partner. Recognizing that in life, as in art, the present all too rapidly becomes the past, Vera reminds me that the future is now. This book is dedicated with much love to her.

Maxwell K. Hearn
Douglas Dillon Chairman, Department of Asian Art,
The Metropolitan Museum of Art

LENDERS TO THE EXHIBITION

Anonymous lenders

Chen Shaoxiong

Guo Zhen

Hong Kong Museum of Art

Li Huasheng

M+, Museum for Visual Culture, Hong Kong

Marian Goodman Gallery

Alexandra Munroe

The Museum of Modern Art, New York

Christopher Phillips

Qiu Anxiong

The San Diego Museum of Art

Sigg Collection

David Solo

André Stockamp and Christopher Tsai

Sun Xun

Xu Bing

Yale University Art Gallery, New Haven

Akiko Yamazaki and Jerry Yang

Yang Fudong

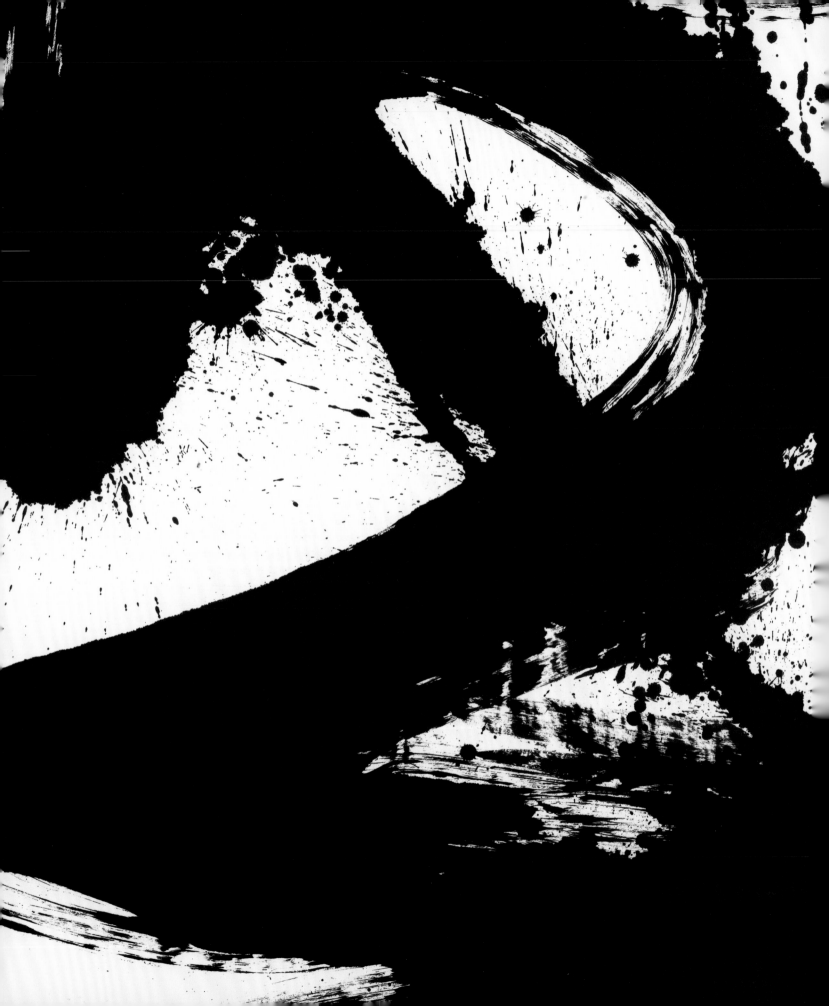

INK ART: AN INTRODUCTION

MAXWELL K. HEARN

For more than two millennia, ink — carbon derived from lampblack or pine soot that has been formed into cakes, then turned into liquid by grinding on an inkstone and mixing with water — has been the principal medium for painting and calligraphy in China. Artists have used ink to write or draw on virtually every conceivable surface, although most often the preferred format has been silk or paper mounted as vertical or horizontal scrolls or albums. Exploring the enormous expressive potential of this medium, artists have experimented with the full range of ink tonalities — the endless "colors of ink," from jet black to the palest, transparent gray — as well as with the dynamic qualities of line, dot, and wash using the uniquely responsive supple-tipped brush. Indeed, the indivisibility of tool and medium is acknowledged in the term *bimo*, "brush and ink," which in traditional Chinese art is virtually synonymous with the arts of painting and calligraphy. The more knowledgeable the practitioner, the greater number of earlier precedents one might draw upon to enrich his or her personal style or "brush method" (*bifa*), much the way a poet might embellish a verse with an array of embedded references. In this way, every trace of the brush carries the autographic handprint or "heartprint" of the individual, reflective of his or her intellect, emotions, and connection with the past (**FIG. 1**). Thus have Chinese cultural traditions been sustained and renewed.

Since the early twentieth century, the primacy of the "ink art" tradition in China has increasingly been challenged by new media and practices introduced from the West. These foreign influences have led to a division in the Chinese art world between *guohua* (Chinese-style painting) and *xihua* (Western-style painting).[1] To this day, Chinese art academies segregate *guohua* and *xihua* into separate departments with distinct curricula. Since the 1980s, however, a third type of "globalized" art has arisen in China that can no longer be categorized by either of these two terms. Some Chinese artists have identified this new art form as "experimental ink painting" (*shiyan shuimo*). Typically, its practitioners have sought to "modernize" Chinese art through references to Western models while retaining the use of traditional Chinese painting tools and materials — brush, ink, and paper. Another group of artists, however, has abandoned traditional Chinese formats and techniques to experiment freely with various new media and postmodern strategies in pursuit of their expressive goals. Wu Hung, in his contribution to this volume, characterizes these two approaches as transforming China's cultural heritage from within and from without.

The goal of this study is to examine that subset of art created by mainland Chinese artists from the 1980s to the present that has fundamentally altered inherited Chinese tradition while maintaining an underlying identification with the

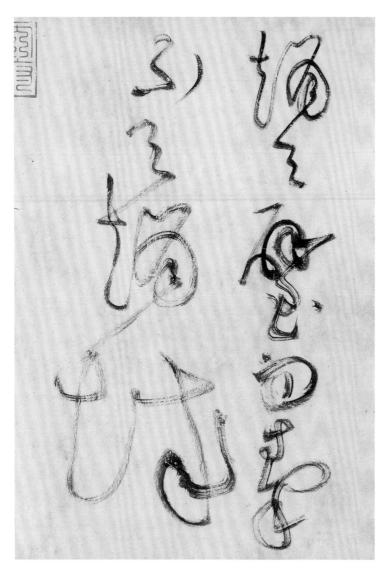

Fig. 1. Huang Tingjian (1045–1105). Detail of *Biographies of Lian Po and Lin Xiangru*, Northern Song dynasty (960–1127), ca. 1095. Handscroll; ink on paper, 13 ¼ in. × 60 ft. 4 ½ in. (33.7 × 1840.2 cm). The Metropolitan Museum of Art, New York, Bequest of John M. Crawford Jr., 1988 (1989.363.4)

expressive language of ink art.[2] While most of the artists included here have continued to work with ink as their principal medium, the selection has not been limited to such works. Instead, this book seeks to define a contemporary "ink aesthetic" in which references to traditional pictorial and calligraphic concepts remain a defining feature of an artist's vision without limiting that artist's formal solutions. As the artist and theorist Zhang Yu (b. 1959) describes it, "The most important thing [in defining this aesthetic] is the ink and wash spirit! This spirit is peculiar to us Chinese. Contemporary works with such ink and wash spirit are what we should pursue. Therefore, ink and wash cannot be regarded simply as equal to materials, techniques and forms, or so-called brushwork and ink applying technique."[3] Thus, in support of this theory asserting the primacy of spirit over technique, woodblock prints; oils and acrylics; photography, film, and video; installation and performance art; and even furniture and sculpture have been included when those works are seen to embody aesthetic choices or stylistic references that are indelibly linked to China's cultural past. It is this more inclusive definition of ink art that is examined here.

There are several reasons why this discussion begins in China of the mid-1980s. The death of Mao Zedong (1893–1976) and the arrest of the Communist leaders known as the Gang of Four brought to an end the decade-long Cultural Revolution. Universities and art academies reopened, and in

Fig. 2. Tang Xiaohe (b. 1941). *Strive Forward in Wind and Tides*, 1971. Oil on canvas, 68 ¹⁵⁄₁₆ in. × 9 ft. 8 in. (172.5 × 294.5 cm). Private collection

1978 a backlog of eager applicants matriculated into undergraduate and graduate programs. No longer were students exposed almost exclusively to Soviet-style Socialist Realist art (**FIG. 2**) as Western texts on philosophy and art were translated into Chinese, lending movements such as Surrealism and Dada, long superseded in the West, new immediacy in China. Complementing these changes, Deng Xiaoping's (1904–1997) new priorities opened up a period of exploration, self-examination, and questioning about China's place in the world as artists were able to live abroad for extended periods.

In more recent years, with the growing affluence brought about by a booming art market, artists may now travel with relative freedom; many have residences both in China and abroad. As Chinese artists have become increasingly conversant with global art trends, one may fairly ask, Do they see themselves as Chinese artists or as artists who are Chinese by birth but can live and work anywhere? I suspect that most see themselves as moving between two personae: global citizens whose expression is not constrained by their place of birth, and Chinese by birth, residence, and cultural heritage — or, as Cai Guo-Qiang (b. 1957), who has lived outside China for nearly three decades, describes it, "I always feel as though I am swinging like a pendulum between Chinese and Western culture."[4] For those artists who choose to live in China, their lives and art are subject to the constantly shifting lines of what is politically

acceptable. Many of those who live abroad, though they are able to work in relative freedom, do so with the recognition that their art is distinct from that of other cultures. After visiting the United States for the first time in 1998, the performance artist Zhang Huan (b. 1965) discovered that "whenever Chinese contemporary art is discussed in a Western cultural context, 'Chinese' always comes before 'art,' which says a lot about its status in international forums."[5]

Like Cai and Zhang, all the artists considered here have been profoundly influenced by political and cultural developments in their home country, and, in support of Zhang's assertion that "artists are also representatives of their culture," their work is strongly inflected by their use of media and imagery that are preeminently Chinese (**FIG. 3**).[6] Indeed, forming part of a minority has led Chinese artists who live abroad to confront their "Chinese-ness" in ways that may serve to enhance their consciousness of national and racial identity. This may in turn guide their choice of materials, media, tools, or cultural references.

Such questions of cultural identity challenge the entire field of modern and contemporary art, which for much of the twentieth century was defined narrowly as works produced in Western Europe and America; artists living outside this cultural sphere were largely ignored unless they embraced the artistic idioms of that mainstream. But contemporary

Fig. 3. Qiu Anxiong (b. 1972). Still from *New Classic of Mountains and Seas I*, 2006. Three-channel animated video with sound; 30 min. Collection of the artist [Exhib.]

practitioners are now active across the globe, and forms of expression no longer develop solely from Western artistic traditions or from the preceding modernist past.[7] Consequently, while it is no longer possible to understand contemporary Chinese art without recognizing its practitioners' awareness of Western concepts and art forms, one cannot ignore the culturally specific traditions from which it developed.

As Chinese artists began to show their work at the Venice Biennale, they attained a new global stature that has since been confirmed by commercial success (FIG. 4).[8] Yet most of the artists considered in this book have not been widely collected by Western museums, suggesting that their work, which continues to espouse distinctly Chinese themes arising from either the ancient or the recent past, possesses an identity that is less accessible to Western critics and collectors. As such, it has been harder to integrate their production into exhibitions of global contemporary art.

During the three decades chronicled in this volume, China has undergone an astonishing economic and political transformation, emerging as the world's second largest economy and as a military and political force that cannot be ignored. These dramatic changes often have appeared contradictory — most notably the unique fusion of Marxist philosophy and capitalist economics that Deng Xiaoping labeled "socialism with Chinese characteristics." But while China has absorbed many

Western technologies and methodologies, their application will inevitably be shaped by the unique features of China's land and people.

So too in the arts, the past thirty years have witnessed many bold appropriations of and experiments with Western concepts and techniques, as well as an ongoing interest in self-definition. As Chinese artists have become fully conversant with global art trends, some have demonstrated a desire to explore and reinvigorate the cultural memories and heritage that continue to define China and its people. The artists presented here cannot be fully explained or understood by a single set of criteria; many may be viewed with equal validity as "ink art" innovators and as international artists. Either way, it is hoped that this assemblage of works will provide a sense of the creative potential embedded in a tradition that has never been dormant, and that is constantly being reimagined and reborn.

Fig. 4. Yang Jiechang (b. 1956). *Crying Landscape,*
2002. Installation view, 50th Venice Biennale, 2003.
Private collection, New York [Exhib.]

TRANSCENDING THE EAST / WEST DICHOTOMY: A SHORT HISTORY OF CONTEMPORARY CHINESE INK PAINTING

WU HUNG

From the early twentieth century to this day, art students in China have had to choose between *guohua* (Chinese-style painting) and *xihua* (Western-style painting) when entering the field.[1] These two types of painting are first of all determined by their different media. Chinese-style painting is executed predominantly with ink on *xuan* paper;[2] the term *guohua* is thus often interchangeable with *shuimo hua*, meaning "water-and-ink painting" or simply "ink painting." *Xihua* technically refers to oil and watercolor paintings, but the term is also used broadly for any art form, technique, and style that originated in the West. The difference between Chinese- and Western-style painting, however, is much more profound than their divergent materiality. In fact, after the systematic introduction of Western art to China in the early twentieth century, the dichotomy between *guohua* and *xihua* came to determine not only the structure of art education and the artist's professional identity but also the criteria of art criticism and the venues of exhibition and publication.[3] The same dichotomy provided a basis for a persistent discussion around two fundamental questions: How can Chinese-style painting be modernized, and how can Western-style painting become Chinese? Answers have been sought in both theory and practice but for a long period rarely challenged the dichotomy itself. An oil painter might incorporate technical elements and aesthetic principles from traditional art, and an ink painter might enrich his or her work with perspective and shading, but they remained oil painters and ink painters professionally. A third group of artists, represented by Lin Fengmian (1900–1991) and Xu Beihong (1895–1953), has advocated erasing the boundary between Chinese and Western painting, but their idea of "fusion" (*ronghe*) is still predicated on the East/West dichotomy.

Against this historical background, the development of contemporary art over the past thirty years has reshaped the relationship between the two art forms in two important ways. First, to a group of ink painters, the issue at stake is no longer how to Westernize *guohua* but how to make it contemporary and global. In pursuit of this goal they have since the 1980s conducted many experiments and undertaken persistent discussions, succeeding in inventing a new field in Chinese art with its own agendas and history. Second, the proliferation of modern and contemporary art in the 1980s and 1990s dismantled the medium-based division between *guohua* and *xihua*. Compared with ink and oil painting, newly introduced contemporary art forms — installation, performance, body art, etc. — are not strictly culturally specific. When modern and contemporary Chinese artists embraced these forms, their purpose was not to create new counterparts to either *guohua* or *xihua* but to subvert the established norms of Chinese art, including the rigid division between Chinese- and Western-style painting. As a result, contemporary art in China transcended the historical entanglement of these two traditions by connecting itself to other regional branches of international contemporary art. In the global sphere new art forms provided artists of heterogeneous origins with an "international language," allowing them to address both local and global issues in a versatile, individualized manner. From this perspective contemporary Chinese artists have devised different ways to negotiate with traditional art in order to demonstrate their own contemporaneity.

This understanding explains two kinds of works discussed in this volume. The first is a new type of ink painting that transformed *guohua* from within. The other kind reflects contemporary artists' utilization and transformation of China's cultural heritage from without. Experimenting with installation, performance, photography, and video, and adopting postmodern strategies of deconstruction, appropriation, and bricolage, these artists defy the framework of *guohua* and assimilate Chinese elements into dynamic interactions between the local and the global. Since important artists and works in the second category are discussed elsewhere in this book, this essay focuses on the first type of artwork, to provide a short history of contemporary Chinese ink painting, or "experimental ink painting" (*shiyan shuimo*), as it is called by the majority of Chinese art critics.[4]

THE ORIGIN OF EXPERIMENTAL INK PAINTING

Experimental ink painting can be traced back to the 1980s, when the Chinese art world was in turmoil and the state of *guohua* was inevitably brought into question. The 1980s witnessed a vibrant cultural movement, which in a short period disseminated a huge amount of information about Western art and ideas among young Chinese artists and led to the emergence of numerous unofficial art groups and exhibitions during the '85 Art New Wave.[5] Although this avant-garde movement had the central agenda of modernizing Chinese art based on Western models, it prompted all artists, including Chinese-style painters, to reexamine old premises, goals, and taboos in their respective fields. Three events especially incited critical reflections on *guohua*. The first was the publication of Wu Guanzhong's (1919–2010) series of essays in 1979 and 1980 in which he attacked the heavy emphasis of socialist art on content over form, and declared that abstract beauty is at the core of artistic creation.[6] Although Wu studied oil painting in his early years, by the 1980s he had become accustomed to traditional brush painting on Chinese paper. His writings thus had a more direct impact on the field.

Adding fuel to the debate around Wu's writings was the solo exhibition of experimental ink painter Liu Kuo-sung (b. 1932) at Beijing's National Art Museum of China in 1983. Liu was born in China but moved in 1949 to Taiwan, where he studied both traditional brush-and-ink painting and Western-style painting at National Taiwan Normal University. From the 1960s, he devoted himself to transforming Chinese-style painting into a branch of modern art, challenging its national identity and rejecting its traditional reliance on brushwork (*bi*). Instead, he promoted broad ink wash and invented new painting methods and tools that allowed him to combine ink, color, and collage in a single composition. Pushing the boundary even further, he fused ink painting with abstract art and Pop: his *Space* series (1960–1970s), for example, juxtaposes photographic images of the Apollo 8 space mission with a circular earth spray-painted purple. He was invited by the Research Institute of Chinese Painting in 1980 to lecture at various Chinese art academies, and his exhibition traveled to eighteen Chinese cities after its Beijing debut. Wherever his bold, unconventional works were shown, they generated curiosity among young *guohua* painters, who had been frustrated by the prevailing conservatism in their field and saw in Liu's work possibilities to modernize *guohua*.

The third event was a debate instigated by Li Xiaoshan's (b. 1957) essay "My View of Today's Chinese-Style Painting." Published in 1985, it offered a startlingly negative picture of *guohua*.[7] In Li's view, because of the narrow, formalistic interest of traditional literati painters and their escapist mentality, Chinese-style painting had begun its decline before the twentieth century. He claimed that modern painters had tried to revitalize the art form with only limited success and that even the four most influential *guohua* artists in the second half of the century either returned to tradition or adopted the socialist model to depict "politically correct" subjects.[8] He thus concluded: "Under such historical conditions, what today's theory of Chinese-style painting needs cannot just be revision and improvement, but must be a fundamental remake. We must abandon old theoretical systems and ossified ideas about art, and must stress the conceptual issues that make a painting modern."[9] Li's essay attracted wide attention, especially after *Chinese Fine Arts Weekly* published a condensed version under the title "Chinese-Style Painting Has Reached the End of Its Days."[10] An intense debate erupted among critics; although their opinions differed widely, most recognized the need for change.

Unrelated as they were, these three events constituted a general intellectual context for a new trend in 1980s Chinese art, called "modern ink painting" (*xiandai shuimo*) by some critics. Artists in this trend distinguished their work both from traditional literati art and from officially sponsored Socialist Realist art, and articulated their identity based on this double-edged refusal. Because they rejected literati aesthetics, they separated themselves from contemporaneous New Literati painters (*Xin wenren huajia*) such as Zhu Jianxin (b. 1953) and Xu Lele (b. 1955), who advocated restoring the spiritual independence of premodern scholar-artists. Their refusal to politicize socialist painting, on the other hand, prompted them to explore the aesthetic potential of ink and paper. Inspired by modern Western art and the pioneering examples of experimental ink painters, some of them tried to dissolve images into abstract and semiabstract forms, and to make bold "ink play" in the manner of Abstract Expressionism. Among these artists, Wang Gongyi (b. 1946) made some impressive works that contrast ink wash with geometric shapes while balancing linear and circular patterns (**FIG. 5**). Wang Chuan (b. 1953), a promising oil painter in the Scar Art (*Shanghen meishu*) movement in the late 1970s, now transformed himself into an abstract ink painter, expressing philosophical concepts in minimalistic "ink-flows." Whereas these two artists renounced pictorial forms entirely, a second group of modern ink painters,

Fig. 5. Wang Gongyi (b. 1946). *Time and Space*, 1986. Ink on paper, 82 ⅛ × 78 ¾ in. (210 × 200 cm). Private collection

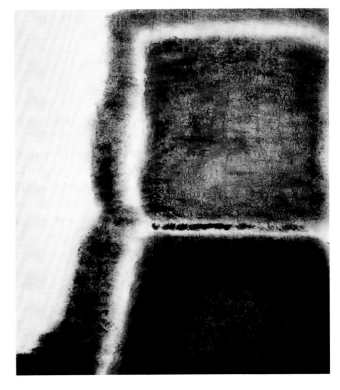

Fig. 6. Yan Binghui (b. 1956). *Primordial Image*, 1996. Ink on paper, 38 ⅝ × 34 ⅝ in. (98 × 88 cm)

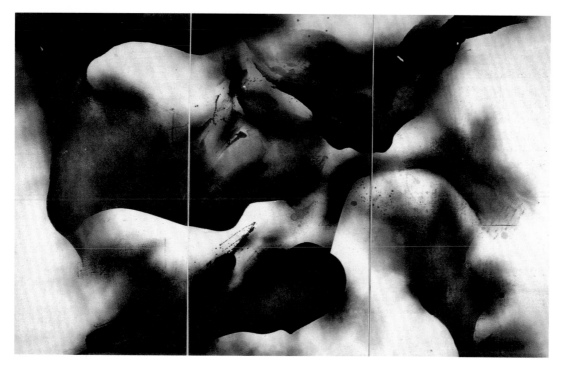

Fig. 7. Shen Qin (b. 1958). *Landscape*, 1986.
Ink on paper, 70 ⅞ × 102 ⅜ in. (180 × 260 cm)

including Li Shinan (b. 1940), Yan Binghui (b. 1956; **FIG. 6**), Shen Qin (b. 1958; **FIG. 7**), and Li Jin (b. 1958), traversed the boundary between representation and abstraction in depicting landscape and figure. A third group of modern ink painters, including Shi Guo (b. 1953), Zheng Chongbin (b. 1961), and Chen Xinmao (b. 1954), experimented with enriching ink painting with other materials and techniques to create new visual effects.

The most adventurous and ambitious experimental ink painter of the 1980s was, without question, Gu Wenda (b. 1955). It is significant to note that in the first half of the 1980s, Gu transformed himself from a Westernized "modern painter" to a challenger of Western modernism. One aspect of this transformation concerns art media: as late as 1985 he still made oil paintings in a Surrealist spirit, but his 1986 solo exhibition in Xi'an consisted entirely of ink works.[11] In particular, works in the exhibition's "internal" section (closed by the authorities to the general public) demonstrated a radical departure from conventional ink painting. The critic Guo Yaxi finds four kinds of experimentation in these works: constructing bold "ink blocks" as an abstract field of visual expression; using a variety of unorthodox painting methods such as "splashing," "flushing," "washing," and "spraying"; distorting established *guohua* schemata and borrowing elements from modern Western art; and breaking down the boundaries

between ink painting, installation, performance, and other forms of Conceptual Art.[12]

Although other ink painters made similar attempts in the 1980s and even earlier,[13] Gu stood out with the intensity and complexity of his visual experiments. He did not simply abandon brushwork and representation but broadened the space to negotiate with tradition. For example, in *Mythos of Lost Dynasties Series — Tranquility Comes from Meditation* (1985), the five compositions of this monumental series mix ink splash and brushwork, abstraction and concrete images (**SEE FIG. 24**). The first composition, *Primitive World*, is imageless; the shifting ink tones allude to the undifferentiated *qi* (cosmic energy) in the newborn universe. The remaining four compositions, subtitled *Composition of Words*, *Synthesized Words*, *Deconstruction of Words*, and *Overlapping of Words*, integrate calligraphy, landscape, and abstract ink wash in different ways. *Synthesized Words*, the best known of the five, presents a landscape scene near the bottom of the painting, with water and rocks executed in a traditional literati manner (**SEE FIG. 25**). Shapeless ink wash fills the rest of the picture and can be read as the cloudy sky above the landscape or as an abstract background for a large, made-up character written in fluid and energetic brushstrokes. Combining the character for "unhindered" or "unobstructed" (*chang* 畅) with that for "spirit" (*shen* 神) into a single ideograph, the grand and elegant calligraphic image sums up the message of the painting, that the interaction and interpenetration of images and words generate infinite possibilities for their mutual transformations.

The relationship between experimental ink painting and the '85 New Wave is complex. Although scholars have linked Gu, Ren Jian (b. 1955), Liu Zijian (b. 1956), and some other academically trained ink painters to the avant-garde movement, a careful examination of these cases reveals instead a conceptual conflict between the two. For example, Ren Jian was a founding member of the Northern Art Group, the first avant-garde collective in China, established in 1984. His most famous work, *Primeval Chaos*, is an ink painting measuring nearly one hundred feet long (**SEE FIG. 50**). He used ink in this instance, however, because it was his graduation work for the department of Chinese-style painting at the Lu Xun Academy of Fine Arts and had to adhere to the department's requirements. His other works from the mid-1980s were predominantly oil paintings because, in his words, he "was experiencing a 'modern phase' at the time."[14] In Gu's case, he refused to associate himself with any collective activity during the '85 New Wave.[15] Other ink artists like Liu Zijian did participate in group activities but only in minor roles.[16] Most tellingly, the "China/Avant-Garde" exhibition in 1989, conceived as a general review of the '85 New Wave movement, featured only a very small number of ink paintings among the more than eight hundred works on display.[17]

Two basic conditions underlay the uneasy relationship between the nascent experimental ink painting and New Wave movements. The first was the general agenda of the New Wave to modernize Chinese art based on Western models. Not only did most New Wave artists derive inspiration from Western modernism, but the very notion of an avant-garde movement came from the West. This general direction ran counter to that of experimental ink painting, the goal of which was, at least to most outsiders, to revitalize an indigenous art tradition. The second condition was, once again, the deeply rooted dichotomy between *guohua* and *xihua*, which remained a general framework of art practice and criticism in 1980s China. Ink painters, including most experimental ink painters, studied and taught in various departments of Chinese-style painting and belonged to related professional associations. They had their circles of friends and admirers, and exhibited and published their works through specific venues. It is thus understandable why the first group appearance of experimental ink painting took place under the general umbrella of *guohua*. This event, the "Invitational Exhibition on New Works of

Chinese Painting," organized by Zhou Shaohua (b. 1929) in 1985, included experimental works by Li Shinan, Gu Wenda, Yan Binghui, Li Jin, Shi Hu (b. 1942), and Tang Jixiang (b. 1939).[18] The remaining twenty-five invited artists, however, either belonged to older generations or were associated with other tendencies in the field of *guohua*, such as New Literati painting.

These two conditions together posed a persistent question to advocates of experimental ink painting: Could ink painting become a branch of modern and contemporary art in its own right? Liu Kuo-sung recognized in the 1960s that to achieve this goal, ink painting had to shake off its associations with national identity. The critic Li Xianting addressed this topic again in 1986. In an essay published in the journal *Fine Arts*, he argued that to free ink painting from the East/West dichotomy, Chinese artists and critics had to do away with the concept of *guohua* and develop ink painting into "pure abstraction" (*chuncui chouxiang*).[19] In making this argument he contrasted experimental ink painting with two types of mainstream *guohua*, one continuing the literati tradition and the other following the Socialist Realist model.

Related to such efforts to detach experimental ink painting from conventional *guohua*, another debate surfaced in the early 1990s and focused on the utility of *bimo* (brush and ink), two visual elements long considered the backbone of traditional ink painting. Wu Guanzhong, in his characteristic brusque manner, announced in 1992 that "*bimo* counts for nothing!"[20] To this Wan Qingli (b. 1945) countered: "There is nothing left without *bimo*!"[21] When the "Second International Exhibition of Ink Painting" was held at the Shenzhen Painting Academy later that year, Liu Kuo-sung and Lang Shaojun (b. 1939) again invoked these opposite positions, with Liu squarely negating the significance of brushwork in modern ink painting and Lang insisting on the fundamentality of brushwork to any kind of Chinese-style painting. Although this debate would continue, some artists and critics took a more pragmatic approach, developing experimental ink painting into an independent field with its own network of practitioners, publications, and exhibitions. They achieved this goal in the 1990s.

ESTABLISHING THE FIELD

A key figure in establishing the field of experimental ink painting is Zhang Yu (b. 1959). After graduating from the Tianjin Academy of Arts and Crafts in 1988, he became an editor at the Yangliuqing Painting Institute. While developing a personal style of modern ink painting, he also brought fellow experimental ink painters and art critics into an interactive network by compiling a series of publications and by organizing conferences to discuss the state of experimental ink painting. His first edited volume, *Modern Chinese Ink Painting*, appeared in 1991 and featured works by thirty-eight artists — the largest showcase of experimental ink paintings to date.[22] His next project produced the multivolume series *Tendencies of Chinese Modern Ink Art at the End of the Twentieth Century*. Differing from the previous volume, this publication aimed to provide an ongoing venue in which to study individual experimental ink painters and to deepen theoretical discussions.[23]

Also in 1993, Huang Zhuan and Wang Huangsheng compiled a special issue for the journal *Guangdong Artists* in which they introduced the term "experimental ink painting" to characterize this emerging field.[24] The two editors applied the label to any experimental ink work, whether the images were representational or abstract. While this broad application of the term would become standard in Chinese art criticism,[25] a group of abstract painters felt that the word "experimental" best described their own efforts to reinvent the language of ink painting. They thus took the term as their own and excluded nonabstract images.[26] This second definition of experimental ink painting was sometimes adopted by curators and critics. For example, when Huang Zhuan had an opportunity to organize an exhibition in San Francisco in 1996, he selected eight experimental ink painters, all but one favoring abstraction.

Huang's exhibition, "Homecoming: Contemporary Chinese Experimental Ink Painting Group Exhibition,"[27] was one of several organized outside China in the mid-1990s to focus on this type of painting.[28] Despite their moderate size and sometimes obscure venues, these international events played an important role in raising the profile of experimental ink painters, left somewhat behind when other kinds of contemporary Chinese art began attracting global attention in the early 1990s. Understood in this light, the catchwords "contemporary" and "experimental" reflect the artists' desire to join a globalized contemporary art world. The same desire also characterized a large conference/exhibition project held in 1996 in Guangzhou, "Contemporary Chinese Ink Art on the Eve of the Twenty-first Century." Co-organized by Zhang Yu and Pi Daojian (b. 1941), it had three central themes: "contemporaneity and globalism in 1990s ink art," "culture clash and artistic strategy in contemporary ink art," and "the trend of deconstructing easel painting and contemporary ink art." Once again, a strong effort to connect experimental ink painting with international contemporary art is indicated.[29]

The period from 1995 to 1998 was a turning point in the development of experimental ink painting, which finally emerged as a vibrant field in China with its own network of artists and independent venues of exhibition. During this period, there also appeared a considerable body of critical writings on experimental ink painting. Huang Zhuan, in his 1996 "Experimental Chinese Ink Painting at the Beginning of the 1990s," analyzed the historical conditions of experimental ink painting and its multiple directions.[30] Pi Daojian, Liu Xiaochun, Lu Hong, Yin Shuangxi, Yi Ying, Gu Chenfeng, and Wang Nanming all contributed to a lively discussion on the nature and dimensions of experimental ink painting.[31] Meanwhile, this type of painting appeared in large exhibitions in major public museums, such as the "Grand Exhibition of Chinese Art: Contemporary Chinese Painting," which was sponsored by the Ministry of Culture and held at the National Art Museum of China in 1997; and the Third Shanghai Biennale in 1998, which had the goal of reflecting "the newest state of an ancient art tradition." Also in 1998, the official China Central Television (CCTV) broadcast the special program *Conflict in Ink* to showcase works by six abstract ink painters, and Hong Kong's World Culture and Art Publishing House put out a hefty volume entitled *1990s Chinese Experimental Ink Painting*.[32] By this point, experimental ink painting had clearly established a strong position within China's mainstream art. The critic Yin Shuangxi thus stated in 2002: "The basic components of Chinese-style painting since the 1990s can be summarized as belonging to three large fields: 'experimental ink painting,' 'academic realist ink painting,' and 'traditional ink painting.'"[33]

TRENDS IN EXPERIMENTAL INK PAINTING

As a field, experimental ink painting was not a specific art genre but should be understood as a broad spectrum of artistic experimentation. Artists at one end of the spectrum continued to engage with landscape and figuration; those at the other end connected themselves with Conceptual Art and other contemporary art forms and media. This understanding provides a general framework to survey experimental ink painting in three areas, namely experimental landscape and figure painting, abstract ink painting, and contemporary art projects utilizing ink and paper as integral visual elements.[34]

Representative artists in the first area include Li Xiaoxuan (b. 1959), Shao Ge (b. 1962), Huang Yihan (b. 1958), Tian Liming (b. 1955), Wang Yanping (b. 1956), Cui Jian (b. 1963),

Fig. 8. Li Xiaoxuan (b. 1959). *Stocks! Stocks!*, 1999. Set of five panels; ink and light color on paper, each 9 ft. 1 ½ in. × 48 ⅞ in. (278 × 124 cm)

and Wu Yi (b. 1966). Most of them are figure painters. Some, such as Li Xiaoxuan, Shao Ge, and Huang Yihan, have been labeled New Realist (*Xin xieshi*) ink painters, owing to their interests in contemporary life, urban environment, and youth culture. One finds interesting parallels between their works and the New Generation (*Xinshengdai*) oil paintings of the early 1990s. Li, for example, depicted street scenes with a heightened sense of chaos and fragmentation; the broken brush lines, distorted size relationship, and crowded composition all contribute to the feeling of suffocation and disorientation (**FIG. 8**). Huang was the central figure of the Cartoon Generation (*Katong yidai*). With his brightly colored pictures of young people and cartoon images, he hoped to rescue ink painting from the "old geezers" and to make this art form accessible to young people who had grown up in a commercial society strongly influenced by Western culture (**FIG. 9**).

Other figure painters explored the psychological interiority of their subjects or an imagined time/space beyond history. Wang Yanping, one of a few female experimental ink painters, depicted women's private space with a subtle palette of pink and blue. Tian Liming likewise used color to blur the distinction between Chinese- and Western-style painting. His subdued, nearly indistinguishable figures sharply contrast with Wu Yi's sketchy, fractured images. Then there is Liu Jin'an (b. 1957), whose allegorical figures seem to emerge from mountain cliffs and fossilized clouds; their powerfully shaded bodies merge into an eternal landscape inscribed with history and memory (**FIG. 10**). A rare landscapist in this group is Cui Jian (b. 1963). Extracting images of mountains, trees, and streams from traditional literati painting, he weaves such visual

Fig. 9. Huang Yihan (b. 1958). *The Cartoon Generation: Very Charming*, 2000. Ink and color on paper, 70 ⅞ × 38 ¼ in. (180 × 97 cm)

Fig. 10. Liu Jin'an (b. 1957). *The Tao of Ink*, 1993. Ink and color on paper, 43 ¼ × 43 ¼ in. (110 × 110 cm)

Fig. 11. Cui Jian (b. 1963). *Mountain Views No. 2*, 2001. Ink and light color on paper, 95 ⅝ × 48 ⅜ in. (243 × 123 cm)

elements into a mosaic-like texture, creating a picture plane reminiscent of Jackson Pollock's drip paintings (**FIG. 11**). Works resulting from such deconstruction and reconstruction collapse representation and abstraction and blur the boundary between Eastern and Western art.

Turning to the area of abstract ink painting, one finds Wang Chuan, Liu Zijian, Zhang Yu, Yan Binghui, Shi Guo, Fang Tu (b. 1963), Wang Tiande (b. 1960), Li Huasheng (b. 1944), Liang Quan (b. 1948), Hu Youben (b. 1961), Wei Qingji (b. 1971), and Chen Xinmao. Some Chinese critics have distinguished two kinds of abstract ink paintings, labeling them "hot" and "cold." "Hot abstraction" (*re chouxiang*) refers to dynamic, powerful "ink images" (*moxiang*) charged with strong emotion and/or metaphysical significance. Liu Zijian, for example, developed the concept of *moxiang* in the late 1980s to replace the traditional term *bimo*. Shortly afterward, his works began to display a distinctive personal style, combining fragmentary symbols, clashing shapes, and intersecting positive and negative spaces to insinuate conflicting cosmic forces (**FIG. 12**). In contrast, examples of "cold abstraction" (*leng chouxiang*) employ repetitive, geometric elements; the painting process resembles meditation that demands great mental concentration. A representative artist in this category is Li Huasheng. For a long time he painted literati landscapes in an untrammeled style. But in 1998 he abruptly abandoned this style and covered papers with vertical and horizontal lines (**SEE FIG. 116**). The term "abstraction" may be misleading in describing these works because the artist did not perceive the gridwork as a

total image. Rather, the painstakingly drawn lines signify the passage of time, visualized through the slow movement of the brush as an extension of the artist's body and mind.

The classification of "hot" and "cold" abstraction can be too simplistic, however, because many examples do not fit in these polar categories, and few artists created works with these concepts in mind. In most cases, artists changed their style or visual mode over time. Wang Chuan's paintings through the mid-1990s, for example, are strikingly assertive, contrasting dense calligraphic images with an empty ground (**FIG. 13**). Serious illness altered his life and changed his art after 1998, when he began using painting as a curative device to

Fig. 12. Liu Zijian (b. 1956). *Memory · The Cross*,
1999. Ink on paper, 32 ¼ × 63 in. (82 × 160 cm).

purify his own mind. Rhythmic and with rich tonal variations, these later works mirror what he saw introspectively as his inner self. In another instance, Zhang Yu's fingerprint paintings may be considered "cold" for their prolonged creative process and contemplative quality. Repeatedly pressing his index finger on soft *xuan* paper with ink or color, he united paintings, objects, and architectural spaces with a single body-sign. But his *Divine Light* series is nothing if not turbulent and explosive. Inspired by the Big Bang theory, some works in this series depict circular shapes, like dark suns, suspended in the galaxy and emitting rays of light from the depth of a bottomless space (**SEE FIG. 121**). Another painter who escapes the confines of "hot" and "cold" abstraction is Chen Xinmao. His paintings feature distorted historical texts — woodblock prints that are incomplete and partially smeared as a result of misprinting (**FIG. 14**). The blurred characters appear dilapidated, like ruins of ancient monuments that have become sources of modern visual experience.

By combining ink painting with printing and collage, Chen's works lead us to the third category of experimental ink painting, which enriches contemporary art forms such as installation and performance. Gu Wenda and Wang Gongyi had already combined ink painting and installation as early as the 1980s. Wang Chuan continued such experimentation with "Ink · Dot," an exhibition held from 1990 to 1991 at the Shenzhen Art Museum. Conceived as a single installation, the show repeated large and small dots on all surfaces of the gallery. Drawn without traces of brushwork, these circular shapes

Fig. 13. Wang Chuan (b. 1953). *Untitled*, 1988.
Ink on paper, approx. 70 ⅞ × 38 ⅛ in. (180 × 97 cm).
Private collection

Fig. 14. Chen Xinmao (b. 1954). *Misprinted Historical Texts*, 2001. Mixed media on paper, each 18 ⅛ × 18 ⅛ in. (46 × 46 cm)

Fig. 15. Wang Tiande (b. 1960). *Ink Menu*, 1996. Multimedia installation, dimensions variable. Hong Kong Museum of Art, donated by Ms. Wong Ying-Kay, Ada

betrayed a different notion of ink painting, one devoid of skill. Wang Chuan's experiment was followed by Wang Tiande's *Ink Menu* in the mid-1990s. The installation consisted of a round dining table surrounded by six Ming-style chairs, which, along with the bowls, dishes, glasses, and wine bottles on the table, were all covered with ink-painted *xuan* paper (**FIG. 15**). Later in the decade, the Hebei painter Hu Youben fashioned huge murals that showed nothing but layered black paint on a wrinkled surface. In this way, he applied the concept of "ink image" not only to painting but also to architecture.

These three aspects of experimental ink painting, namely, experimental landscape and figure painting, abstract ink painting, and art projects combining ink painting and new, contemporary art forms, all reached maturity around the mid- to late 1990s. As a result, they constituted a new subfield of Chinese-style painting, as Yin Shuangxi claimed in the statement cited above. This development, on the other hand, also reveals that the success of experimental ink painting came with a price, that in order to be accepted by mainstream museums and media, this newly emerging field had to be reinstalled into the general field of *guohua*. Herein lies a dilemma faced by experimental ink painters: after years of struggling to modernize ink painting, their works were still labeled "Chinese" and separated from global contemporary art. In other words, although they were able to open up a new vista within Chinese painting, they nevertheless failed to dismantle the deep-rooted dichotomy between *guohua* and *xihua*. This problem, however, has had less impact on ink painters and installation artists living in places outside China, where Chinese-style painting does not exist as a general field in art education and practice. It is much easier for these artists to develop a double identity as experimental ink painters *and* as globalized contemporary artists, regardless of whether their works feature landscape and figures, favor abstract images, or combine ink painting with other art forms.

A number of Chinese artists working today approach the tradition of two-dimensional ink painting in markedly different ways. Zheng Chongbin (b. 1961) has divided his time between Shanghai and San Francisco for the past two decades; his lyrical, elegant compositions are appreciated in the West as abstract art but fall readily into the category of experimental ink painting in China. From his perspective, however, he has been exploring the subtle tension between shades of ink tones and abstract shapes for twenty to thirty years, finding endless possibilities in contrasting yet harmonizing these two visual elements (**FIG. 16**). Bingyi (b. 1975) is a relative latecomer to the field. She received a Ph.D. in Chinese art history from

Fig. 16. Zheng Chongbin (b. 1961). *Slanted Light*, 2011–12. Ink on paper, 12 ft. 9 ½ in. × 74 ⅞ in. (390 × 190 cm). Private collection

Fig. 17. Bingyi (b. 1975). *Cascade*, 2010. Ink on paper, 42 ft. 7 ¾ in. × 65 ft. 7 ½ in. (1300 × 2000 cm). Installation view, David and Alfred Smart Museum of Art, The University of Chicago, 2010. Collection of the artist

Yale University in 2005, but soon sought to transpose her knowledge of literati art into paintings instead of scholarly publications.[35] Inspired by traditional masters like Shitao (1642–1707), she creates intimate handscrolls as well as mural-size compositions to convey her experience of traveling through famous Chinese mountain ranges. One of these works, the enormous ink painting *Cascade* (2010), which she created for the Smart Museum of Art in Chicago, combines both macroscopic and microscopic visions of the universe with abstract, unceasingly transformative ink images (FIG. 17).

Influenced by Zen Buddhism and Daoism, Yang Jiechang (b. 1956) began to make ink abstractions even before leaving China for France in 1989. In Paris he reconceptualized ink painting as a temporal art, obsessively applying layers upon layers of dark ink to make his *100 Layers of Ink* series (1989–98). The unfathomable "black holes" that resulted from this process betray a notion of absolutism, reminding people of the Daoist idea of a primordial chaos (*hundun*). Some works in the series contrast two kinds of ink surfaces: floating above a smooth, muted dark background is an angular shape, which, owing to the excessive layers of ink, has acquired a metallic, nearly reflective appearance (SEE FIGS. 118–120). The implicit sculptural quality in such layering is further accentuated in works like *100 Layers of Ink — Vast Square*, a cube of ink painting created by piling up several blackened boards inside a metal frame. To Yang, the piece "is a conceptual work, related to time, space, and the material of ink. An important factor is repetition, the aspect of multiple layers."[36]

Liu Dan (b. 1953) first studied Chinese-style painting before he left China in 1981, and then received training in America. He returned to the medium of ink in 1988 and started to paint scholars' rocks in traditional Chinese gardens. Following the Ming dynasty (1368–1644) artist Wu Bin (active ca. 1583–ca. 1626), Liu portrayed a single rock in twelve compositions to capture the animated quality of the object. His debt to traditional painting, however, should be understood in a spiritual rather than an iconographic or a stylistic sense. For one thing, although his works often have a strong literati flavor, he consistently eschews explicit brushwork, focusing instead on an image as an organic whole. A typical example is his 1991 *Dictionary* (SEE FIG. 47). Measuring nearly seven feet high and ten feet long, it magnifies an ordinary dictionary hundreds of times its original size. By depicting the dictionary in a painstaking, photorealistic style, Liu stresses its vulnerability to time and human touch: the book's yellowish paper and worn pages arouse nostalgia, testifying to an intimate relationship with a human subject.

Fig. 18. Yun-Fei Ji (b. 1963). *Below the 143 Meter Watermark*, 2006. Ink and color on paper, 9 ft. 10 ½ in. × 56 ⅜ in. (301 × 142.6 cm). Worcester Art Museum, Massachusetts

Fig. 19. Fan Kuan (active ca. 990–1030). *Travelers among Mountains and Streams,* Northern Song dynasty (960–1127), early 11th century. Hanging scroll; ink and colors on silk, 81 ⅛ × 40 ½ in. (206 × 103 cm). National Palace Museum, Taipei

Fig. 20. Zhang Jianjun (b. 1955). *Nature*, 1987.
Ink on rice paper, 68 ⅞ in. × 9 ft. 5 ³⁄₁₆ in. (175 ×
288 cm). Private collection

Like Liu Dan, Yun-Fei Ji (b. 1963) developed a particular brand of "Chinese-style painting" in America. Executed on *xuan* paper and taking traditional landscape painting as the point of departure, his images can be read as a kind of mindscape populated by human, semihuman, and nonhuman creatures from both real and fantasy worlds. Before 2002, most of his works were inspired by traumatic events in China's modern history, especially the Cultural Revolution. His engagement with the Yangzi Gorges Dam Project — the largest hydroelectric project in human history, which was announced in 1992 — marked a crucial reorientation in his historical imagination. Although trauma continued to dominate his mind, he shifted his gaze from the past to the present. His travels through the Yangzi Gorges area, from one demolished village to another, became the basis for *The Empty City* series (2003) and a long scroll entitled *Water Rising* (2006). In these works, human figures and their environment are both displaced and fragmented. Hills, rocks, and trees appear as disjoined spatial elements, intermingled with destroyed houses, scattered furniture, and

dislocated people. Strong connections can be found between Ji's hanging scrolls (**FIG. 18**) and Northern Song (960–1127) monumental landscape art (**FIG. 19**). But if Northern Song images manifest a visual logic devised to glorify great mountains, Ji twists and distorts such logic to depict a world that has been decimated by tempest: it is a broken-down utopia.

Other ink painters reinvented themselves as Conceptual artists after leaving China while maintaining a conversation with the tradition of ink painting. Gu Wenda, for one, started two large installation projects in the United States, *Forest of Stone Steles* and *United Nations Monuments*, but he has never stopped making ink painting and calligraphy on two-dimensional surfaces. The Shanghai artist Zhang Jianjun (b. 1955) caught critics' attention during the '85 New Wave with his *Mankind and Their Clock* (1987), an epic Surrealist-inspired oil painting with the subtle tonality of an ink painting. He continued to explore the richness of ink after immigrating to New York in 1989 but turned to Chinese philosophy and aesthetics for inspiration. A series of experiments led to the creation of two impressive works in 1992. The first consisted of a set of two-dimensional compositions, each juxtaposing two circular forms, one above and one below. He torched the paper to make the upper disk, and drew the lower disk with a diluted ink wash that looks wet even after it dries. Whereas the two circles clearly evoke the notions of yin and yang in Chinese cosmology, Zhang employed this symbolic framework to explore the potential of water and fire as art media. A second work from 1992 was the installation *Fog Inside*. Influenced by Minimalism, he filled a flat, round cylinder with ink-infused water to the brim. The sharp contour of the cylinder conveyed the sensibility of a steel sculpture, but the water inside it generated a sense of impermanence — a feeling reinforced by the steam that slowly rose from the liquid surface and disappeared into the air. For the past twenty-five years he has continuously produced works in two- and three-dimensional forms, with ink as a constant component. His 1987 triptych *Nature* combines ink drawing and collage to restage his memory of river views in South China (**FIG. 20**). His installation *Ink Garden of Re-Creation* for the 2002 Shanghai Biennale featured a Chinese scholars' rock made of solid black ink (**FIG. 21**). In a version of this work, water flowed from its interior, gradually dissolving the rock into a trickling black stream. At this point, Zhang has joined another group of artists who, in their effort to refashion traditional Chinese art under the umbrella of international contemporary art, have embraced new forms such as installation, video, and performance, and have thus ventured into other territories beyond ink painting.

Fig. 21. Zhang Jianjun (b. 1955). *Ink Garden of Re-Creation*, 2002. Installation of sumi-ink rock, bricks, wood, water, fish, and pump system; dimensions variable. Installation view, Fourth Shanghai Biennale, Shanghai Art Museum, 2002. Private collection, Shanghai

PAST AS PRESENT IN CONTEMPORARY CHINESE ART

MAXWELL K. HEARN

Rather than attempt a comprehensive survey of the diverse art forms produced in China during the last three decades, the selection of artworks presented here endeavors to make narrative sense, however provisional, of the newness and complexity of that portion of contemporary art production in China that remains indelibly Chinese.[1] The included artists were all born in mainland China — all but three after the founding of the People's Republic of China in 1949. All came to maturity after the Cultural Revolution (1966–76), and all have experienced China's opening up to the West under the reform policies of Deng Xiaoping; the bloody suppression of the demonstrations in Tiananmen Square on June 4, 1989; and the contradictory circumstances of the past two decades in which increased economic opportunity and greater access to information and international travel have been accompanied by a growing schism between the wealthy and the poor, and by greater efforts on the part of the government to monitor and infringe upon freedom of expression.

To narrate this story, works have been organized by subject matter into three broad categories: the written word, landscape, and abstraction. A fourth category looks "beyond the brush," encompassing works that fall outside these thematic groupings but retain significant cultural associations with the notion of an ink art aesthetic, a definition of which is offered in my introduction to this volume (see pp. 13–17).

Writing, China's highest form of artistic expression as well as its most fundamental means of communication, conveys both personal and public meaning. Ubiquitous, it is valued for both its semantic content and its aesthetic significance. Authors have long exploited the multiple, even contradictory meanings of many ideographs to create veiled commentaries on political and personal issues, while calligraphers have adopted specific styles to reflect their mental state or point of view. Given the inherent power of this universal medium, the written word has been a rich terrain for artistic exploration in China.

For more than one thousand years, landscape imagery has been used to convey values and moral standards, both of an individual and of society as a whole. In the eleventh century, court-sponsored mountainscapes with a central peak towering over a natural hierarchy of hills, trees, and waterways might be read as a metaphor for the emperor presiding over his well-ordered state. And by the fourteenth century, when the learned elite of China were denied access to official service under the Mongol Yuan dynasty (1271–1368), images of blasted pine trees, windblown bamboo, or rustic retreats nestled in wilderness settings conveyed notions of survival, endurance, and withdrawal from the dusty world of politics. Today, as China is transformed by modernization and urban development, artists continue to mine the symbolic potential of landscape imagery to comment on the changing face of China and explore the "mind landscape" of the individual.

Abstraction is at the very heart of Chinese painting and calligraphy. Because the brush mark, in addition to performing a descriptive or semantic role, has always been recognized as a record of the artist's hand, both painting and calligraphy have been valued for their abstract expressive potential. Since scholar-officials began to dabble in painting as early as the eighth century, the most elite forms of that art have been understood as vehicles for self-expression rather than serving a representational function. Likewise, calligraphers often employed their art as a way of showcasing their personal brush styles. In such works (often transcriptions of well-known literary pieces), the real subject became the dynamic qualities of composition, gesture, and ink tonality. Benefiting from such a rich tradition of exploiting the abstract and symbolic qualities of painting and writing, contemporary Chinese artists have been able to selectively adopt Western notions of Conceptual Art and abstraction to augment and expand their expressive goals.

"Beyond the Brush" examines works that neither fit into the above three thematic categories nor derive their primary identity from traditional forms of ink art, yet they exhibit an ink art aesthetic through their rich associations with Chinese literati pastimes or patronage.

THE WRITTEN WORD

No aspect of Chinese culture carries greater significance than the written word. Chinese characters convey both semantic meaning and aesthetic value. Traditionally written with a supple-tipped brush, every character is an image with a rich set of formal associations. Developing across four millennia, written Chinese evolved in five basic script types and an infinite number of stylistic variations as key masters created individual interpretations that became paradigms to study and emulate. A person's command over one or more of these models was regarded not only as a reflection of his erudition and ideals but also as an indication of his character and personality. If Englishmen once judged their fellow countrymen by how they spoke, in China one was judged by how he wrote.[1]

Given the layers of cultural meaning that adhere to calligraphy, it is hardly surprising that contemporary artists have sought new ways to confront the power of the written word. Even as modern technology has made traditional brush writing an avocation rather than a necessity, the written language remains central both to China's cultural identity and to the identity of each individual.

The indivisibility of the semantic and aesthetic aspects of Chinese writing has to do with what might loosely be called its pictographic or, more correctly, ideographic origins.[2] Unlike alphabetic languages that merely indicate a word's pronunciation, the form of each Chinese character often signifies something of its meaning. Each character is made up of discrete components, one of which (the radical) usually serves as a semantic marker. For example, all characters for trees have a tree radical, 木 (*mu*), along with a component — a phonetic marker — that may suggest how the character is pronounced: the word for cedar tree, 柏 (*bai*), is made up of the tree radical plus a character that is pronounced "bai" (白); that for cassia tree, 桂 (*gui*), of the tree radical plus a character that is pronounced "gui" (圭); and that for pine tree, 松 (*song*), of the radical plus a character that is now pronounced "gong" (公).

The "graphic" identity of the Chinese language means that, to an extent far greater than with alphabetic languages, the written word is an object of aesthetic appreciation. The earliest form of Chinese writing, used in inscriptions on stone and bronze, is still in use in the seals applied to documents and artworks (hence it is called seal script). This script gradually evolved into a form of scribal writing that shows the use of a flexible-tipped brush (clerical script) that led, in turn, to a fully articulated "standard" script as well as abbreviated versions of these forms (semicursive and cursive scripts). All remain in use today. Command over these different script types was an important way for gentlemen to demonstrate their learning. With the standardization of the written language about the fourth century, the handwriting of certain individuals came to be recognized and emulated as paradigms of excellence — calligraphy became an art form. When the Tang emperor Taizong (r. 627–49) selected the writing style of Wang Xizhi (303–361) as his paramount calligraphic model, he defined an orthodox manner that rulers in all subsequent dynasties endorsed as a way of demonstrating their legitimacy. But in every generation, other masters creatively reinterpreted the Wang style, allowing for a broad range of "hands" that came to be associated with the personalities and traits of their practitioners. Furthermore, those who sought to distance themselves from court politics might reject the Wang style in favor of more archaic, "primitive" forms of writing. How one wrote was understood to reflect one's character, but it might also be read as a subtle mode of manifesting one's dissatisfaction with or dissent from the status quo. Challenging the status quo is fundamental to the works presented here, as politically motivated transformations of the form and usage of the Chinese language have engendered a profound skepticism in the trustworthiness of words.

In a country where even today there are numerous regional dialects, the written language has played an essential role in unifying a landmass larger than Europe. Widespread functional literacy meant that anyone who could read also had some sense of what constituted "good" writing. For more than one thousand years, the written language has been a ubiquitous part of China's visual landscape (**FIG. 22**). In the West figurative art has played a dominant role in civic spaces: rulers' profiles have long been stamped on coinage, and sculptures of gods, men, or beasts have decorated buildings and public squares. Shop signs — the White Horse Tavern — traditionally bore an image rather than a name. But in China, the written word was everywhere: official buildings

Gu Wenda (b. 1955). *Synthesized Words*, 1985
(fig. 25, detail)

Fig. 22a, b. The ubiquity of written signage in Chinese cities, as demonstrated in twelfth-century (above) and twenty-first-century (below) views. Zhang Zeduan (1085–1145). Detail of *Spring Festival along the River,* Northern Song dynasty (960–1127), 12th century. Handscroll; ink and color on silk, 9 ¾ in. × 17 ft. 4 ⅛ in. (24.8 × 528.6 cm). The Palace Museum, Beijing. Keith Macgregor. Detail of *Neon Fantasy, Nathan Road,* 2002. Archival pigment print, 30 × 30 in. (76.2 × 76.2 cm)

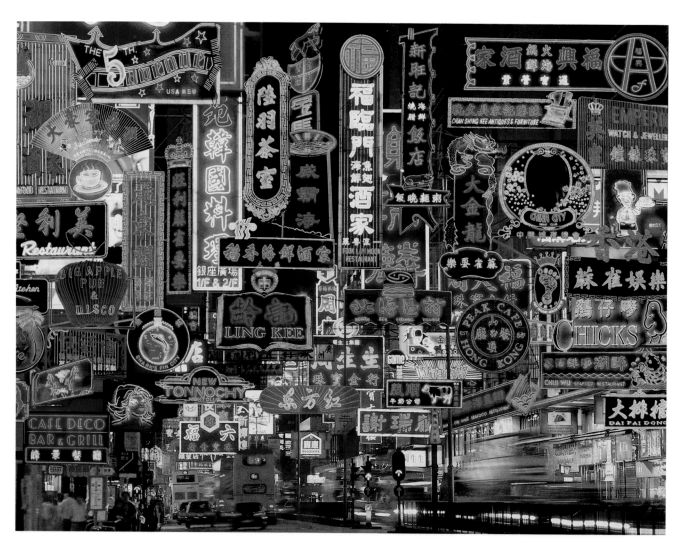

and temples, memorial arches and commemorative steles, shops and vendors' stalls, the halls and pavilions of private residences, and even the boulders and cliffs of scenic mountains and historic sites were identified by or embellished with inscriptions, which in most cases preserved the handwriting of a ruler or noted calligrapher. It was only in the twentieth century that Chinese leaders adopted the Western tradition of placing their portraits — not just their written words — in public spaces.[3]

The complexity of written Chinese, despite its ubiquitous presence, has mediated against its easy mastery or dissemination. With more than forty thousand characters in the Chinese language, typewriters were not practical, and printed books involved vast fonts of movable type or, prior to the modern era, woodblocks for each printed page. Consequently, until the advent of computers, the propagation of texts was largely accomplished through handwritten copies.

In the twentieth century, the graphic complexity of the written language was viewed as an obstacle to literacy. Under Mao Zedong, there was even an effort to abandon Chinese characters entirely in favor of an alphabet. This initiative failed, but the government did succeed in instituting simplified forms for many characters.[4] Many of the simplified forms derive from traditional cursive modes of writing and have undoubtedly made easier the task of learning to write, but it also has meant that traditional texts printed using more complex character forms have become less accessible. The visual richness of the written language has been diminished.

The consequences of this radical transformation of China's written language in the 1960s and 1970s together with the concomitant prevalence of big-character posters (*dazibao*) — large-scale political slogans that were pasted onto walls all across China, proclaiming a succession of governmental initiatives that changed with every shift in party politics (**FIG. 23**) — made language a ripe subject for artistic exploration. Beginning in the 1980s a number of Chinese artists began to experiment with the form and content of Chinese writing, using language as a visual medium often at odds with the semantic meanings of the words represented. Using miswritten, invented, or actual but randomly collected characters, these artists' works all subvert the function of the written language as a form of communication in order to disrupt viewers' preconceptions. The result was to undermine language as a vehicle for mass culture — whether for political, commercial, religious, or artistic ends — and, instead, to empower individual interpretation.

Among the artists represented in this book, Gu Wenda (b. 1955), who in the early 1980s emerged as one of the

Fig. 23. A wall plastered with big-character posters, ca. 1969

pioneering figures of experimental ink painting (*shiyan shuimo*) is perhaps the most thoroughly trained in the traditional arts of ink painting and calligraphy. As such, he is uniquely poised to challenge it from within.[5] Born in Shanghai to a middle-class family with strong cultural roots, Gu's interest and aptitude in art emerged early.[6] About 1971, while he was still in middle school, a teacher introduced him to the traditional landscape painter Xu Genrong (b. 1944), who encouraged him "to make new creations as his foundation" rather than to copy old styles.[7] At the time, he also admired the works of Li Keran (1907–1989).[8] Though he trained initially as a maker of woodblock prints, Gu continued to practice calligraphy and painting with a private tutor who had studied with the leading Shanghai painter-calligrapher Wu Changshuo (1844–1927).[9] In 1976 the Shanghai Art Gallery exhibited two of Gu's landscapes depicting "appropriate" revolutionary themes. These attracted the attention of China's most progressive art school, the Zhejiang Academy of Fine Arts (now the China Academy of Art), in Hangzhou, and in 1979 Gu was one of only five applicants accepted into the department of traditional Chinese painting (*guohua*). There, he studied with the renowned landscape master Lu Yanshao (1909–1993).[10] However, by his own account, Gu was a rebellious student who was drawn to the ideas being explored by his schoolmates in the department of oil painting — Huang Yongping (graduated in 1981), Wang Guangyi, and Zhang Peili (both graduated in 1984) — where most of the artists who were part of the '85 Art New Wave were training.

Fig. 24. Gu Wenda (b. 1955). *Mythos of Lost Dynasties Series—Tranquility Comes from Meditation*, 1985. Set of five hanging scrolls; ink on paper, each approx. 9 ft. ½ in. × 69 ⅛ in. (275.6 × 175.6 cm). Scrolls 1–3: Collection of Guo Zhen [Exhib.]; scroll 4: DSL Collection; scroll 5: Hong Kong Museum of Art

In 1985 Gu took part in the "Invitational Exhibition on New Works of Chinese Painting" in Wuhan.[11] In this exhibition devoted to *guohua*, Gu's works stood out, owing to their large scale and provocative conceptual rather than pictorial subject matter. It was here for the first time that Gu displayed examples of his pseudo-characters, recontextualized ideographs that are further subverted by being "faked, modified, miswritten, dripped," and executed in different script types and at different scales.[12] Among the earliest works in this series is *Mythos of Lost Dynasties Series — Tranquility Comes from Meditation*, five oversize hanging scrolls datable to 1985 (**FIG. 24**). The pentad features characters hovering over or within surreal "splashed ink" landscapes or cloudscapes. The center scroll, subtitled *Synthesized Words*, with its single invented ideograph suspended over a landscape, established the pattern for most of Gu's later works in the series (**FIG. 25**). In it, the elongated vertical stroke of the ideograph's central element (*shen* 申) bisects the composition along its vertical axis and extends suggestively toward a watery passage framed by rocky promontories (Gu was reading Freud at the time and frequently embedded sexual imagery in his works).[13] The full ideograph is unreadable, but Gu has pointed out that its cursive-script components (易, 申, 示) may be interpreted (from right to left) as the character for "unobstructed" (*chang* 畅) and that for "spirit" (*shen* 神).[14] While Gu's overriding purpose may have been to subvert the semantic function of calligraphy, his creation of a "new" symbol embodying the notion of an unfettered spirit is a powerful emblem of his wish to escape cultural stereotypes: "To me, illegible script is more creative, more illusionary and imaginative than normal script. I felt so free when working with illegible words. I thought, 'There must be a meaning, I just don't understand it yet.'"[15]

Like his fellow students at the Zhejiang Academy, Gu was influenced by newly available translations of Western texts, including Wittgenstein, Freud, and Nietzsche, and he cites the impact of Western philosophy on his pseudo-characters: "Studying the language of philosophy from [Bertrand] Russell and [Ludwig] Wittgenstein coincided with my study of seal script. Seal script is an ancient form of writing that isn't used today; you can't understand it at all. So I thought of seal script as a fake language. I became really interested in Wittgenstein's theory of the mystery of the universe that cannot be described by language."[16] If, according to Wittgenstein, what lies outside language is nonsense, then Gu's pseudo-characters are explicit explorations of an illogical world of images and emotions that can be pictured but not adequately articulated through words alone.

Despite acknowledging the influence on his work of big-character posters, which as a child he had helped the Red Guard create, and of his time making folk art (popular prints)

Fig. 25. Gu Wenda (b. 1955). *Synthesized Words,*
from *Mythos of Lost Dynasties Series—Tranquility
Comes from Meditation,* 1985. Hanging scroll from
an original set of five; ink on paper, 9 ft. ½ in. ×
69 in. (275.6 × 175.3 cm). Collection of Guo Zhen
[Exhib.]

Fig. 26. Xu Bing (b. 1955). *Book from the Sky,* ca. 1987–91. Hand-printed scrolls and books; ink on paper, overall dimensions variable. Installation view, Seattle Asian Art Museum, 2007. Collection of the artist [Exhib.]

in a woodblock-printing factory, Gu has refuted the idea that his pseudo-characters are a statement against Maoist-era propaganda.[17] Rather, he asserts that his primary motivation was not to make a strong political statement but to challenge and redirect traditional painting and calligraphy.[18] By contrast, Gu's contemporary Xu Bing (b. 1955) has confirmed the influence of Maoist doctrine and policies on his work, particularly the transformation of written Chinese:

> When each member of the Chinese cultural community first begins his or her education, he or she must spend years memorizing thousands of characters. This process is a sort of ceremony in homage to the culture, and it leaves all Chinese with an extreme sense of respect for the "written word." My generation, however, was irreparably affected by the campaign to simplify characters. This remolding of my earliest memories — the promulgation of new character after new character, the abandonment of old characters that I had already mastered, the transformation of new characters and their eventual demise, the revival of old characters — shadowed my earliest education and left me confused about the fundamental conceptions of culture.[19]

Further complicating Xu's relationship to the written word was his witnessing firsthand of its destructive potential at the outset of the Cultural Revolution. In 1966 he saw big-character posters criticizing his father, a history professor at Peking (Beijing) University, who was labeled a reactionary and imprisoned in the campus "cattle shed," while his mother, a library administrator at the university, was sent to a reeducation camp. The eleven-year-old Xu, an older brother, and two younger siblings were left in the care of their fourteen-year-old sister.

Against the backdrop of this childhood trauma, *Book from the Sky* (*Tianshu*) is the artist's remarkable response to the often blatant contradiction between propaganda and reality, words and actions, in a China where doctrine, news, and history were continually being rewritten and texts could no longer be trusted (**FIG. 26**). While the work is inspired by the form and typography of traditional Chinese woodblock publications, faithfully replicating every stylistic detail of traditional Chinese printing, not a single one of its invented characters is intelligible.[20] If Gu's ideographs, looming over an amorphous landscape, hint at new meanings, then Xu's text conveys the illusion of legibility but remains defiantly undecipherable.

The work's basic unit is a four-fascicle book stored in a wood case. Each fascicle comprises between 61 and 96 folded

Fig. 27. Xu Bing (b. 1955). Set of four woodblock-printed volumes from *Book from the Sky*; ink on paper, each, open, 18 ⅛ × 20 in. (46 × 51 cm); wood case, 19 × 13 × 4 ¹¹/₁₆ in. (49 × 33 × 11 cm). Collection of the artist [Exhib.]

Fig. 28. Xu Bing (b. 1955). Hand-carved pearwood blocks used to print *Book from the Sky*: frontispiece (left) and movable type with individual characters within a gridded frame (right). Single frontispiece block 12 ½ × 8 ½ × ½ in. (31.8 × 21.6 × 1.3 cm); racked type 17 × 20 × 1 ½ in. (43.2 × 50.8 × 3.8 cm); small type block ¼ × ¼ × ¾ in. (.6 × .6 × 1.9 cm); large type block ¾ × ¾ × ¾ in. (1.9 × 1.9 × 1.9 cm). Collection of the artist [Exhib.]

and stitched sheets, each page printed using hand-carved movable type (**FIGS. 27, 28**). The finished book, with a total edition of 120 sets, is a virtual compendium of earlier printing conventions: identifiable by their type size and distribution within a standard nine-column format are a preface, table of contents, a narrative text divided into chapters with commentaries and notes in the margins above, catalogue entries, a glossary, an afterword, and a printer's colophon. The typeface, based on Ming dynasty (1368–1644) interpretations of a Song dynasty (960–1279) printing style (*songti*), has an impersonal, almost mechanical, appearance; not intended to resemble brush writing, it is made up of squared lines with angular

accents that make the carving of the characters more efficient.[21] Xu "picked out three 'characters' that seemed to [him] most to resemble real Chinese characters and used them as a general title."[22]

Having accompanied his mother through the stacks of the university library as a child, Xu had an intimate knowledge of premodern publications, and his ability to create so many imaginary characters reflects both an early interest in typefaces and a formative encounter with Chinese folk art: one year after graduating from Peking University High School, where he had worked part-time as an art instructor and as a member of the school's propaganda unit, Xu was sent to a remote

commune in the Taihang Mountains of rural Yanqing County, northwest of Beijing, to be cleansed of his "polluted" family background. In addition to his farmwork, Xu started a mimeographed newsletter celebrating rural culture, and because of his knowledge of calligraphy, he was asked to contribute to traditional village celebrations by writing talismanic glyphs composed of auspicious four-character phrases (**FIG. 29**). These composite images required the integration of disparate components into a single calligraphic figure — the same process he employed to create his imaginary characters for *Book from the Sky*.[23]

Xu magnifies the impact of his text by creating an environment that immerses the viewer in a sea of imaginary words, with an array of open books spread across the floor and long sheets suggestive of handscrolls and hanging scrolls suspended from the ceiling and walls. But while the installation evokes Chinese canonical writings — presumably paying homage to the millennium-long heritage of printing in China, to the widespread literacy that this invention engendered, and to the ancient veneration for the written word — the traditional appearance of the books and scrolls mocks viewers. Frustrating all efforts at decipherment, *Book from the Sky* implies that China's literary and historical legacy in the aftermath of the Cultural Revolution is no longer accessible, and that even contemporary texts, though seemingly intelligible, may in fact be incomprehensible or meaningless.

The work's original title, *Mirror to Analyze the World: The Century's Final Volume* (析世鉴－世纪末卷), suggests that it was meant as a commentary — indeed, the century's "last word" on the state of affairs in China — on the growing inaccessibility of traditional Chinese culture.[24] But the title the work ultimately acquired, *Tianshu* (天书), is more ambiguous.[25] *Tian* may signify "sky," "heaven," or "emperor"; *shu* can mean either "book" or "writing." Thus, *Book from the Sky* may be viewed either as heaven-sent — but written in a mystical form that is indecipherable — or as a proclamation from on high that so obfuscates the truth that it can be neither understood nor interpreted.

Book from the Sky was the result of a multiyear process that began in 1986, after Xu had spent a decade at the May Seventh College of Arts, Beijing, which reverted to its earlier name, the Central Academy of Fine Arts (CAFA), shortly after Mao's death. First as a student and then as an instructor, he worked in the college's printmaking department, creating woodblock images of rural life. He also authored the book *Teaching Notes for Basic Drawing* (1981) and "I Picture What I Love" (1981), an essay describing his creative practice that became a standard art-school text.[26] At the time, the gradual

Fig. 29. This composite glyph (right) by Xu Bing reconfigures into a single character the auspicious four-character phrase (left) "Bringing in wealth and riches" (*Zhao cai jin bao*)

opening up of Chinese society after the Cultural Revolution enabled Xu to immerse himself in newly available translations of Western and Chinese texts. The experience proved overwhelming: "The more I read, the more muddled my thinking became, until I felt as if something had become lost to me. I was like a starving person who all at once has too much to eat and winds up so uncomfortable that he is filled with disgust."[27] By 1986 Xu had begun experimenting with a handwritten version of *Book from the Sky*, then in 1987 spent a year hand carving a woodblock typeface of more than 1,200 invented characters to create a printed version. Characters for the books were smaller than those for the wall hangings, so the entire installation necessitated carving more than 4,000 pieces of type. After exhibiting this version of *Book from the Sky* in 1988, Xu decided to make a more finished set of books with more refined characters, which he had printed and bound with the help of a small factory outside Beijing. This is the set he has exhibited as *Book from the Sky* since 1991.[28] The work created a sensation when it was first shown, in October 1988, at the National Art Gallery in Beijing as part of an exhibition devoted to Xu's art of printmaking. It was also included in the "China/Avant-Garde" exhibition, which opened at the National Art Gallery in February 1989.[29] That exhibition was closed down almost immediately by the authorities, and in the aftermath of the brutal suppression of democracy demonstrations in Tiananmen Square, *Book from the Sky* was singled out for public criticism. Writing in the officially sanctioned *Literature and Art Newspaper* (*Wenyi bao*) in June 1990, one CAFA professor stated, "If I am asked to evaluate the *Book from the Sky*, I can only say that it gathers together the formalistic, abstract, subjective, irrational, anti-art, anti-traditional . . . qualities of the Chinese New Wave of fine arts, and pushes the New Wave towards a ridiculous impasse. . . . The essence of the Chinese New Wave of fine arts is to oppose the laws of art and to oppose society."[30]

In July 1990, Xu accepted a fellowship from the University of Wisconsin. After residing in the United States for several years, he found that, by treating individual letters like the components of an ideograph, he could recompose English words to resemble brush-written characters. Just as Chinese characters, no matter how simple or complex, are visualized inside squares of uniform size, each of Xu's English words conforms to an imaginary square — hence its name: square word calligraphy (**FIGS. 30, 31**).

Xu's invented word system, while drawing attention to formal differences between Chinese and English, underscores the malleability of language, with works such as *The Song of Wandering Aengus by William Butler Yeats* — in which the classic poem is recomposed into a pair of hanging scrolls using square-word calligraphy — blurring the linguistic and cultural boundaries between East and West (**FIG. 32**). Bafflement on the part of both Western and Chinese audiences gives way to clarity as the logic and readability of Xu's system come to light. Perhaps in the effort to facilitate comprehension, Xu has installed mock classrooms with copybooks and computers to teach audiences how to read and write his reconfigured English (**FIG. 33**). His didactic approach to the subject, reflecting his longtime role as a teacher, is best conveyed in *An Introduction to Square Word Calligraphy,* which offers detailed directions on how to prepare ink, hold a brush, and execute individual

Fig. 30. A comparison of Xu Bing's square word calligraphy (left) and standard-script calligraphy by Zhao Mengfu (right). Left: Xu Bing (b. 1955). *An Introduction to Square Word Calligraphy,* 1994–96 (fig. 35, detail); right: Zhao Mengfu (1254–1322). Detail of *The Record of the Miaoyan Temple,* ca. 1309. Handscroll; ink on paper, 13 ½ in. x 11 ft. 11 ½ in. (34.2 x 364.5 cm). The Princeton University Art Museum

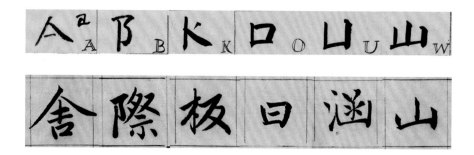

Fig. 31. Examples of Xu Bing's square word alphabet (above) and Chinese characters by Zhao Mengfu (below)

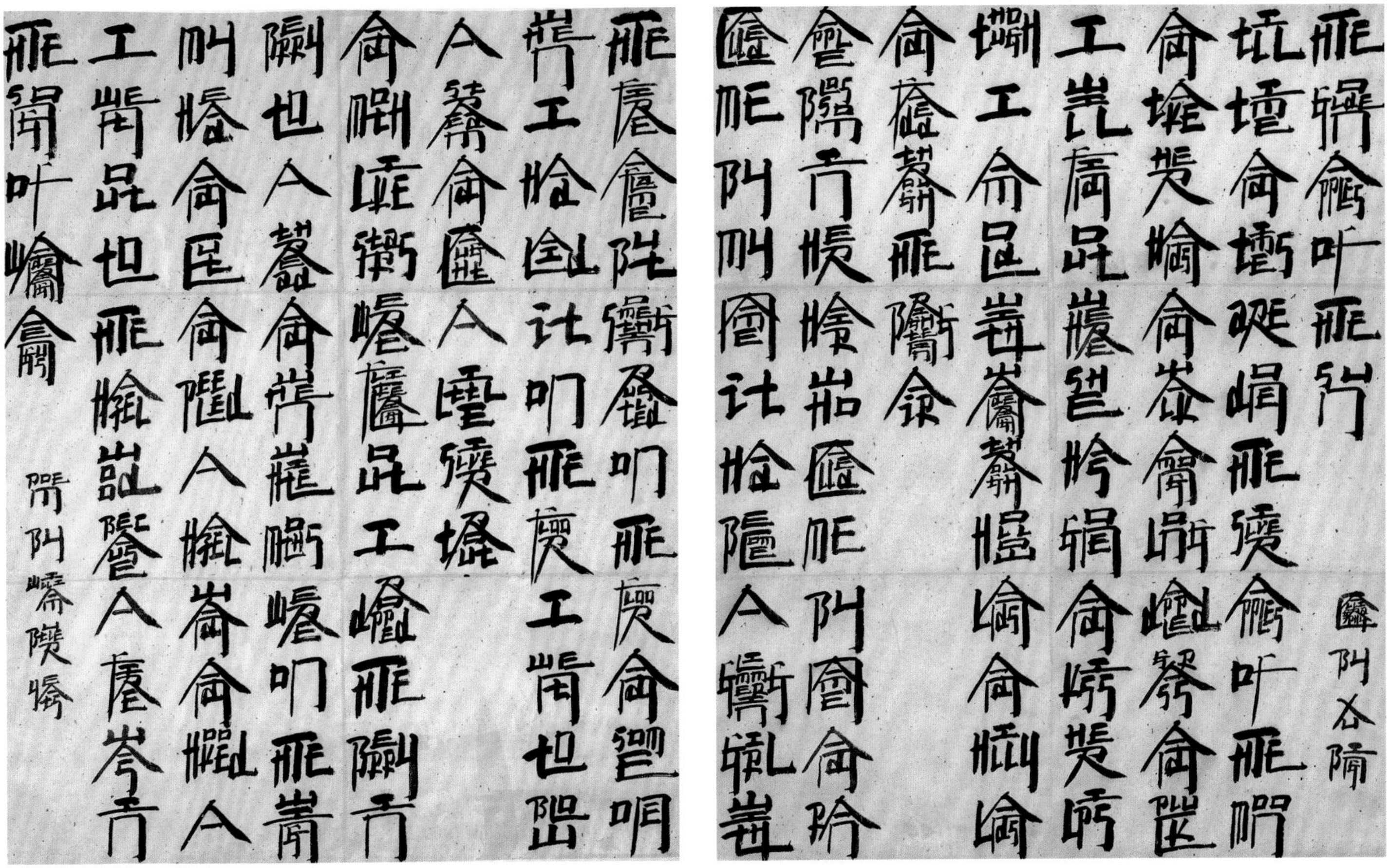

Fig. 32. Xu Bing (b. 1955). *The Song of Wandering Aengus by William Butler Yeats*, 1999. Pair of hanging scrolls; ink on paper, each 63 ¼ × 51 ½ in. (160.5 × 130.8 cm). Private collection, New York [Exhib.]

Fig. 33. Installation view of Xu Bing's square word
calligraphy classroom, Copenhagen, 1994

brushstrokes (**FIGS. 34, 35**). In contrast to *Book from the Sky*, which presents the written word as a barrier to understanding, *An Introduction to Square Word Calligraphy* communicates writing's power to bridge cultural differences.[31] As Xu has observed, "The main purpose of my work is . . . to change people's way of thinking about culture. . . . When looking at Square Word Calligraphy, you need to get beyond any preconceived notions and develop a new conceptual understanding."[32]

An Introduction to Square Word Calligraphy is more than a primer on how to write English in a new way; it asserts the value of practicing calligraphy as a means of self-realization:

> "Calligraphy" is by nature different from "writing." It is
> not merely a tool of communication, but also an activity
> that combines both artistic expression and spiritual
> energy. From the first stroke of a word to its completion,
> our entire bodies are involved. It is a process of com-
> muning with nature, of experiencing consummate
> beauty, and of discovering our inner selves.

Xu's sentiments are in keeping with the notion that the physical act of writing has long held an essential significance in Chinese culture. The hand writing of religious texts was considered an act of merit, while transcribing a secular text was a way of committing it to memory. Moreover, copying a text by a famous calligrapher was a way to master both its content and a particular calligraphic style. Both goals were viewed as a form of self-cultivation.

Qiu Zhijie (b. 1969) embraced calligraphy at an early age, and having begun his schooling just as the Cultural Revolution was ending and traditional culture was enjoying a revival, he felt none of the ambivalence toward Chinese culture that slightly older artists such as Xu Bing and Gu Wenda experienced: "My calligraphy teachers . . . were more or less the last generation of traditional Chinese scholars. They had a huge influence on me. I never experienced that complete rejection of tradition, nor a complete return to tradition. As far back as I can remember, Chinese tradition has just been a part of my life."[33] As a teenager in the late 1980s, however, he was deeply affected by his encounter with contemporary art. On a visit to the nearby city of Xiamen, he viewed works by the Xiamen Dada group, led by Huang Yongping (b. 1954). The group's rejection of traditional approaches to art and their engagement with Western modernism had a profound impact on Qiu.

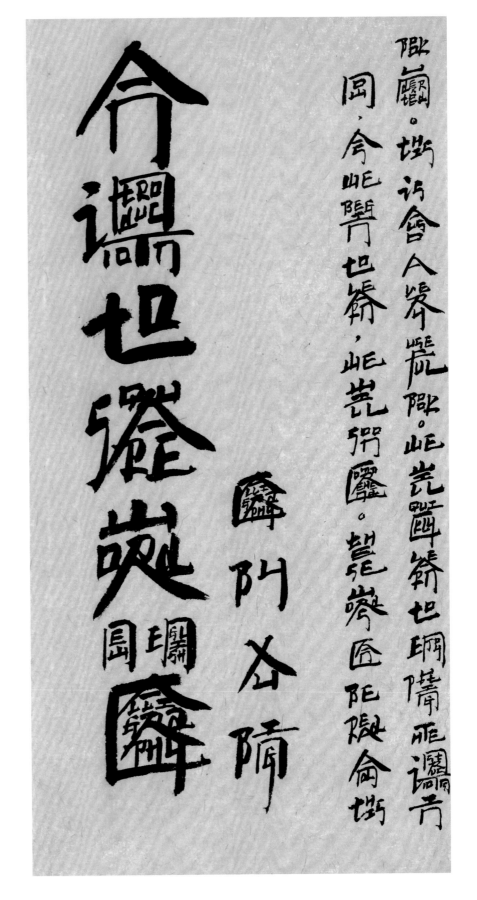

49

Fig. 35. Xu Bing (b. 1955). *An Introduction to Square Word Calligraphy*, 1994–96. Handscroll; ink on paper, 19 in. × 17 ft. (48.3 × 518.2 cm). Private collection, New York [Exhib.]. Xu's scroll ends (at lower right) with the well-known children's rhyme that begins, "Rain, rain, go away . . ."

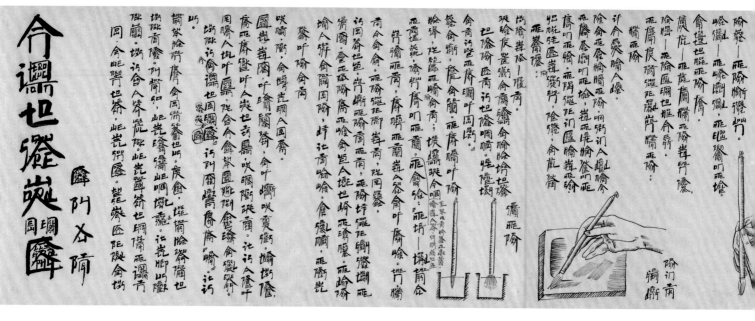

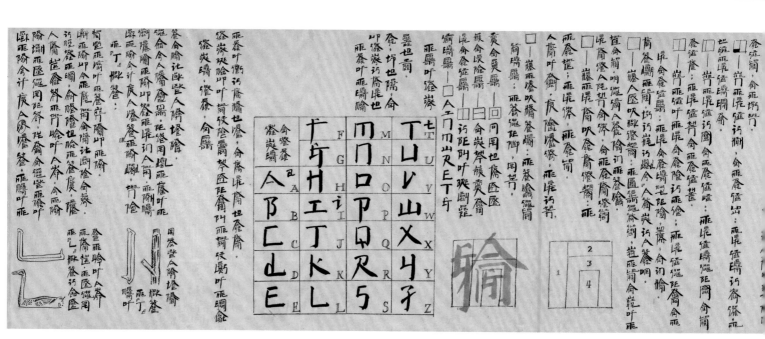

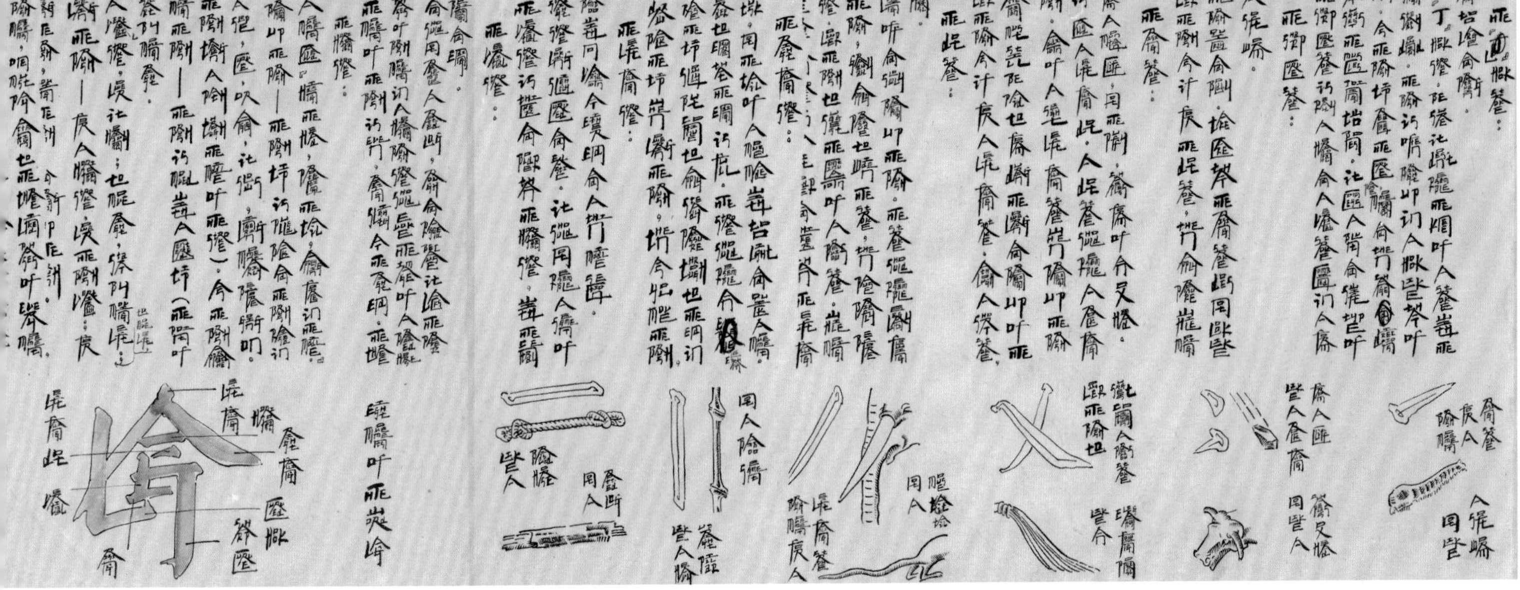

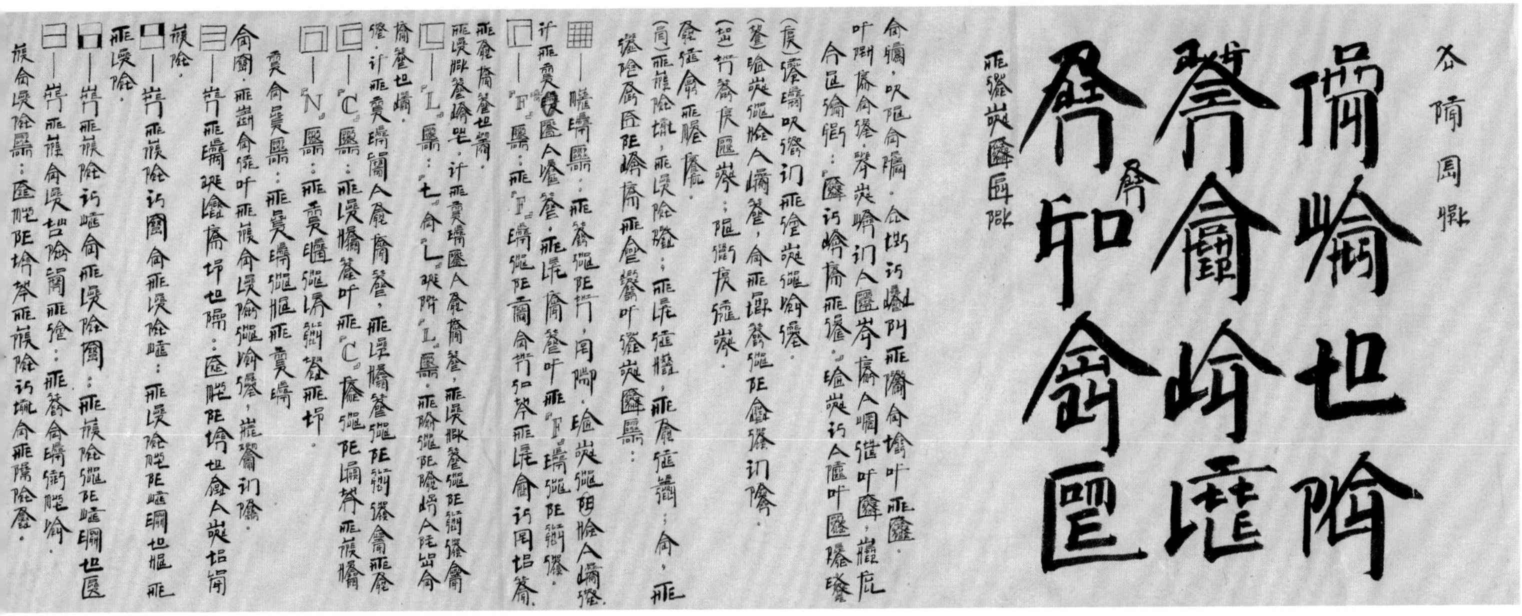

Fig. 36. Qiu Zhijie (b. 1969). *Writing the "Orchid Pavilion Preface" One Thousand Times*, 1990–95. Five chromogenic prints, each 19 ¼ × 39 in. (49 × 99 cm). M+ Sigg Collection, Hong Kong [Exhib.]

Shortly thereafter, in 1988, Qiu was admitted to the Zhejiang Academy, where he was assigned to the printmaking department. There, he continued to explore Western trends such as Fluxus and to examine "process in art."[34]

A striking example of Qiu's interest in process, particularly the performative aspect of calligraphy, is his *Writing the "Orchid Pavilion Preface" One Thousand Times* from 1990–95 (FIG. 36). The "Orchid Pavilion Preface" was written by Wang Xizhi to introduce a group of poems composed at a springtime gathering held at the Orchid Pavilion in A.D. 353. Fueled by bonhomie and free-flowing wine, Wang wrote the preface in a burst of spontaneous emotion. When he transcribed his draft the next day, he could not reproduce the inspired naturalness of the original. Although Emperor Taizong commanded that this legendary piece of writing be buried with him, a number of versions survive as tracings or freehand copies, and the text has long been enshrined as the ultimate model of running-cursive script that every aspiring calligrapher has copied.[35]

Qiu began by writing the famous text on a blank sheet of paper in a freehand interpretation of the original. He then wrote over his first transcription again and again. The first fifty transcriptions were filmed and are preserved as a video. Well before the fiftieth writing, however, the paper turns into a saturated black field, the original content entirely indiscernible. According to Qiu, "Within the classical forms of calligraphy, the original hand of the literatus is a kind of measure of one's artistic identity and attainment of internal perfection. For this reason, the text of the *Orchid Pavilion* is presented as an unsurpassed classic that epitomizes the value of a certain unselfconscious, carefree spirit that ultimately denies formal elaboration." By writing the same text repeatedly, Qiu not only focused on the *process* of writing but also eliminated "the literary nature of calligraphy" and asserted the ultimate goal of calligraphic practice "as a form of 'written meditation.'"[36] Far from belittling the repetitive act of writing the same text over and over as meaningless drudgery, however, Qiu reasserts the traditional Confucian ethic of self-cultivation through the discipline of gradual mastery. His words also suggest an appreciation for Chan (Zen in Japanese) Buddhist notions of attaining enlightenment, even as one engages in the mundane routines of daily life.

Qiu has identified in the work of his friend Wu Shanzhuan (b. 1960) a similar effort to remove the inflections of an identifiable calligraphic style, describing Wu's handwritten quotations of typographic script as anonymous, with no discernible trace of an individual hand.[37] Wu's diverse body of work has consistently challenged the boundaries and

Fig. 37. Installation view of "75% Red, 20% Black, 5% White," Zuyin Temple, Zhoushan, 1985

definitions of what constitutes a work of art, and in his engagement with the written word, he has succeeded in repudiating the semantic, calligraphic, and symbolic functions of characters, reducing them to independent works of graphic art. In 1985, after graduating from the Zhejiang Academy, he and six classmates mounted an exhibition entitled "75% Red, 20% Black, 5% White" at a temple in Zhoushan, Zhejiang Province (subsequently installed at the Zhejiang Academy in 1986; **FIG. 37**). The exhibition, featuring about seventy works with characters written in red, black, or white in the proportion indicated by the title, juxtaposed seemingly random phrases from advertisements, poetry, religion, politics, and daily life ("the Last Supper," "public toilet," "serve the people," "good treatment of skin disease"), selected from examples found posted on the street. These discordant fragments of popular language evoked the ideological confrontation of the Cultural Revolution, when a succession of manifestos and slogans competed for attention, while the color red was associated with good Communists, black with enemies of the people, and white with the nonaligned.[38]

The following year, Wu created a second installation as part of what he has called his *Red Humour* series (**FIG. 38**). Using black, red, and white ink in an assortment of brush styles, Wu completely covered the walls, floor, and ceiling of his Zhoushan studio with an array of big characters and phrases excerpted from literature and daily life. The resulting collage of words overwhelms the senses and defies interpretation, excepting the four immense characters arranged in a grid on the floor,

which exploit traditional Chinese wordplay. When the words are read "*wu shuo ba dao*" (无说八道), they may be understood as "don't speak nonsense." This phrase also brings to mind a common expression for "nonsense," "*hu shuo ba dao*" (胡说八道), literally, "barbaric speech, eight ways." Since the character *wu* (无) is homophonic with the character for Wu's surname (吴), one may also interpret the phrase to mean "Wu speaks nonsense." Finally, by reading the character *ba* (八) as *ren* (人), one may read the four characters as "*wu ren shuo dao*" (无人说道), or "nobody can interpret this."[39] By writing the character *dao* (道), the eponymous word for Daoism (also spelled Taoism), using a more simplified form (辺) that was subsequently withdrawn from usage, Wu further undermines the logographic meaning of this text. What we are left with is the artistic equivalent of Babel.

In *Character Image of Black Character Font* of 1989, Wu's stated goal was to liberate the written word from both the creative manipulation of the calligrapher and its linguistic meaning so as to emphasize the character's inherent artistry (**FIG. 39**). As this title makes clear, Wu's characters are both words (*zi*) and images (*xiang*) composed of crisp lines of uniform width that most resemble printed examples of boldface type.[40] Four of the six images included in this survey are legible — "yes, this, crowd, yet" (是此丛而) — while the characters in the other two images have been effaced or torn so as to render them undecipherable. But even the legible characters defy semantic interpretation.[41] By selecting words that function as prepositions,

Fig. 38. Wu Shanzhuan (b. 1960). *Red Humour Series—Today No Water,* also known as *The Big Characters (Dazibao),* 1986. Multimedia installation, dimensions variable. Installation view at the artist's studio and Institute for Mass Culture, Zhoushan, 1986

Fig. 39. Wu Shanzhuan (b. 1960). *Character Image of Black Character Font*, 1989. Six unmounted sheets; ink and color on paper, each 33 × 26 ⅜ in. (84 × 67 cm). Private collection, Hong Kong [Exhib.]

conjunctions, or other grammatical particles, Wu removes the possibility of reading meaning into them.

Wu calls these glyphs "deficit (red) characters" (*chi zi* 赤 字). The word *chi* (赤) can mean either "red" or "empty," just as in the West "in the red" is synonymous with running a deficit. In Wu's ironic usage, large-character images — at one time powerful expressions of Red (Communist) ideology — satirize both political censors' and art critics' efforts at interpretation (hence his rubric for this body of work, "red humor"). In his friend Qiu Zhijie's view, Wu's insistence on the viewer's freedom to explore multiple possible interpretations "is the true foundation of an open society."[42]

The artist has cited his debt to Dada and Surrealism,[43] but he has distinguished his approach to language to that taken in Western art: "If we are [creating] conceptual art, it is based on the concept that the aesthetic forms of Chinese typography in themselves exist as works of art; rather than on the concept of Chinese characters as linguistic expressions. In this way our conceptual art differs from Western conceptual 'Word Art,' which emphasizes the concepts expressed by language."[44] He further notes: "When we realize Chinese characters as forms of pure beauty on the canvas, the audience still recognizes them as a language that expresses a concept . . . but it is a language that does not correspond to the established codes of meaning for Chinese characters."[45]

He also has acknowledged the influence of the ubiquitous big-character posters of the Cultural Revolution though, like Gu Wenda, maintains that his works should not be read merely as commentaries on that era: "A work of art is a physical object, not a social state of mind, so a society's ideology cannot be used as the final standard by which to judge it."[46] Gu, too, has experimented with traditional Chinese wordplay to undermine semantic meaning. In June 1986, less than a year after he first exhibited his pseudo-characters at the Wuhan Invitational, Gu held his first solo exhibition at Xi'an Artist Gallery. Among the works on display were two additional works from the series *Mythos of Lost Dynasties*: *I Evaluate Characters Written by Three Men and Three Women* (FIG. 40) and *Negative and Positive Characters* (FIG. 41). Though the authorities banned the exhibition before it opened (they later allowed a few professional artists limited access), the exhibition attracted national attention.[47]

In *I Evaluate Characters* (1985), six of Gu's students at the Zhejiang Academy, where he taught from 1981 to 1987, each wrote on a sheet of paper a large-scale variation of the character "quiet" (*jing* 静). No two characters are written the same way. To these characters Gu added spatters of ink, then

used red pigment either to cross out the characters with an X or to indicate approval with a circle. Such marks were a traditional way for teachers to indicate whether a character had been written correctly, but they also were a powerful reminder of the Cultural Revolution when, in Gu's words, "You cross out the bad person, and leave the good person."[48]

Some characters resemble early seal script, while others are written backward or have had their components reversed. Varying intensities of ink have been added to the six sheets of paper, including a shadowy image of newspaper print on the upper right sheet. Gu's alternating sequence of Xs and Os creates a balanced pattern that unifies the otherwise disparate forms while leaving no indication of why certain pictographs have been crossed out and others not. The decontextualization of the word "quiet" problematizes the characters by detaching them from semantic meaning, but in a telling gesture that acknowledges the power of tradition, Gu has signed and dated the piece and impressed his seal in the conventional manner along the scroll's lower left edge.[49]

Gu's *Negative and Positive Characters* (1984–85) is an even more ambitious work. In it, three large hanging scrolls are each inscribed with the characters *zheng* and *fan*. When juxtaposed, the words can mean "correct" and "contrary," "proper" and "improper," "front" and "back," "orthodox" and "unorthodox," thus calling into question what is correct or incorrect in art or in social behavior. In all three scrolls the two characters are written one above the other, starkly silhouetted in black ink against a white ground. Gu uses a variety of techniques to undermine their graphic and lexical force, including reversing the order of the characters or writing them backward, literally contradicting their semantic sense. The characters in the flanking scrolls are also partially obscured by dark forms that resemble standing figures; the one on the left appears to extend its right arm and open hand, and the characters *fan* and *zheng* are legible among its swirling drapery folds. Some of these brushstrokes are suggestive of other ideographs; the character for "female" (*nü* 女) is discernible on the figure's head.[50]

Fung Mingchip (Feng Mingqiu, b. 1951) has also sought to subvert the primacy of the written word as a vehicle for semantic meaning, but rather than veil characters under layers of meaning like Gu Wenda, Fung elicits ghostlike vestiges of language from layers of water and ink. An entirely self-taught calligrapher, Fung creates what he calls "new scripts" that expand the visual experience of the written language: "Creating calligraphy is not just about how to write. More importantly, it is about how to see and how to treat the art of calligraphy."[51]

Fig. 40. Gu Wenda (b. 1955).
*Mythos of Lost Dynasties
Series—I Evaluate Characters
Written by Three Men
and Three Women*, 1985.
Hanging scroll; ink on paper,
9 ft. 4 ¼ in. × 70 in. (285 ×
178 cm). Private collection,
Hong Kong [Exhib.]

Fig. 41. Gu Wenda (b. 1955). *Mythos of Lost Dynasties Series—Negative and Positive Characters*, 1984–85. Three hanging scrolls; ink on paper, each 9 ft. 4 ⅝ in. × 68 ½ in. (286 × 174 cm). Private collection, Hong Kong [Exhib.]

Fung became an artist in spite of the many obstacles he encountered during his early years. His family moved from a small village in Guangdong Province to Hong Kong and then, in 1977, to New York, where he worked as a deliveryman in Chinatown: "By the time I approached thirty, I saw my future, like a movie I had seen so many times before. Everything was fixed, predictable, and very depressing."[52] Moving to Taiwan in 1986, Fung was able to devote himself more fully to the arts and during the next decade moved between Taipei, Hong Kong, and New York, writing and directing plays, composing poetry, and publishing a novel before focusing on his career as an artist. He now works primarily out of Hong Kong.

Heart Sutra, dated 2001, a pair of hanging scrolls that transcribes identical portions of a major scripture in the Buddhist canon, illustrates how Fung manipulates ink and water to create a unique fusion of calligraphy and abstraction (FIG. 42). On the "transparent" scroll, sixty-four characters are written in such pale, wet ink that they blur into faint shadows against the white paper.[53] Fung rendered these characters, which he describes as "transparent script" (*touzi*), by first making circles with water, then writing onto the dampened surface in very dilute ink so that each character appears to be surrounded by a halo. Because Fung left the center of each circle dry, the middle of each character appears darker. On the "luminous" scroll, the same characters are arrayed against a black ground so that they appear to emit light, in what Fung refers to as "luminous script" (*guangzi*). The characters were written first with water on a blank sheet of paper. They became visible only after Fung applied a layer of dark ink over most of each character. Where the water had already saturated the paper, the ink was only partially absorbed, leaving ghostlike traces. The artist left a triangular area uninked at the center of each character to heighten the effect of light emanating from the characters.

The square format of these paired images, the organization of the text into a grid, the contrast of light and dark elements, and the equal emphasis given to figure and ground demonstrate how Fung's sensibility has been shaped by his work as a seal carver. Further, by impressing a different seal with the same legend, *xiang* 相 ("form" or "phenomenon"), near the center of each composition, he has accentuated the yin-yang contrast of this pair of scrolls. The seal on the transparent scroll is carved with the character *xiang* in relief (yang), so that it appears red against a blank white ground, while the *xiang* on the luminous composition is in intaglio (yin), so that it appears uninked against a dark red ground.

The visual impact of the work so overwhelms its narrative function that it is impossible to read this pair of scrolls

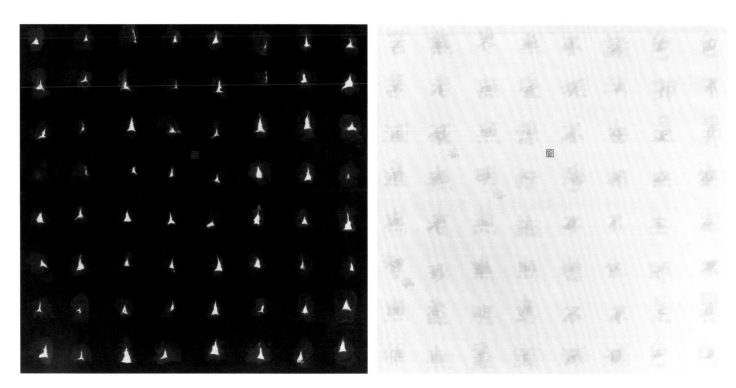

Fig. 42. Fung Mingchip (b. 1951). *Heart Sutra*,
2001. Pair of hanging scrolls; ink on paper, each
26 ⅝ × 27 ½ in. (67.6 × 69.8 cm). The Metropolitan
Museum of Art, New York, Gift of Susan L.
Beningson and Steve Arons, in memory of Renée
Beningson, 2011 (2011.527.2a, b) [Exhib.]

merely as texts. As in the works of Gu Wenda, Xu Bing, and Wu Shanzhuan, Fung's calligraphy exists primarily as an image. His emphasis is on the form of the composition rather than the structure of individual characters, and indeed, his process of merging forms with the emptiness of blank paper or the darkness of saturated ink may be understood as a visual equivalent of the transcribed sutra passage:

> Form does not differ from emptiness; emptiness does not differ from form. Form itself is emptiness; emptiness itself is form. . . . All Dharmas are empty of characteristics. They are not produced, not destroyed, not defiled, not pure; and they neither increase nor diminish. Therefore, in emptiness there is no form, feeling, cognition, formation, or consciousness . . . no field of mind consciousness; and no ignorance or ending of ignorance, up to and including no old age and death or ending of old age and death. There is no suffering, no accumulating, no extinction, and no Way, and no understanding and no attaining.[54]

Using visual rather than lexigraphic means, Fung's work seeks to induce a state of consciousness equivalent to what is advocated by the text: a meditative state in which the viewer transcends both the text and the medium to achieve a new level of awareness — the higher consciousness that is also the goal of the sutra.

By privileging process and visual effects over semantic content, Wang Tiande (b. 1960) has also sought to redefine ink painting and calligraphy, rejecting both traditional subject matter and formats. Since the early 1990s he has consistently explored the tactile qualities of ink on paper in which brushed or splashed applications of ink emphasize texture, pattern, and the artist's touch rather than representational or semantic legibility.[55]

Born and raised in Shanghai, Wang has never acknowledged the impact of the Cultural Revolution on him or his family. In 1978 he enrolled in the Shanghai School of Arts and Crafts and in 1984 was admitted to the highly competitive graduate program in *guohua* at the Zhejiang Academy, where Gu Wenda was then an instructor.[56] Like Gu, Wang had had little exposure to Western art. Commenting on these formative years, Wang has observed: "I was cut off for years from the West, and developed my craft in relative isolation. I struggled to find creative inspiration from deeply rooted traditions. While my friends turned to oil painting, I redefined ink painting and calligraphy, the most value-laden of China's art

forms."[57] He rapidly embraced the new abstract expressive potential of the ink medium that Gu and others were advocating.

A literal layering of imagery and material is a principle feature of Wang's *Digital* series, exemplified by his imposing triptych *Digital No. 02HP01–03* (FIG. 43). Each of the work's three vertical panels consists of two sheets of paper layered one atop the other. Each bottom sheet is inscribed, to varying degrees, with what the artist insists is a random assortment of Chinese characters, loosely arrayed in columns (FIG. 44A). Some characters overlap or are smudged, rendering them illegible. The top sheets are made of translucent paper into which the characters have been burned with a cigarette or incense stick (FIG. 44B). These calligraphic traces — which recall Fung Mingchip's pale vestiges of characters — arrayed in parallel columns, reveal flickering glimpses of the inked and uninked surfaces that are otherwise only dimly visible below. Wang developed this method of "writing" after he accidentally dropped ash onto paper while lighting a cigarette in his studio and observed the resulting perforations. According to Wang, the process resembles that of burning information onto DVDs and digital drives — hence the title of this series. Appropriately, each work is identified using letters and digits that resemble a serial number or computer code to give the date, format, and number within the series. Thus, *Digital No. 02HP01–03* may be read as "2002: hanging paintings one through three."

While Wang acknowledges his bonds to traditional art, his work cannot be evaluated on the same terms. One of the fundamental characteristics of calligraphy is that one can vicariously retrace the act of creation. Wang's layering of ink and paper obscures his characters to the point that it is no longer possible to follow how each was composed. Yet the vivid physical traces of the artist's hand, wielding both a brush and a burning implement, assert the primacy of the creative process and the materiality of the object. While representational or semantic content has been rendered inaccessible, what remains is an enhanced awareness of the fragility of these unmounted sheets as the bearers of the artist's vigorous brushwork and singed traces, reminding us that much of Chinese culture is preserved through a medium that is inherently fragile and vulnerable, and that our grasp of past traditions is similarly elusive.

For the calligrapher, as with an athlete or musician, proficiency comes through disciplined practice — the repetition of the same movements until they become second nature. Only then can the writer begin to push beyond the style of his models to experiment with his own creative interpretations. The daily regimen required to maintain one's skill was seen as a

Fig. 43. Wang Tiande (b. 1960). *Digital No. 02HP01–03,* 2002. Three pairs of unmounted sheets; ink and burn marks on paper, each sheet 8 ft. 8 ¾ in. × 26 ¾ in. (266.1 × 67.9 cm). Private collection, New York [Exhib.]

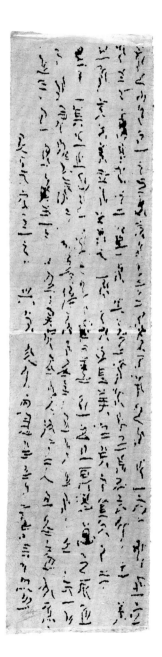

Fig. 44a–c. From left to right: calligraphic characters executed in ink on paper; calligraphic characters burned into translucent paper; the layered sheets, constituting the left-hand scroll of Wang Tiande's triptych *Digital No. 02HP01–03*

Fig. 45. Song Dong (b. 1966). *Printing on Water (Performance in the Lhasa River, Tibet, 1996)*, 1996. Thirty-six chromogenic prints, each 23 ¾ × 15 ¾ in. (60.5 × 39.9 cm). The Metropolitan Museum of Art, New York, Promised Gift of Cynthia Hazen Polsky (L.2011.70.6) [Exhib.]

character-building act, a way of recentering oneself that might be likened to the practice of meditation. Song Dong (b. 1966) has long viewed calligraphy as a kind of ritual in which the act is more important than the physical trace. This attitude is reflected in his performances, which are by nature evanescent and epitomized by his *Water Diary*.[58] Since 1995, Song has kept a diary written in water on a stone. As the water dries, the text vanishes. As a child Song first learned calligraphy in this manner to conserve paper; as an adult he has revived this practice as a form of meditation.

Although born in the same year that the Cultural Revolution began, Song was nonetheless able to take painting lessons as a child and eventually studied oil painting at Capital Normal University, Beijing.[59] There, his academic style of figural painting attracted attention, and Song had a work exhibited in the "China/Avant-Garde" exhibition in 1989, the year of his graduation. But the suppression of the pro-democracy demonstrations in Tiananmen Square that June coupled with his increasing exposure to Western contemporary art led him gradually to abandon his classical training and to experiment with performance and installation art.

Like *Water Diary*, Song's *Printing on Water (Performance in the Lhasa River, Tibet, 1996)* explores the impact of transcribed words that leave no semantic trace (**FIG. 45**).[60] This site-specific performance was recorded in a set of thirty-six photographs that show the artist repeatedly stamping the Lhasa River in Tibet with a large wood seal carved with the Chinese character for water (*shui* 水).[61] According to the artist, the idea for this work came to him while attending an artists' symposium in Lhasa that examined the human impact on the natural world. He learned from speaking with local residents of an annual ritual held on the fourth day of the fourth lunar month, when small statues of the Shakyamuni Buddha are immersed in the river. When the statue is in the water, the river bears the image of the Buddha; when it is removed, the essence of the Buddha remains.

Song adapted this idea by first writing out a large regular-script version of the character *shui*, then having local craftsmen carve it into wood. In his mind, stamping the river with this symbol, which was meant to represent the pure concept of water, became a way of ritually purifying it as it made its way from the Tibetan highlands to Beijing, where it arrives much polluted owing to man's intrusions. In actuality the Lhasa River joins the Yarlung, or Brahmaputra, River, which flows into the Bay of Bengal, but in the artist's conception, it represented the headwaters of China's great rivers that, figuratively at least, flowed to Beijing — from whence political control flowed back to Tibet.

Fig. 46. Zhang Huan (b. 1965). *Family Tree*, 2001. Nine chromogenic prints, each 21 × 16 ½ in. (53.3 × 41.9 cm). Yale University Art Gallery, New Haven, Leonard C. Hanna, Jr., Class of 1913, Fund [Exhib.]

Song carried out this performance twice: first, before a large audience; then, in front of a camera operated by his wife, the artist Yin Xiuzhen (b. 1963). To stage this second performance, Song and Yin rode bicycles to a spot about ten kilometers outside the center of Lhasa, where the camera would capture an image that included water, mountains, and traces of man's presence — power lines and a broadcasting tower visible on the far shore. He stamped continuously for one hour — enough time to meditate on man's impact on the natural world — without knowing when Yin would hold down the shutter release. The pictures represent thirty-six of thirty-eight sequential frames on a single roll of film that was exposed over about thirty seconds. This sequence of images recalls a cinematographic record that has been slowed down to the point that one sees the individual frames.

Song went on to explain that his posture, seated cross-legged in a shallow portion of the river, echoes that of the Buddha, while the replication of his image recalls the Thousand Buddhas motif — a metaphor for the potential of all sentient beings to achieve Buddhahood.[62]

Printing on Water is one of a number of the artist's performances that invoke Buddhist or Daoist concepts, and like Fung Mingchip's *Heart Sutra* serves as a striking reminder that both Chan Buddhism and Daoism, which advocates harmonizing the self with natural principles, have been important sources of inspiration for contemporary Chinese artists. Song's intention may have been to link traditional religious practice with a greater awareness of and reverence for the natural environment, but by eschewing didacticism in favor of "a gentle, if not absurd sense of subversion," *Printing on Water* offers an effective commentary on words as powerful linguistic markers that place objects and people within a specific cultural context.[63] Thus, the act of stamping the Chinese word for "water" onto a Tibetan river may be read as a response to China's efforts to assert its cultural hegemony over Tibet. When asked about this piece in an interview in 2009, Song's response was elusive: "Large seals often symbolize power. I exerted great force [in stamping the seal on the water,] but in the end left no trace."[64]

The power of the Chinese language to assert political claims over a region's identity finds a parallel in *Family Tree* by Zhang Huan (b. 1965), a work that suggests how language and culture can intrude upon personal identity to such a degree that they obscure individuality (**FIG. 46**). Born in Anyang, Henan Province, Zhang was raised almost entirely in the countryside, and in high school an aptitude for sketching enabled him to receive after-school training in what he has described as "Soviet-style" art. He went on to study painting at Henan University, graduating in 1988, and moved to Beijing in 1991, where he earned his master's degree from the Central Academy of Fine Arts in 1993. For the next several years, Zhang engaged in a number of powerful performance pieces featuring his naked body, including *12 Square Meters* (1994) in which he sat for an hour — covered with honey and fish oil — in a public latrine full of flies, and *65 Kilograms* (1994), in which he was suspended in chains from a ceiling while a nurse drew his blood and allowed it to drip onto a hot skillet.[65] In 1998 an invitation to participate in Asia Society's "Inside Out" exhibition enabled Zhang to move to the United States, where, constrained by both racial stereotyping and his inability to speak English, he confronted the need to define both himself and his art within a new cultural milieu. He discovered that "whenever Chinese contemporary art is discussed in a Western cultural context, 'Chinese' always comes before 'art,' which says a lot about its status in international forums." But he recognized that "artists are also representatives of their culture." Limited in his ability to articulate his identity through spoken language, Zhang invoked the primacy of his body as a medium of communication: "The body is the proof of one's identity, so the corporeal self is the most essential component in my works. But the way my body is presented in an artwork and the message it carries is entirely determined by my mind. My objective is to establish the relationship between the body and life."[66]

With *Family Tree*, made less than two years after his move to New York, Zhang offered his face as a surface on which words, names, and stories connected to his cultural heritage are, literally, written. The result is a trenchant commentary on how the individual is conditioned and categorized by his inherited culture. This performance piece is documented in nine photographs that record the gradual obscuring of Zhang's face with inked words until it is completely blackened. Among these words and phrases, which were specified by Zhang and transcribed by three calligraphers, are those that have overt cultural or political associations, including four characters on his forehead that refer to a well-known fable often invoked by Mao Zedong.[67] Most, however, derive from the ancient Chinese art of physiognomy, which seeks to map personality traits and divine the future based on the shape of one's facial features. For example, a line of characters marking the location of moles on his lower forehead includes those for "wife" (*furen* 夫人), "prosperity" (*lu* 禄), "good fortune" (*fu* 福), and "guest" (*keren* 客人), while on the bridge of his nose is the character for "auspicious" (*ji* 吉). But rather than elucidate Zhang's character and fate, these traditional divinatory marks ultimately obscure his identity beneath a dense layer of culturally conditioned

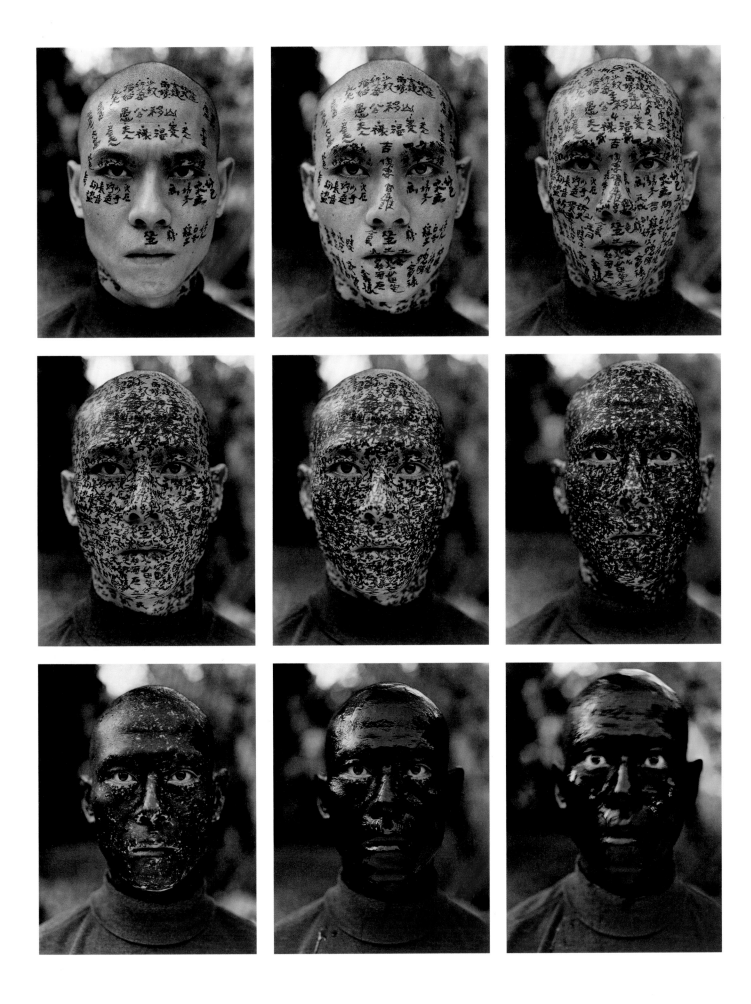

Fig. 47. Liu Dan (b. 1953). *Dictionary*, 1991. Ink and watercolor on paper, 81 ⅛ in. × 10 ft. (206 × 304.8 cm). Collection of Akiko Yamazaki and Jerry Yang [Exhib.]

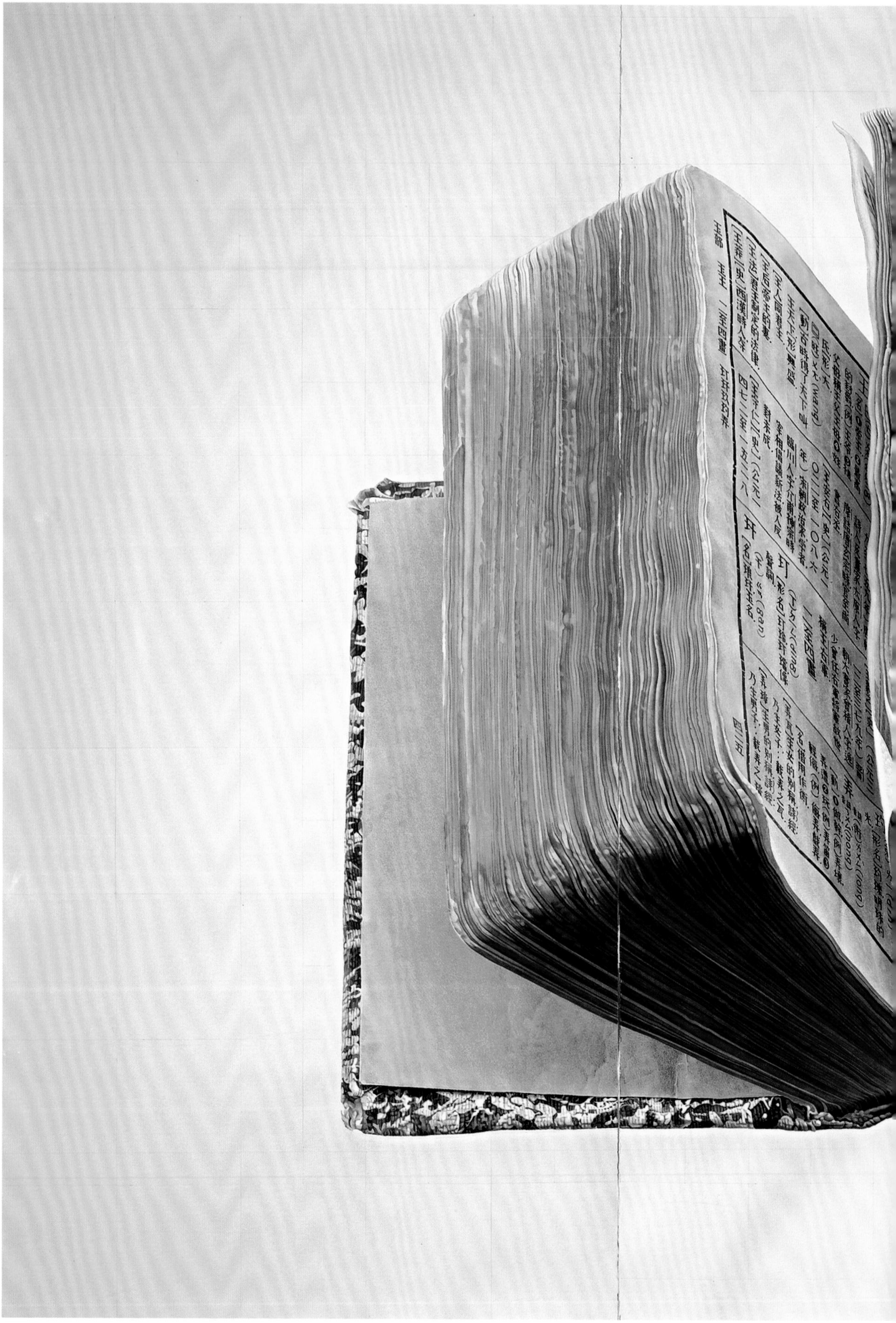

references: "My face turned black. My appearance disappeared as well. Nobody knew the color of my skin, and it was as if my identification no longer existed. I disappeared."[68]

Because both his body and mind have been conditioned by his race and his upbringing, Zhang's autonomy as an individual is constantly in danger of being overwhelmed by his heritage. His dilemma is that of all artists: How does one continually redefine oneself and reinvent one's art to escape from mere imitation of past models, or the even more insidious danger of self-imitation, in which an artist merely perpetuates his "brand"?

A final subtle commentary on how language influences the cultural identity and personal freedom of its users is emblematically displayed in Liu Dan's (b. 1953) monumental image of a dictionary from 1991 (FIG. 47). Born in the cosmopolitan city of Nanjing, Liu brings an entirely different sensibility to the treatment of words that reflects his combined passion for both Western and traditional Chinese art. Liu's father was a college chemistry professor, and his mother taught high school English. Their heavy teaching schedules meant that Liu and his three siblings were left in the care of their paternal grandfather, a Confucian-style gentleman who instilled in them a sense of moral rectitude and discipline, in part through the rigorous study of calligraphy, which he regarded not as art but as a way of training the mind.[69] At the same time, Liu developed an early interest in Western art, which he encountered entirely from books. A pencil drawing he made at the age of thirteen after an illustration in *Cyrano de Bergerac* reveals a precocious talent (FIG. 48), but the outbreak of the Cultural Revolution that year interrupted his artistic pursuits.[70] He joined the Red Guard and engaged in struggles with rival factions for two years before being sent to the countryside to be "reeducated" by the peasants. For nearly ten years Liu lived in rural surroundings but found ways to return intermittently to Nanjing, where he met the noted artist Ya Ming (1924–2002) about 1973, becoming his assistant in 1976.[71] When the Cultural Revolution ended, Ya Ming resumed his post as vice director of the Jiangsu Painting Academy in Nanjing; Liu was admitted to the program in 1978, becoming a star pupil in *guohua*. In 1981 he married Elizabeth Wichmann, a scholar of Chinese theater and the first Westerner permitted to perform with a Beijing opera troupe. The couple soon moved to Honolulu, and Liu, suddenly free of political constraints but newly burdened with creating a viable career in the West, accepted portrait commissions and made landscapes inspired by the volcano Haleakala. His breakthrough came in 1987–88, when he applied his meticulous drawing style to a greatly enlarged landscape composition inspired by the monumental imagery of traditional Chinese painting.[72]

Fig. 48. Liu Dan (b. 1953). *Copy of Book Illustration from "Cyrano de Bergerac,"* 1966. Pencil on paper, 7 ⅞ × 5 ⅞ in. (20 × 14.8 cm). Collection of the artist

A similarly meticulous aesthetic informs Liu's *Dictionary*. At the time he had just finished his monumental *Ink Handscroll* (SEE FIG. 52) and decided to try using watercolors for the first time, choosing a small family dictionary as his subject. Published about 1937, the dictionary contained neither simplified characters nor Communist-inflected rhetoric. As Liu has observed, "It was *pure* in its explanations. No ideological references in its definitions! That's why I liked it so much."[73] He claims that, rather than selecting which pages of the book to illustrate, he allowed it to fall open naturally, to one page that mentions Wang Xizhi, the patriarch of Chinese calligraphy, and the poet-painter Wang Wei (699–759); and to another page with words that use the water radical (*shui* 水), including those that make reference to Liu's home province of Jiangsu and to Napoleon (one may see the word "Waterloo" reproduced in English).

To create such a precise rendering of the book, Liu squared a six-by-nine-inch pencil drawing for transfer to a larger format.[74] Characters were sketched first in pencil, then filled in with light ink. Gradually, Liu added color — subtle washes to suggest the yellowed tones of the paper; darker tones for the red endpaper and the frayed textile cover — effects that establish temporality and indicate use.[75] Finally, he went over the characters in dark ink. While the resulting image appears almost hyperrealistic, Liu insists he was not interested in capturing how an object might look through a camera lens. Rather, his artistry lies in shifting from a macroscopic to a microscopic way of looking — examining an ordinary object methodically and painstakingly, then using his art to transform it into something monumental.[76] Juxtaposed with Xu Bing's *Book from the Sky* and other works that subvert the semantic power of the written word, Liu Dan's *Dictionary* presents a nostalgic view of the Chinese language before the interventions of the Maoist era — before language was both uncoupled from its past and, through censorship and propaganda, forced to adopt definitions imposed by strictly enforced dogmas that nonetheless changed constantly with shifting Communist party agendas.

NEW LANDSCAPES

China is arguably the most human landscape on earth. Continuously inhabited from the dawn of prehistory, it is impossible to sink a spade into the earth without turning up some artifact from the past. Since the rise of agriculture, China's loess hills have been terraced into fields and its lowlands honeycombed with rice paddies — interventions that required the labor of generations to build walls, excavate canals, and tame flood-prone rivers. This manpower also built a formidable array of urban environments — walled cities that were the centers of distinctive regional cultures. Rising above the expanse of farmland and cities are the mountains: revered dwelling place of immortals, reservoirs of cosmic energy (*qi*), and the ideal site for temples, tombs, and spiritual renewal. For more than one thousand years, Chinese depictions of landscape have taken mountains and the streams and rivers that flow from them as their principal motifs — the ultimate expression of nature's majesty. But the natural hierarchy envisioned by Chinese artists was incomplete without a human presence. Farmers, fishermen, travelers, monks, and scholars or their traces — pavilions, retreats, boats, or pathways — are an integral part of most landscape imagery, while in more symbolic works elements such as pines, bamboo, and plum, but also flowers, rocks, birds, and animals, were adopted by artists as metaphors for human values, either their own or those of the painting's recipient. Thus, a painting of a pine might be understood as a "portrait" of an individual's steadfast convictions and character. And while the transience of individual lives is mirrored in the cycle of seasons or in the growth, maturity, and decay of a tree, the mountains and rivers represent the eternal face of nature to which humankind also belongs. This natural hierarchy was the model of the well-ordered state, and so landscape imagery long served as a metaphor for the political world and the individual's place within it — either prospering in a summer scene or living as a recluse through a desolate winter.

Today the landscape of China is being transformed in ways that were unimaginable for most of its history. Cities have morphed into multimillion-person metropolises; highways and high-speed railways crisscross the country; mountains have been leveled; great rivers have been dammed; and the proliferation of power plants, factories, and commercial enterprises has led to an explosion in both prosperity and pollution. These dramatic changes to the environment have engendered a new consciousness that has found expression in a diversity of art forms.

All the artists considered here have invoked traditional media or imagery in ways that anchor them to a distinctly Chinese vision of nature. Those working with the most traditional of these formats — ink on paper — have responded to its considerable challenges, establishing individual styles that extend the legacy of earlier masters, most successfully by quoting visionary landscapes or redeploying the forms and brush conventions of literati painting. Others have transcended their models to create startling new images that bespeak the expressive potential of this ancient medium.

Vast in scale, subject matter, and ambition, Ren Jian's (b. 1955) *Primeval Chaos*, completed in 1988, sought to define a new role for traditional painting commensurate with the opportunities heralded by Deng Xiaoping's political and economic initiatives following the bleak days of the Cultural Revolution. Ren spent much of his early life in China's northernmost provinces, and this had a profound effect on his work; one might say that his vision was shaped quite literally by his environment. Ren and his family moved from Huazi, Liaoning, to Harbin, Heilongjiang, when he was in elementary school. He remained there through college, earning undergraduate and graduate degrees in *guohua* at the Lu Xun Academy of Fine Arts. After graduating in 1983, he was assigned to the Heilongjiang Painting Academy. The next year, Ren helped found the Northern Art Group. Comprising artists working in Harbin and led by Ren's schoolmate Shu Qun (b. 1958) along with fellow Harbin native Wang Guangyi (b. 1957), the group advocated the revitalization of China's traditional culture by declaring "a revolt against the art of the temperate zones."[1] They recognized in Northern Civilization an inherent "masculine strength" and sought to make works that embodied this quality, which they saw as the antidote to the "effeminate" traditions in both Eastern and Western civilizations. In their writings the group asserted the need for a new kind of "rational painting" that exhibited the same cool purity and austere objectivity as the stark landscapes of northern China. In Wang Guangyi's series *Northern Wastelands* (1985), for example, abstracted figures move through mysterious, bleak environments that are strongly reminiscent of Surrealist imagery (**FIG. 49**).

Liu Dan (b. 1953). *Ink Handscroll*, 1990
(fig. 52, detail)

Fig. 50. Ren Jian (b. 1955). *Primeval Chaos*, 1987–88.
Handscroll; ink on polyester, 59 in. × 98 ft. 5 in.
(150 × 3000 cm). Hong Kong Museum of Art, donated
by Ms. Wong Ying-Kay, Ada [Exhib.]

Fig. 49. Wang Guangyi (b. 1957). *Frozen North Pole*,
from the series *Northern Wastelands*, 1985. Oil on
canvas, 26 ¾ × 33 ⅞ in. (68 × 86 cm). Private collection

Visions of an amorphous world with vaguely defined figures also characterize Ren's *Primeval Chaos* (**FIG. 50**). Measuring nearly five feet tall and one hundred feet long, the scroll has been described as depicting the creation of the universe from its philosophical conception (*daohua*) to its materialization (*wuhua*) to its humanization (*renhua*).[2] Ren's cosmic vision follows the format and medium of traditional painting, but the scale and subject matter owe nothing to earlier Chinese art forms. The scroll blends Eastern and Western imagery — cosmic spheroids and mandala-like drawings; swirling vortices and hovering clouds; bearlike beasts (**FIG. 51**) and a confronting phoenix and dragon — in a succession of crescendos as it unrolls from left to right, a departure from the right-left orientation of traditional handscrolls.[3] Further distancing the work from Chinese precedents is the use of Western-style chiaroscuro to describe the clouds, hills, and other landscape elements. Having created the painting to fulfill his graduation requirement from the department of *guohua,* Ren has worked predominantly in oil ever since, and has returned only recently to ink as a medium.

Liu Dan's *Ink Handscroll* of 1990 is similar in scale, medium, and ambition, and applies Western techniques and imagery to a Chinese medium and format (**FIG. 52**). He began work on the painting, which is more than fifty-eight feet in length, shortly after the demonstrations in Tiananmen Square

were crushed by military intervention; it took more than a year to complete.[4] Liu is said to have been inspired by the form of a flickering candle flame, which may be why he chose to begin the scroll with roiling jets of cinnabar pigment and plumes of white, as if the landscape were erupting from a volcano or forged in fire.[5] As the scroll unfurls, the red dissipates into grays and blacks, while the white areas morph into shapes suggestive of clouds, watercourses, jagged ice outcrops, or crystalline inclusions but, almost never, patches of sky. Here, Liu presents an uninhabitable world with no sign of human occupation.

To create this convoluted vision, Liu began by squaring a small pencil sketch (**FIG. 53**) for transfer to the full-size scroll, which he affixed to the walls of his studio (**FIG. 54**). He used thread stretched between pins to re-create the grid at a larger scale and then transferred the design using faint ink lines or dots (**FIG. 55**). Only then did Liu begin the slow process of filling in the forms with texture strokes and pale washes: "First I must prepare the stage, then I can dance on it."[6] The landscape is modeled using marks of uniform thickness created by applying a constant amount of pressure to the brush tip, which remains centered in each line (*zhongfeng*) — a method derived from calligraphy. While the hatch marks recall Western methods of shading, there is no consistent light source. Instead, the shifting tonalities of ink represent a rhythmic interplay of positive and negative patterns that defy any logical reading of mass or

Fig. 51. Detail of *Primeval Chaos*

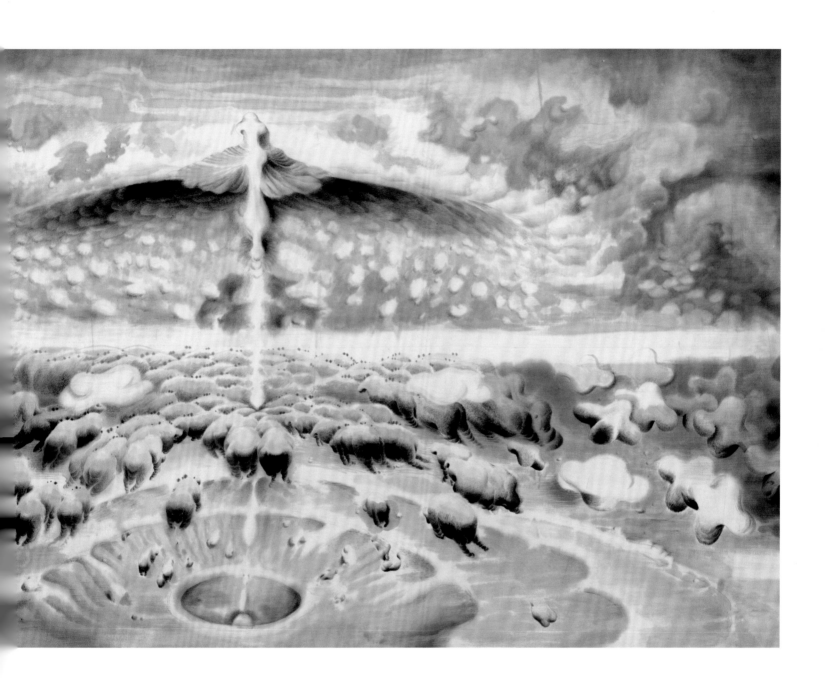

Overleaf: Fig. 52. Liu Dan (b. 1953). *Ink Handscroll*, 1990. Handscroll; ink and color on paper, 37 ¾ in. × 58 ft. 4 in. (95.6 × 1780 cm). The San Diego Museum of Art, Museum purchase (1998.1) [Exhib.]

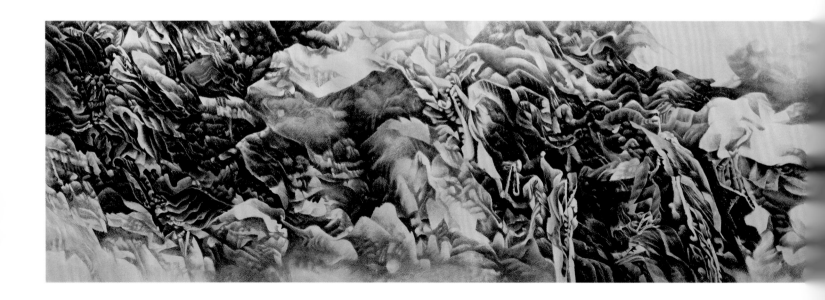

Fig. 53. Liu Dan (b. 1953). Detail of study for *Ink Handscroll*, 1990. Pencil on paper, 3 ½ × 65 ¾ in. (9 × 167 cm). Collection of Alexandra Munroe [Exhib.]

Fig. 54. Installation view of *Ink Handscroll* (in progress) in Liu Dan's studio, Honolulu, ca. 1990

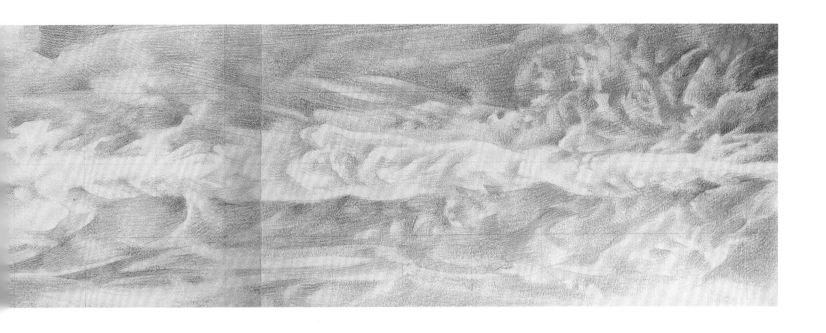

Fig. 55. Detail of *Ink Handscroll* showing
traces of underdrawing

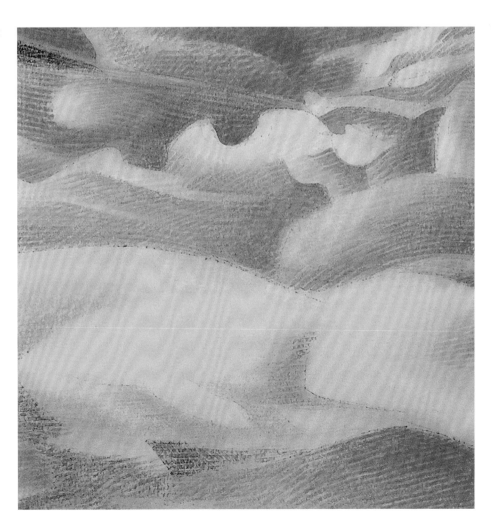

space. Liu's intense focus on the individual brush marks allows him to "shift the perspective of landscape painting . . . to the microcosmic level," thereby revealing its "inside complexity."[7]

The painting is often compared to the work of the Nanjing artist Gong Xian (1619–1689), whose brooding landscapes are likewise methodically built up of monochrome hatch marks (FIG. 56). But Liu claims that Gong is not an artist he has studied in particular, and that he has found greater inspiration in the fantastic landscapes of the late Ming artist Wu Bin, who was active in Nanjing from about 1583 to 1626 (FIG. 57). While one may see certain resonances with past masters in his work, Liu's landscapes remain uniquely his own. He has said, "I don't think I'm part of the literati tradition. . . . I belong to myself, I belong to my art. Being part of a legacy has no limitations."[8]

Shao Fan's (b. 1964) *Landscape* of 2009 shares many of the attributes that define the works of Ren Jian and Liu Dan (FIG. 58). Large in scale, *Landscape* combines meticulous technique, compositional complexity, and a tension between representation and abstraction. It also evokes a traditional style and subject without relying on the direct appropriation of an earlier master's idiom.

Shao was exposed to art from an early age: both his parents taught Soviet-style oil painting at the Central Academy of Fine Arts, and his father had a collection of traditional painting, calligraphy, and furniture, which he was able to retain during the Cultural Revolution owing to his high status in the Communist party. Shao's talent led him first to the Beijing School of Applied Arts, then to the Art and Craft Research Institute (*Gongyi meishu yanjiusuo*) in Beijing, where he studied wood carving and porcelain making.[9] Much of what he studied at school, however, he subsequently began to rethink: "I realize now that my education was Western. As I got older I wanted to move away from a Western aesthetic — the aesthetic that academics in China teach and which is espoused by most contemporary artists. I had to learn by myself how to be a Chinese artist, by trial and error."[10]

Landscape, a monochrome composition of heavily foliaged trees and looming cliffs shrouded in cloud, is unique in Shao's oeuvre. According to the artist it was inspired by *Summer Mountains amid Mist and Rain* by Wang Hui (1632–1717), particularly its middle section (FIG. 59).[11] Like that work, *Landscape* is concerned with the expressive potential of painting rather than the realistic representation of nature — a literati ideal succinctly expressed a generation before Wang's time by Dong Qichang (1555–1636), who declared, "In discussions of wondrous scenery, painting is no match for nature, but if what one is discussing is the wonders of brush and ink, then nature cannot compete with painting."[12]

Despite the influence of these precedents, Shao's painting subtly subverts the customary literati context for judging his work and betrays the influence of Western art forms. Its large scale and square format are decidedly Western, and, more significantly, instead of using brush and ink, it is painstakingly built up of thousands of pencil marks applied, over two months' time, like the hatch marks of a Western engraving (FIG. 60).[13] In effect, Shao has created a traditional Chinese image using an entirely Western medium. A further departure from traditional sources is the fact that Shao has inverted one of Wang Hui's picture elements so that when the painting is turned upside down, it remains equally legible as a depiction of a looming cliff and cloud-filled grotto: what previously appeared to be the white trunks of trees now reads as rivulets and waterfalls (FIG. 61). This attribute not only points up the essential abstraction of literati painting but also may imply the fundamental uncertainty and ambiguity of life during troubled times, when established values and assumptions are upended — just as they were in the time of Wang Hui, when the Ming dynasty was overthrown and the Manchus established the Qing dynasty (1644–1911). But Shao's hybrid vision, which combines old and new, East and West, may also promise a way to transcend life's uncertainties. Describing a secluded vale beyond the reach of the modern world, *Landscape* conceals an alternative universe that, like a Daoist paradise, awaits discovery amid our mundane existence.[14]

The influence of Daoist thought pervades the work of Qiu Shihua (b. 1940), whose minimalistic paintings elude categorization just as their liminal content evades easy detection. Executed in oil — often on unprimed canvas — with barely detectable brushstrokes, each is created through the application of many layers of dilute, semitransparent paint until the underlying landscape details that Qiu has painted in black or colors all but vanish in the overall whiteness of the composition. And while this monochromy — sometimes glowing, sometimes muted — might recall a late Turner seascape or an Impressionist evocation of light, the paintings do not represent retinal views of the external world. Rather, they are "mind landscapes" — images that have materialized from the artist's imagination and are meant to induce meditative engagement.[15]

Born in Sichuan in the midst of World War II, Qiu attended the Xi'an Art Academy, where he studied Socialist Realist oil painting. After graduating in 1962, he spent the next twenty-two years in Tongchuan, a bleak coal-mining town north of Xi'an, where he painted posters and large-scale billboards for the local cinema. In 1984 he was offered a job in Shenzhen, a special economic zone near Hong Kong, and three

Fig. 56. Gong Xian (1619–1689). *A Thousand Peaks and Myriad Ravines*, Qing dynasty (1644–1911), ca. 1670. Hanging scroll; ink on paper, 24 ⅜ × 40 ⅛ in. (62 × 102 cm). Museum Rietberg, Zurich, Gift of Charles A. Drenowatz

Fig. 57. Wu Bin (active ca. 1583–ca. 1626). *Frontal View*, from *Ten Views of a Fantastic Rock*, Ming dynasty (1368–1644), dated 1610. Section of a handscroll; ink on paper, scroll 21 ⅞ in. × 31 ft. ¼ in. (55.5 × 945.8 cm). Private collection

Fig. 58. Shao Fan (b. 1964). *Landscape*, 2009.
Pencil on paper, 62 ¼ × 62 ¼ in. (158 × 158 cm).
The Metropolitan Museum of Art, New York, Gift
of Frank Kong Siu Ming, 2011 (2011.100) [Exhib.]

Fig. 59. Wang Hui (1632–1717). *Summer
Mountains amid Mist and Rain*, Qing dynasty
(1644–1911), dated 1681. Ink on paper,
54 × 24 ¾ in. (137.2 × 63 cm). Tianjin Museum

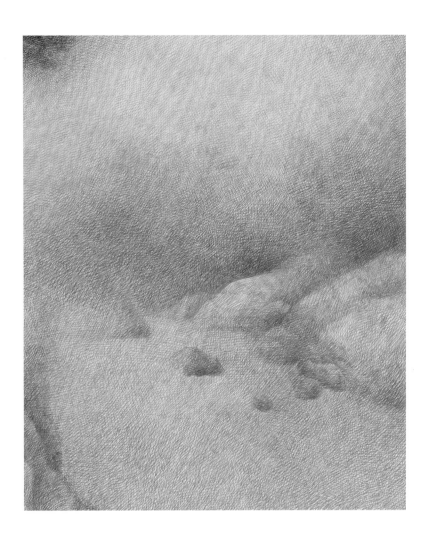

Fig. 60. Detail of *Landscape* showing hatch marks

Fig. 61. *Landscape*, inverted

years later went to Europe for the first time. There, he sought out not contemporary art but the French Impressionists, whom he appreciated for their ability to convey qualities of light. But Qiu, who had been introduced to Daoism by his father, was more influenced by a subsequent trip to the Gobi Desert, and by a Daoist master whom he met in 1991 and credits with helping him open new vistas in his artistic vision.[16]

Unlike Western-style landscapes, which are usually "windows" on to a scene, Qiu's timeless compositions reveal themselves incrementally; there is no single vanishing point or mathematical perspective.[17] They are built up of complementary opposites such as light and dark, yin and yang, mass and void, all of which have been reduced to traces.[18] Qiu has described these works as "simple and pale, calm and empty. All being and non-being is hidden in them, completely self-contained."[19] Qiu achieves this heightened state of perception through Daoist meditation, the practice of which he finds possible in both the making and the viewing of a painting: "When I paint I do not think of structure or theme, what I seek is a certain 'flavour' — a rhythm of spirit and energy, so that the soul drifts in the painting, like a shadow of the mind. Everything is flat and calm. 'Form' is unimportant. It is like being in meditation, when the entire cosmos looks like a white mist, and one finds oneself in a world of white light. Here, time and space seem to be annihilated. Human passions do not matter."[20] A work dated 1996 resembles the dimpled slope of a mountain rising steeply from a level foreground in a manner that recalls a traditional "high distance" perspective (FIG. 62).[21] Another, datable to about 2001, might be read as a grove of trees along a lakeshore (FIG. 63). In a third work, dated 2002, there is a strong intimation of the sun shining through a dense fog and reflecting off a foreground expanse of water (FIG. 64). All three share the aesthetic of "serene blandness" (*pingdan*), a quality most famously admired in the works of Ni Zan (1306–1374).[22] Ni's spare, monochrome paintings, brushed in pale, dry ink on paper, evoke stark wilderness settings with little or no indication of human habitation (FIG. 65). But Ni's minimal compositions are achieved by the restrained application of ink on blank paper, whereas Qiu obscures his pictorial content beneath layers of thin white paint. Never titled, Qiu's paintings remain purely visual experiences.

At the other extreme from the imaginary landscapes of Ren Jian, Liu Dan, Shao Fan, and Qiu Shihua are works that record the real world, to varying degrees of verisimilitude, through highly descriptive, even photorealistic, imagery. In traditional Chinese painting these two approaches were categorized as "drawings of ideas" (*xieyi*) and "drawings from life" (*xiesheng*). The former are identified with literati artists whose

Fig. 62. Qiu Shihua (b. 1940). *Untitled*, 1996. Oil on canvas, 45 ¼ × 71 ⅝ in. (115 × 182 cm). Sigg Collection [Exhib.]

Fig. 63. Qiu Shihua (b. 1940). *Untitled*, 2001?
Oil on canvas, 36 ¼ × 66 ¹⁵⁄₁₆ in. (92 × 170 cm).
M+ Sigg Collection, Hong Kong [Exhib.]

Fig. 64. Qiu Shihua (b. 1940). *Untitled*, 2002. Mixed
media on canvas, 31 ⅞ × 68 ½ in. (81 × 174 cm).
M+ Sigg Collection, Hong Kong [Exhib.]

Fig. 65. Ni Zan (1306–1374). *Wind among the Trees on the Riverbank*, Yuan dynasty (1271–1368), dated 1363. Hanging scroll; ink on paper, 23 ¼ × 12 ¼ in. (59.1 × 31.1 cm). The Metropolitan Museum of Art, New York, Bequest of John M. Crawford Jr., 1988 (1989.363.39)

calligraphic, nonrepresentational styles are fundamentally self-expressive, while the latter are most often associated with professional painters adept at highly descriptive representational styles. In both traditional and contemporary Chinese art, however, the recording of observed reality has always involved the intervention of artists, and how they manipulate and transform imagery ultimately becomes the defining feature of their creativity.

In contrast to Qiu Shihua's commitment to a kind of cerebral minimalism, Yang Jiechang (Yang Jiecang, b. 1956) has experimented with both abstract and meticulous photorealist works executed in a hypercoloristic palette. A prime example of the latter is *Crying Landscape*, Yang's 2002 series of five huge triptychs depicting modern landscape scenes (**FIG. 66**).[23]

Yang was schooled in traditional Chinese art as a child and has continued to explore the medium of ink throughout his career. Born and raised in Foshan, Guangdong Province, Yang applied his knowledge of *guohua* and calligraphy to writing big-character posters for the Red Guard during the Cultural Revolution. He continued his studies at the Foshan Folk Art Research Institute (1974–78) and the Guangzhou Academy of Fine Arts (1978–82). After graduating, Yang taught Chinese painting in the meticulous style (*gongbi*) at the academy until 1988, but his mastery of traditional craftsmanship was counterbalanced by the rebellious, iconoclastic spirit of the Red Guard. Rejecting the mere perpetuation of inherited methods, Yang recognized that, "psychologically speaking, Chinese ink painting students had a bit of an inferiority complex, because they felt that, compared to students studying sculpture or oil painting, it was much more difficult for them to be in sync with contemporary art trends." He "soon realized that you had to find your own path."[24] In 1989 he was invited to participate in the exhibition "Magiciens de la terre" at the Centre Georges Pompidou in Paris, which, together with his marriage to Martina Köppel, a residency permit from Germany, and the suppression of the democracy movement in Tiananmen Square, led Yang to remain in Europe. He currently resides in Paris and Heidelberg.[25]

Since the 1980s, Yang has worked in a variety of forms and media — painting, collage, installation, performance, and sculpture — but an overriding concern has been "how to implant Chinese traditional painting, traditional Chinese aesthetics and thought into a contemporary context."[26] Throughout, Yang has remained committed to "individual expression and self-improvement," an ideal that resonates with Confucian values: "I am very interested in the idea of traditional literati. They thought about art, not about specific works. They used art to refine themselves."[27]

Fig. 66. Yang Jiechang (b. 1956). *Crying Landscape*, 2002. Set of five triptychs; ink and color on paper, each triptych 9 ft. 10 ⅛ in. × 16 ft. 4 ⅞ in. (300 × 500 cm). Private collection, New York [Exhib.]

Fig. 66a. *Crying Landscape: BASF*

Fig. 66b. *Crying Landscape: Yangzi Dam*

Fig. 66c. *Crying Landscape: London*

Fig. 66d. *Crying Landscape: Las Vegas*

Fig. 66e. *Crying Landscape: Pentagon*

Fig. 67. Yang Jiechang (b. 1956).
Sketch for *Crying Landscape: Nuclear Power Plant*, 2002. Ink on paper

In *Crying Landscape* Yang deploys a *gongbi* version of the antique "blue-and-green" painting style on a grand scale to depict iconic buildings that connote political, industrial, or military power. Intended as a series of six triptychs, Yang had time to complete only five, but a sketch for the sixth image (**FIG. 67**) — number three in the envisioned sequence — makes possible a reconstruction of his original idea. First displayed at the 2003 Venice Biennale, the triptychs were hung from the ceiling in a sequence specified by Yang and accompanied by Johann Strauss's *The Blue Danube* waltz, punctuated by the sound of the artist's screams (**SEE FIG. 4**). While the *gongbi* technique and lush colors are visually ingratiating, the content, revealed gradually as one views each triptych in turn, leaves the viewer unsettled.[28]

As originally conceived, the first three triptychs present images of industrial power: an oil refinery, the great dam at the mouth of the Yangzi Gorges, and a nuclear power plant. The next three highlight emblems of political, commercial, and military power: the Houses of Parliament, a Las Vegas casino, and the Pentagon. Only in his final triptych — an image of the Pentagon as it appeared some weeks after the September 11 attack, together with a schematic image of the airliner at the moment of impact — does Yang's intention become explicit. While the damaged Pentagon renders palpable the threat of

terrorism, the vulnerability of the other buildings is hinted at more subtly. The refinery is silhouetted against a fiery sunset that could easily be mistaken for an actual conflagration; the Yangzi Gorges dam appears threatened by the arcing contrail of an incoming missile; Parliament is framed by the boughs of a blossoming tree, but the bursts of light from the streetlamps on the Westminster Bridge might be confused for bomb blasts; and the casino reduces New York City landmarks — the Statue of Liberty, Ellis Island, Grand Central Terminal, and the Empire State Building — from symbols of Western cultural and economic might to mere imitations, encircled by a roller coaster and the streaking lights of traffic. Yang, who witnessed the enormous suffering brought about by Mao's utopian vision of socialism, here undermines the promise of stability, prosperity, and security symbolized by these iconic buildings. Rendered in the saturated pigments associated with the "blue-and-green" landscape style, traditionally used in China to evoke an idyllic past, they appear, like so many of man's monuments to permanence and power, vulnerable, ephemeral, and subject to political or commercial (or artistic) exploitation.

In *30 Letters to Qiu Jiawa*, Qiu Zhijie similarly adopts a highly descriptive painting style to present an iconic image — the Nanjing Yangzi River Bridge — as an ironic commentary on

Fig. 68. Installation view of Qiu Zhijie's "Breaking the Ice," Ullens Center for Contemporary Art, Beijing, 2009

for Contemporary Art in Beijing in late 2009 (**FIG. 68**). Responding to the nine sets of pillars inside the space, Qiu created *30 Letters to Qiu Jiawa*, a series of thirty monumental ink paintings — ten triptychs — to hang within the intervening spaces defined by the columns along one side of the hall. Each triptych depicts one span of the bridge plus additional imagery that echoes the three-dimensional works that complete the installation (**FIG. 69**). Each painting also bears a terse statement directed to his daughter, who spent the first month of her life in the hospital, at the same time the artist was framing his proposal for the Ullens Center installation. It was amid such personal uncertainty and vulnerability, qualities at the fore of his research into suicide and the Nanjing Bridge, that Qiu conceived the work.[33]

The triptych featured here is the third in the series (**FIG. 70**). Above, below, and intermingling with a rendering of the bridge, unclear as to whether they compound or compromise its integrity, are images including magnets, pulleys, and coils; shells, seagulls, and rootlike strands; hourglasses; a conveyor belt; and naked children. Against this backdrop are the following messages to his daughter: "The future they describe is only towers in the sky"; "Don't try leaving the present"; and "You constantly need to go back to the past."

In the left-hand painting, which bears the first of the three phrases, is a whirling tower that recalls Vladimir Tatlin's (1885–1953) never-realized *Monument to the Third International* (1920) — an icon of Soviet Utopian ideals and a fitting complement to a structure that symbolized the same ideas of progress for China (**FIG. 71**). In Qiu's reimagining, Tatlin's tower appears to have spun into the bridge's structure, dissolving into strands that dangle above the water. That the monument and the bridge have become entangled might be an ironic comment on Mao's wish to elevate the status of the bridge to that of popular art — a criticism that Naum Gabo (1890–1977) leveled at Tatlin when his work first appeared: "Either build functional houses and bridges or create pure art or both. Don't confuse one with the other."[34]

Together, this triad of paintings presents a complex meditation on time and the human condition. One cannot envision the future as the Russian Futurists sought to do, but neither can one cling to the past or hold back the passage of time. But while we are destined to remain forever within the present, we can revisit the past in our memories. The arrow above the middle of the bridge points toward the future, but the seagull glances back to the past. Beneath it all, the river flows on. More concretely, Qiu's enormous set of paintings offers a poignant commentary on the changing landscape of

Fig. 69. Qiu Zhijie (b. 1969). *Zeno*, 2009. Roller, conveyor belt, fiberglass, magnet, and electric motor, 85 ft. 3 ⅝ in. × 29 ft. 6 ⅜ in. × 15 ¾ in. (2600 × 900 × 40 cm). Installation view, Ullens Center for Contemporary Art, Beijing, 2009

modern society. Qiu has sought throughout his body of work to reject a narrowly conceptual approach to art: "[Conceptual art] leads our attention to the content of the concept, rather than to the on-the-spot experience of art. Therefore, not only did we oppose bad conceptual art, we fought against 'conceptual art' itself."[29] Instead, Qiu has turned to complex installations that make use of objects and constructions that anchor his work in reality, even as their message remains multilayered and ambiguous. His goal has been to pursue what he calls "total art" (*zongti yishu*).[30]

Part of this exploration is the artist's ongoing project "A Suicidology of the Nanjing Yangzi River Bridge," initiated in 2007. The bridge, which opened in 1968 as the first modern highway and railway bridge to span the Yangzi River, was designed and built entirely by the Chinese and heralded by Chairman Mao as a symbol of New China's independence and progress. Its image became ubiquitous, emblazoned on currency, official documents, and articles of daily use. But the bridge is also the site of the highest number of suicides in China.[31] Qiu's project has led him to research the bridge's construction, to work with suicide-prevention volunteers, and to interview survivors and the families of suicides.

In 2008 Qiu's research culminated in the first of a series of large-scale installations.[32] The second of these, "Breaking the Ice," took place in the main exhibition hall of the Ullens Center

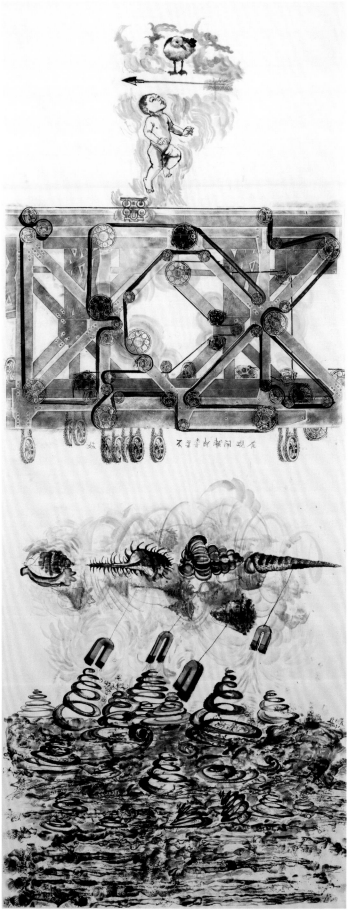

Fig. 70. Qiu Zhijie (b. 1969). *30 Letters to Qiu Jiawa,* 2009. Three hanging scrolls from a set of thirty; ink on paper, each 16 ft. 4 ⅞ in. × 74 ⅞ in. (500 × 190 cm). Private collection, New York [Exhib.]

Fig. 71. Model of Vladimir Tatlin's *Monument to the Third International,* 1920

Fig. 72. Duan Jianyu (b. 1970). *Go Home No. 3*,
2010. Oil on canvas, 47 ¼ × 98 ⅜ (120 × 250 cm).
Private collection

modern China and how national engineering achievements can bring with them unforeseen social consequences.

Iconic vistas excerpted from the Chinese landscape are at the heart of Duan Jianyu's (b. 1970) *Beautiful Dreams*, a series of intimate, unpretentious works that stand at the opposite extreme from the monumental installation art of Yang Jiechang and Qiu Zhijie. Duan grew up in a literary family in Zhengzhou, Henan Province. Her father was a novelist who wrote about his rural background, and her mother worked in a branch of the state-run New China (*Xinhua*) Bookstore, while her elder brother became a painter of local rural life.[35] Duan followed in her brother's footsteps and eventually enrolled in the department of oil painting at the Guangzhou Academy of Fine Arts (1991–95). She currently teaches oil painting at South China Normal University in Guangzhou.

Duan's works often depict rural China in a consciously naive, Westernized representational manner. She typically problematizes these scenes with humorous or provocative additions. In *Go Home No. 3* from 2010, for example, a water buffalo bearing a naked woman on its back stands amid peasants transplanting rice (**FIG. 72**).

Beautiful Dreams, executed in 2008, represents a distinct departure from her usual medium of oil on canvas. Painted in monochrome ink on pieces of flattened cardboard boxes, these images illustrate postcardlike landscape scenes: the "Welcoming-Guest Pine" on Mount Huang, Guilin's spindly karst-formation mountains reflected in the Li River, the Great Wall, and a Yunnanese pavilion juxtaposed with a bird

alighting on a bare tree branch (**FIGS. 73–76**).[36] Duan's treatment of each scene as a flat silhouette emphasizes the picture surface, as does the recycled cardboard, which is often stippled with depressions from its prior use. Like pictures from a tourist brochure, these clichéd images — virtual "brands" for package tours — are further trivialized by being rendered as though they were merely labels stamped onto the cardboard — the quintessential medium used to package commercial goods.

For all their seeming directness and simplicity, however, Duan's paintings challenge easy categorization or interpretation. On one level, the pieces comment on the insertion of traditional Chinese motifs into recycled media and the attendant vulgarization of the spiritual values of that heritage. But the beauty of Duan's carefully crafted paintings transcends their mundane medium and trite imagery. The "Welcoming-Guest Pine" is set within a composition defined by the creases and symmetrical leaves of the unfolded box, resembling a leaf from a traditional album (**FIG. 75**). The Guilin scene is even more artful in its use of the corrugated surface exposed by the ripped-away skin of the cardboard (**FIG. 74**). Set within this torn area as though viewed through a cave opening or revealed in a dream, the reflections of the mountains appear to shimmer and blur in the "waves" of the Li River, where a lone boatman poles his bamboo skiff.

Like Robert Rauschenberg (1925–2008), who first employed discarded cardboard boxes as an artistic medium in 1971, Duan's use of this disposable substance may offer a commentary on the cheap materialism of modern life.[37] Here,

Fig. 73. Duan Jianyu (b. 1970). *Beautiful Dream 3*,
2008. Ink on cardboard, 15 ⅜ × 21 ¼ in. (39 × 54 cm).
Sigg Collection [Exhib.]

Fig. 74. Duan Jianyu (b. 1970). *Beautiful Dream 4*, 2008. Ink on cardboard, 17 ¼ × 13 in. (44 × 33 cm). Sigg Collection [Exhib.]

Fig. 75. Duan Jianyu (b. 1970). *Beautiful Dream 7*,
2008. Ink on cardboard, 11 ½ × 17 ¼ in. (29 × 44 cm).
Sigg Collection [Exhib.]

Fig. 76. Duan Jianyu (b. 1970). *Beautiful Dream 2*,
2008. Ink on cardboard, 10 ¼ × 19 ¾ in. (26 × 50 cm).
Sigg Collection [Exhib.]

however, cardboard may represent more than the importation into China of the most superficial attributes of Western culture — its outer packaging without its original content. This commonplace material might also stand for a universal medium, which, thanks to Duan's intervention, now encompasses attributes of Chinese contemporary culture. Duan's sensitively rendered images ultimately reassert the redeeming value of art within a materialistic world.

The iconic role of landscape as an emblem of cultural identity is the message conveyed by Huang Yan's (b. 1966) *Chinese Landscape Tattoo* of 1999. This series of twelve photographs of Huang's torso and arms painted with a traditional landscape scene exemplifies the artist's "reincarnation" of literati-style painting (FIG. 77). The composition, modeled in ink and colors on a white ground by Huang's wife, the artist Zhang Tiemei (b. 1968), follows the natural form of Huang's body: a broad mountain covers his chest, two trees rising from belly to sternum; tall trees extend along both of his arms from wrist to shoulder; at the base of the trees on his left arm is a small house, while below the willow on his right is a seated gentleman lost in contemplation.

These photographs perform a function different from those of Zhang Huan's face as it becomes progressively darker from the inscriptions written on it (SEE FIG. 46). Huang's images are not a record of a creative performance; they merely present Huang in different poses that show different aspects of the painting — not one of which affords a view of the entire composition. With the artist's face cropped away in each photo, Huang's anonymous torso becomes an emblem of the Chinese everyman who cannot be separated from his cultural heritage, which, like his racial identity, is as indelible as a tattoo.

The issue of identity is fundamental to Huang's decision to have a literati-style landscape painted on his body. For Huang, as for the Chinese literatus, landscape painting is a form of self-expression and is therefore a reflection of who he is: "To paint a landscape is to paint man, to paint oneself. The landscape is the most authentic representation of [the literati] philosophy, of their personal way of conducting themselves in the world. Each mountain, each stone, each blade of grass, each tree acted as a conduit for the expression of their feelings. When I undertook to paint Chinese landscapes on my face, hands, and body, man was the subject, landscape was the object, a landscape painted on the human body was the materialization of the union between subject and object."[38]

For Huang, who grew up in Changchun, Jilin Province, where he studied *guohua* with a local artist from 1978 to 1980, the literati aesthetic still holds relevance. He acknowledges that for a period during his schooling at Changchun Normal University, he became involved in Western-style painting and Conceptual Art.[39] But starting in 1994, he returned to ancient Chinese painting styles for inspiration: "In the early 90s, while at home contemplating traditional versus contemporary art, I realized that they are actually very close. I started painting traditional Song and Yuan dynasty landscapes on the human face (1994), then the body (1995), and finally on canvas (1998). I was inspired by the possibilities of transferring traditional imagery onto 'human canvas,' which I viewed as a way to extend traditional narrative in a contemporary way. The usage of the body image is a reminder that China's artistic heritage is a part of every Chinese person. Combining the physical body with the spiritual landscape further explored the ancient and the intellectual values of the literati art movement."[40]

While Huang professes that China's cultural heritage is an inherent part of every Chinese person, his images also pose a question: Is Chinese culture more than skin deep, or is the adoption of cultural attributes merely a veneer? Just as Ai Weiwei's overpainting of a Han ceramic vessel with the Coca-Cola logo suggests that China's westernization is largely superficial (SEE FIG. 140), Huang's photographs contend that the same may be said of China's efforts to reassert traditional cultural values. Can one really recover the mind-set of the literatus, or do people merely pay lip service to tradition, which modern life makes increasingly inaccessible? Can one simply put on the brand of Chinese culture the way one would put on a pair of designer jeans? The commodification of culture is reinforced by Huang's use of the photographic medium itself, which, like a Warhol parody of a Campbell's Soup label, stresses that art has now become a commercial multiple.

For many Chinese artists, photography — regarded since its inception as the quintessential means by which to record reality — has been a versatile medium for creating powerful landscape images that can either subvert or intensify our perceptions of contemporary China. A striking example of this is the art of Shi Guorui (b. 1964). Shi's monochrome palette, horizontal compositions, and "idealized" images, which both reproduce and interpret the observed world, evince many points of similarity with traditional Chinese landscape painting and create a dynamic tension between the conceptual and documentary functions of this medium.[41]

Shi's interest in photography, which began while he took pictures of foreign visitors to the factory where he worked in his native Shanxi Province, led him to a degree in photography from Nanjing Normal University (1992). But a defining moment in Shi's life came late in 1998: "I had a very bad automobile

Fig. 77. Huang Yan (b. 1966). *Chinese Landscape Tattoo No. 2 and No. 4*, 1999. Two chromogenic prints, each 20 × 24 in. (50.8 × 61 cm). Private collection, New York [Exhib.]

Fig. 78. Shi Guorui (b. 1964). *Shanghai, China,*
15–16 October 2004, 2004. Unique camera obscura
gelatin silver print, 50 ¾ in. × 14 ft. 1 ¼ in. (129 ×
430 cm). M+ Sigg Collection, Hong Kong [Exhib.]

accident that reminded me of how fragile life is. The result was that it made me slow down and contemplate things. I had graduated from a university with a degree in fine arts photography so I knew about its history and early techniques. I was searching for something of a spiritual approach following my accident so the process of having to deal with the amount of time and effort it takes to create these large pinhole photographs seemed like the best approach I could think of."[42] In 1999 Shi spent eight months meditating and taking photographs at a Daoist temple on Mian Mountain; shortly afterward, he began experimenting with the camera obscura.[43] In 2002 Shi began creating monumental landscape panoramas — the Great Wall and Mount Everest — that recall the pristine images of Ansel Adams (1902–1984), whom Shi credits as an early influence.[44]

Shi's use of the camera obscura (Latin for "dark room"), an optical device developed in antiquity to project images, is a conscious return to a premodern stage in the evolution of photography.[45] In contrast to the rapid recording made possible by film and digital cameras, Shi invests a great deal of time in his process. He first determines the "ideal" image he wishes to record and where to site his vantage point, then he prepares a dark chamber with a pinhole for an aperture. The light that passes through this hole casts an upside-down, positive image onto the opposite wall, where Shi has attached a sheet of photographic paper with curved ends to ensure that the focal length — the distance from the aperture to the paper — is consistent. The scale of the image depends on its distance from the aperture, so to create a large-scale panorama Shi must construct a room-size chamber. Once the exposure is complete, Shi closes the aperture, rolls the paper, and places it in a light-safe bag until it can be developed in a specially constructed tank. An exposure may take many hours depending on the quality of the light and the diameter of the aperture. During this time Shi remains inside the darkened room, relying on his experience and intuition to decide when an image is properly exposed; there is no intervening lens or film, and each print is unique, appearing as a negative print in reverse. Shi's direct participation with his process has been likened to time-based art.[46]

Once developed, the resulting images are immediately recognizable and yet strikingly transformed by the twofold effects of the long exposure time: each print possesses a depth of field that is alien to the human eye in its uniform clarity, and any transient phenomena, including all signs of human life, fail to register. Consequently, Shi's prints evoke an otherworldly quietude that recalls Louis Daguerre's (1787–1851) nineteenth-century experiments with large-scale panoramic photographs, a similarity heightened by their high-contrast, black-and-white tonality and dramatic horizontal sweep.[47]

The tranquility of Shi's photographs is the direct result of his slowed-down technique. He deliberately chose this approach in response to the frenetic pace of contemporary China: "This is a spiritual experience for me, sitting inside the camera. I am not a practicing Buddhist but this is my form of meditation. This is my practice. . . . Modern photography is all about speed, capturing a moment in one-hundredth of a second, while the way I work connects me to an ancient process and things that are not fleeting."[48]

In his 2004 panorama of Shanghai (FIG. 78), an exposure time of nearly eight hours meant that none of the city's hyperactivity was recorded.[49] The Huangpu River, a busy shipping route that flows through the heart of the metropolis, appears empty and placid. The sky is without clouds, the highways are devoid of traffic, and the parks are deserted of people. Imposing in scale and timeless in its stillness, Shi's panorama recalls monumental Song dynasty landscapes that present idealized visions or dreamscapes of the natural world. In both art forms, what is conveyed is a vivid sense of the world's eternal aspect. Yet unlike Shi's images of the Great Wall or Mount Everest, which juxtapose man's diminutive presence with the vastness of nature, *Shanghai* presents the viewer with an entirely man-made vista that is a testimony to the explosive growth of China's cities. When Mao Zedong died in 1976, not a single building in China was taller than Shanghai's Park Hotel, which was built in the 1920s. Since that time, an astonishing proliferation of skyscrapers has created an "Architectural Great Leap Forward" or a "Second Cultural Revolution" that has drastically transformed China's urban environment.[50] These structures were created as proud emblems of China's emerging status as a world power, but in Shi's stark image, the intended grandeur of these extravagant structures, rising against a backdrop of faceless high-rises, suddenly feels hollow. The city bereft of human life — a forest of steles or some graveyard of modernity — bears mute testimony to an era that is now lost.

A more subtle but no less powerful vision of the dangers of rapid urbanization characterizes the work of Yang Yongliang (b. 1980). Yang was tutored in traditional Chinese painting and calligraphy from a very young age before receiving formal design training in high school and in the department of visual communications of the Shanghai Arts and Crafts College. After graduating in 2004, he and some classmates set up a studio that created several prize-winning experimental short films and published an instruction manual, *The Cathedral*, which set forth a detailed analysis of 3-D imaging graphics. Since that time, however, Yang has increasingly devoted himself to "painting" with photography.[51]

In contrast to Shi Guorui's "low-tech" approach to the photographic medium, Yang has used his knowledge of computer imaging to "paint" digitally manipulated photographs that evoke traditional Chinese landscapes in both imagery and format. In *View of Tide* from 2008, Yang's composite photograph takes the form of a panoramic handscroll that presents a succession of towering mountains wreathed in mist and surrounded by expanses of open water (FIG. 79). Yang's mountain forms, like those of his Song dynasty models, are conceived frontally and additively as a succession of overlapping light and dark planes arrayed vertically or diagonally to create the illusion of recession. His composition is a faithful re-creation of Zhao Fu's (active ca. 1131–62) handscroll *Ten Thousand Li of the Yangzi River* (FIG. 80).[52] Recession is further suggested by shifts in the scale of picture elements, and by the use of paler ink tones and a diminution in clarity of distant peaks to mimic the blurring effects of a moisture-laden atmosphere. Yang's scroll, like that of his model, ends with a surging wave (FIG. 81) that recalls the famed tidal bore that flows up the Qiantang River by Hangzhou, commemorated in numerous late Song paintings (FIG. 82). In Yang's photomontage, however, the magnified scale of the wave makes it resemble a threatening tsunami — an ominous reminder that nature often overpowers the human order, especially when mankind does not adequately respect it. Beyond this wave Yang has affixed two seals — a final reference to the traditional practice of inscribing one's work. One seal gives Yang's name in both Chinese and English; the other gives the title of the series to which this scroll belongs, *On the Quiet Water*.

Upon closer examination, Yang's majestic mountains are revealed to be composed of countless high-rise apartments and other buildings, while his "trees" are actually power-line

Fig. 79. Yang Yongliang (b. 1980). *View of Tide*, 2008. Inkjet print, 17 ¾ in. × 32 ft. 9 ¾ in. (45 × 1000 cm). M+ Sigg Collection, Hong Kong [Exhib.]

Fig. 80. Zhao Fu (active ca. 1131–62). *Ten Thousand Li of the Yangzi River*, Southern Song dynasty (1127–1279). Ink on paper, 17 ¾ in. × 32 ft. 6 ¾ in. (45.1 × 992.5 cm). The Palace Museum, Beijing

Fig. 81. Detail of the surging wave at the end of *View of Tide*

Fig. 82. Li Song (ca. 1170–1255). *Watching the Tide on a Moonlit Night*, Southern Song dynasty (1127–1279). Album leaf; ink and colors on silk, 8 ¾ × 8 ⅝ in. (22.3 × 22 cm). National Palace Museum, Taipei

Fig. 83. Detail of *View of Tide*

towers and construction cranes — the ubiquitous icons of New China (**FIG. 83**).[53] What initially appears to be a pristine image of nature's grandeur is suddenly revealed to be an entirely man-made environment (only the watery passages comprise images of actual waves and waterfalls). The repetitive buildup of these elements, particularly the apartments with their regular arrays of windows, bears a striking resemblance to the "raindrop" stippling that textures Song rock formations, while the cranes and towers resemble the craggy pines and decidu-ous trees featured in Song paintings. Unlike his Song model, however, Yang's urban environment offers neither a path through its densely packed world nor a single human being to provide companionship. His seemingly harmonious traditional landscape becomes an apocalyptic vision of urbanization — a landscape so overpopulated with anonymous structures that it can no longer support life.

Yang's landscape suggests that both the natural environ-ment and the traditional way in which nature was envisioned are in danger of being overwhelmed by the unchecked growth of a new megalopolis culture — that an ancient culture such as China's risks being transformed irrevocably into a "soulless state that is littered with concrete."[54] As Yang himself has observed: "If I love the city for its familiarity, I hate it even more for the staggering speed at which it grows and engulfs the environment. If I like traditional Chinese art for its depth and inclusiveness, I hate its retrogressive attitude. The ancients expressed their sentiments and appreciation of nature through landscape painting. As for me, I use my own landscape to criti-cize reality as I perceive it."[55]

In *Spring Festival along the River*, an album of thirty-four color images dated 2000, Hong Hao (b. 1965) similarly makes use of Song pictorial imagery, contrasting it with scenes of

Fig. 84. Hong Hao (b. 1965). *Spring Festival along the River,* 2000. Thirty-two leaves from an accordion album of thirty-four; chromogenic print, each leaf 14 ¼ × 12 ¼ in. (36.2 × 31.1 cm). Collection of David Solo [Exhib.]

Fig. 85. Detail of *Spring Festival along the River*

modern life, to comment on China's changing urban landscape (**FIG. 84**). A lifetime resident of Beijing, Hong began taking art classes in 1977, a year after the end of the Cultural Revolution. It was there that he was first introduced to both Western realism and Chinese *guohua*.[56] He went on to study at the Fine Arts High School affiliated with the Central Academy of Fine Arts (1981–85) before being admitted into the academy's printmaking department (1985–89), where he would have met Xu Bing, who graduated from the master's degree program in 1987.

Beginning with a snapshot of the Great Wall taken from an expressway outside Beijing, the album, which unfolds to create a single horizontal composition, documents a journey from suburban Beijing to the city center. These photographs alternate with scenes from the most famous cityscape painting of imperial China, a twelfth-century handscroll that imagines a similar journey from what is thought to be the Song capital of Kaifeng. The side-by-side presentation invites viewers to draw parallels between the ancient past and contemporary life (**FIG. 85**). In so doing, Hong juxtaposes the technology of the brush with that of the camera; ink painting with color photography; and scenes from a twelfth-century Chinese metropolis with contemporary Beijing. The album format highlights dichotomies between the ancient and the modern: his photographs explore monuments and signifiers of the past, including the Great Wall, the Gate of Heavenly Peace (Tiananmen), and the Old Bell Tower, intermingled with modern skyscrapers under construction, signposts and advertisements for local and multinational companies, and vehicles of mass transit. By presenting contemporary images alongside a celebrated example of ancient Chinese art, Hong examines attitudes toward progress and nostalgia, but whether he is championing one over the other remains ambiguous.

Ai Weiwei (b. 1957), on the other hand, is unequivocal in his criticism of China's rush to modernize, particularly the physical destruction and human disruption that have accompanied it. Ai was born in a courtyard house on Tofu Alley in Old Beijing, but his family was forced to move to Xinjiang Province when his father, the celebrated poet Ai Qing (1910–1996), was punished along with many other intellectuals in Mao's Anti-Rightist Campaign. The artist and his family lived in extreme poverty until 1976, when Ai Qing was rehabilitated and they were permitted to move back to Beijing. In 1978 Ai enrolled in the Beijing Film Academy and subsequently joined the artists' collective known as the Stars Group (*Xingxing huahui*), which advocated individuality and experimentation instead of following the prevailing Soviet Socialist Realist style. From 1981 to 1993 Ai lived in New York, studying at the Parsons School of Design and absorbing numerous artistic influences, most notably those of Allen Ginsberg, Andy Warhol, and Marcel Duchamp. Returning to Beijing in 1993 owing to the deteriorating health of his father, he collaborated with Hans van Dijk (1946–2002) and Frank Uyterhaegen (1954–2011) to found China Art Archives and Warehouse in 1998, and in 1999 established his own studio.[57] Since then he has been an outspoken advocate for free expression through blogs, social media, photographic documentation of his life, and exhibitions including "Fuck Off," which he curated as an alternative to the officially sponsored Shanghai Biennale in 2000.[58]

In Ai's view, Beijing has become "unfit for human habitation" because "the city's development lacks a human dimension."[59] His *Provisional Landscapes* vividly document the wholesale transformation of China's landscape by juxtaposing images of the old city as it is being destroyed with views of the new infrastructure that is taking its place (**FIG. 86**). This extensive series consists of long sheets of photographic paper, hung vertically, each of which displays three images. Taken between 2002 and 2008 (years in which the face of China, particularly that of Beijing, was being radically transformed by modernization projects in anticipation of the 2008 Beijing Summer Olympics), most of the photographs in the series juxtapose modern structures with older buildings, largely those that have been demolished, while others chart the transformation of a single site over time. These landscapes are "provisional" because they are in transition, and each group of images both documents and comments on the enormity of these changes. In one trio, the top image, a gridlike expanse of low brick buildings — old barracks? — is a grim reminder of living conditions prior to China's drive to modernize. The middle image, a power plant dominated by smokestacks and cooling towers, is emblematic of the nation's rise as an industrial power. The resulting prosperity is conveyed by the bottom image: new residential towers looming over naked trees and razed houses. A second trio features a leveled construction site in which the gabled roofline of a newly built factory wall echoes that of soon-to-be demolished houses; a third shows receding vistas of a country road lined with fences (presumably erected to screen off new construction sites), the barren underside of an elevated highway, and a gutted building, beyond which stands one of Beijing's restored fifteenth-century city gates — a rare vestige of the wall that once encircled the capital. Like many of the images in this series, all are winter scenes in which leafless trees and gray skies — as well as a complete lack of people — intensify the sense of stark desolation. As is often the case in literati paintings, the intended message is implied by the subject matter and the season without the need to provide an explicit statement.

Trained as a painter in her native Xi'an and later at the Central Academy of Fine Arts in Beijing, Xing Danwen (b. 1967) also uses photography to comment on the changing urban landscape of a rapidly modernizing China. Xing discovered photography through a chance encounter with a photography magazine. Self-taught, she worked first as a photojournalist, playing a key role in documenting China's first generation of performance artists active in Beijing's East Village in the early 1990s.[60] For five years she worked as a commercial photographer in China and Europe before deciding it was not what she wanted: "I understood that I didn't want to be a photographer. I wanted to do art."[61] From 1998 to 2002 she lived in New York, where she earned a master's degree in fine arts at the School of Visual Arts. Since 2002 she has lived and worked in Beijing.

Scroll series, created in 1999–2000, treats two distinct subjects. *Scroll A* series focuses on human activities around Beijing; *Scroll B* series features architectural elements in the Forbidden City and in the alleys (*hutong*) of Beijing's old residential neighborhoods. As their titles imply, these works take the form of long handscrolls, but the artist disavows trying merely to replicate traditional paintings: "My aim is to create an image from similar panorama-like subject material; I shoot them manually without any computer manipulation. . . . I rely on the film's original data without editing either the image or the negative. This raw data becomes part of the final work, which is composed of a long series of images, which together comprise a panoramic vision typical of — and perhaps unique to — Beijing. . . . My vision is always to use one roll of film to create one complete composition."[62]

In *Scroll A1* Xing presents vignettes of people at their leisure in a traditional covered walkway (FIG. 87). Some of the figures are unaware of the photographer, others make eye contact, and two figures are either waving or protesting against the camera's intrusion. In this way the presence of the photographer and, by extension, the gaze of the viewer are acknowledged. By successively melding and juxtaposing her snapshots into a continuous composition, Xing offers an almost cinematic re-creation of the experience of her stroll — a vicarious journey for the viewer that is an essential feature of many handscroll-format landscapes. Indeed, the similarities between a roll of film and a handscroll are inescapable. The printed lines on the top and bottom margins of the film as well as the dark borders at the beginning and end of each composition recall the silk borders that frame traditional scrolls, while the direction in

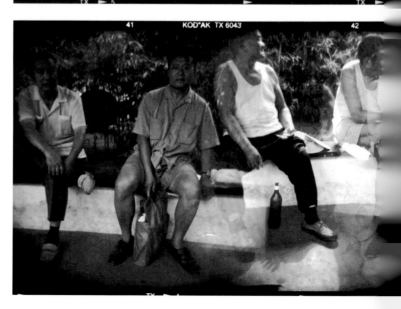

which it is read (in this case, from left to right) is determined by the sequence of numbers printed along the bottom edge. Like the compositional "space cells" in archaic handscroll compositions, the individual exposures often have a circular halo of light to demarcate their boundaries, but by advancing the film less than a full frame, Xing creates double-exposed images that blur and break through these parameters.

Xing's scroll introduces shifting perspectives and changes in scale — again, just what one finds in traditional Chinese painting — which the human eye routinely stitches together seamlessly but no movie camera can replicate.[63] The artist readily acknowledges both sources of inspiration: "I have always been attracted by the world of movies and aim to integrate a filmic sensibility into my photography so that a single still image continues like multiple motion picture images. This places each recorded moment within a continuous timeline. I establish a parallel between the time and dimension of the subject to invent my own panoramic photograph from a multi-vantage-point perspective, which, finally, is much like a study from traditional Chinese painting. I've deliberately broken with the usual way of viewing photography by asking the audience to *read* my work rather than to *look* at my images."[64]

In Xing's *Scrolls* subject matter is less important than how the images combine to form a single composition. This aesthetic quality is even more evident in *Scroll B2*, where the juxtaposition of angles and silhouettes transforms the walls, rooflines, and gates of Beijing's *hutong* and the Forbidden City into a single dramatic abstraction (**FIG. 88**).[65] Made after Xing had lived abroad for a time, both series focus on sites redolent of Chinese heritage — the Old Summer Palace and the Forbidden City — and evince a sense of nostalgia for a world that is rapidly disappearing. Without glamorizing these spaces, Xing's eye captures telling details that evoke a world very different from the modern urban environment that is rapidly overwhelming traditional China.

In her more recent work, Xing has shifted her focus from the walled precincts of the Forbidden City to the modern high-rise "palaces of the people" to reveal that the partitioned cubicles of these megastructures impose their own boundaries on life.[66] The aptly titled *Urban Fiction* series presents large-scale color photographs of real-estate developers' architectural models into which Xing has digitally inserted imaginary human dramas (**FIGS. 89, 90**). These figures form only a tiny part of each image, yet their actions — often carried out by the artist herself — become the focal point in an otherwise sterile environment. Whatever action we are voyeuristically invited to witness — a furtive kiss, a murder, a lady watering her plants — is

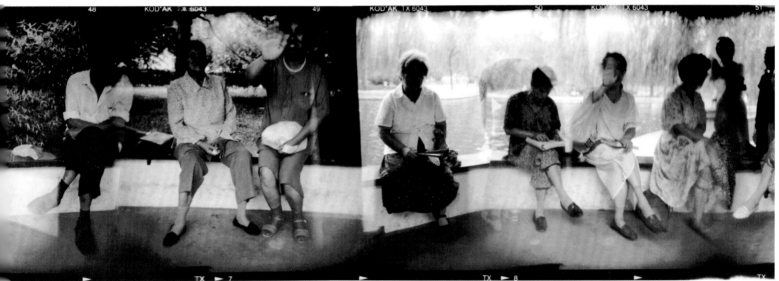

Fig. 88. Xing Danwen (b. 1967). *Scroll B2*, 1999–2000.
Chromogenic print, 4 ⅝ × 62 ⅞ in. (11.8 × 159.7 cm).
Collection of Christopher Phillips [Exhib.]

placed within an imaginary setting in which there is no other trace of genuine human activity. Xing implies that the dream of luxury, modernity, and a better life that these maquettes are intended to convey may actually result in isolation and loneliness.[67]

The growing disjunction between traditional and modern China is a recurring theme in the films of Yang Fudong (b. 1971). Since 2003, Yang has established himself as a leading filmmaker and video artist, exploring in a series of films set amid scenic landscapes or urban environments the restless anomie of educated young urbanites who confront a world that seems unreceptive to their existential plight. After studying art in high school in his native Beijing, Yang earned admission to the department of oil painting at the prestigious China Academy of Art in Hangzhou (1991–95), where he studied Soviet Socialist Realism alongside Qiu Zhijie. Inspired by the example of Huang Yongping and other older graduates who were breaking new ground as contemporary artists, Yang began experimenting with photography and video. In 1997 he moved to Shanghai, where he continues to live and work.

Yang's best-known cinematic work is his *Seven Intellectuals of the Bamboo Grove*, a five-part epic created between 2003

and 2007 that ponders the malaise of seven young people from Shanghai as they seek to define their individual and collective identity.[68] But one of Yang's most seductive films, and the one that comes closest to the sensibility of Chinese painting, particularly the lyrical landscapes of the Southern Song dynasty (1127–1279), is *Liu Lan* (FIG. 91). This fourteen-minute film, completed in 2003, epitomizes how Yang has woven together inspiration from both traditional and modern sources.[69]

Shot in 35 mm black-and-white film, Yang's long, lingering images reveal a sensibility that is more pictorial than cinematic, "like perfectly composed Modernist photographs."[70] The film, wordless but for a poignant song that accompanies the opening and closing scenes, depicts an encounter between a youthful man and woman, the romantic potential of their time together mediated by the very different worlds to which they belong.[71] The girl, Liu Lan, is a simple fisherwoman whose life is circumscribed by a small boat and the surrounding expanse of water. The young man, immaculately dressed in a white suit and carrying a suitcase, may have come from the same environment (he knows how to oar the boat and take fish from a net), but he now belongs to a modern urban culture; his arrival at the isolated landing where the boat is moored remains a

Fig. 89. Xing Danwen (b. 1967). *Urban Fiction
No. 13*, 2005. Digitally manipulated chromogenic
print, 67 × 86 ⅜ in. (170 × 219.5 cm). M+ Sigg
Collection, Hong Kong [Exhib.]

Fig. 90. Detail of *Urban Fiction No. 13*

118

Fig. 92. Wang Fu (1362–1416). Detail of *Joys of the Fisherman*, Ming dynasty (1368–1644), ca. 1410. Handscroll; ink on paper, 10 ⅝ in. × 22 ft. 7 ⅛ in. (27 × 688.7 cm). The Metropolitan Museum of Art, New York, Ex coll.: C. C. Wang Family, Edward Elliott Family Collection, Purchase, The Dillon Fund Gift, 1982 (1982.2.3)

mystery. There is a wistful longing that pervades the encounter as Liu Lan goes about her daily chores. The film ends when she drops the man off at the place from where they departed. Except for the plaintive words of the song — "Why are people in love always apart? . . . Tears in eyes flowing like pearls / in the light of sunset / the Liu Lan girl stands / still on the boat" — there is no acknowledgment of the emotions that the couple may have felt.[72]

Yang's theme may be linked to a long tradition in Chinese art of depicting elegantly dressed gentlemen seeking to distance themselves from the dusty world of politics by dwelling far removed from the cares of urban life, amid humble fishermen — symbols of man's ability to live harmoniously with the natural environment (FIG. 92). But more direct sources of inspiration are two mid-twentieth-century films that allegorize the challenges posed by rapid modernization to China's rural population as a relationship between a fisherwoman of modest circumstance and a "modern man" from a higher social class (the male protagonist in each film appears at times in a Western suit and carrying a suitcase).[73]

In Yang's retelling of this fable, the reticent girl may represent the virtues of a rural past, while the aloof man may stand for an impersonal urban present. In particular, his Western-style clothes, totally out of place in the rustic environment, suggest that social conventions and changed aspirations have become insurmountable barriers to meaningful

communication. But the model-like beauty of both actors undercuts their believability and signals the filmmaker's modernist aesthetic — this is a film, not reality. Rather than developing a plot or delivering a message, Yang's film is about creating a mood of unfulfilled expectation. The slow pace at which the action unfolds and the lingering views of sunlight-dappled waves or reeds veiled in mist evoke a dreamlike state. Presented in a timeless setting, Yang's video is a poignant allegory of modern man's dislocation from, and inability to find his way back to, the eternal verities of a simpler time.

In both subject matter and medium, the videos of Qiu Anxiong (b. 1972) call to mind traditional landscape painting, which he sees as "an artistic presentation of a complete system of Chinese culture, behind which is a spiritual inclination, a kind of value system, an attitude of life, a view of the universe."[74] He works in the horizontal configuration of three-channel video that recalls the handscroll format, and his images, evocative of the style of monochrome ink paintings, frequently draw inspiration from or make references to specific traditional models.

As a student at the Sichuan Academy of Fine Arts (1990–94), Qiu rejected Chinese traditions in his eagerness to embrace new art forms from the West. But after graduation he returned to his native Chengdu, in Sichuan Province, where he rediscovered traditional Chinese art, literature, and philosophy.[75] Six years of postgraduate study at the University of

Kassel (1998–2004) afforded him the opportunity to reflect further on what it meant to be a Chinese artist: "Modern society is under the rule of Western society. . . . The best thing I could do to keep my own identity was to begin reading Nan Huaijin's books and learn traditional things."[76] At Kassel Qiu came into contact with new media and was particularly inspired by the hand-drawn, black-and-white animations of the South African artist William Kentridge (b. 1955), whose *Shadow Procession* of 1999 appeared at the 2000 Shanghai Biennale.[77] Returning to China in 2004, Qiu took a teaching position at Shanghai Normal University and immediately plunged into the production of a series of animations that pointedly evoke the traditional idiom of ink painting. He did not, however, work in ink on paper but instead developed a method of painting in water-soluble acrylic on canvas. This palimpsest medium emulated some of the effects of ink wash but also allowed him to rework the surface of a single composition by adding to, overpainting, or erasing his marks.[78] Photographing each changed state, he reassembled and manipulated these photographs on a computer to create a sequence of moving images to which he then added a soundtrack.[79] Qiu's method of inserting and removing semi-transparent layers of acrylic underscores an underlying message in all his works — the "impermanence of the material world and the inevitability of change."[80]

In the next three years, Qiu produced three allegorical fables cautioning against ungoverned modernization. *In the Sky*, completed in 2005, pictures a landscape shaped by tectonic forces — thrusting mountains like Chinese garden rocks and erupting volcanoes — that emerge and disappear until the growth of a modern cityscape and its accompanying mound of garbage point to humankind's adverse impact on the earth (FIG. 93). The video ends as grass and trees begin to sprout from the mountain of refuse.

Flying South (2006), which contrasts migrating geese with a caged dove, confronts humankind's ultimately futile efforts to manipulate nature and curtail individual freedoms (FIG. 94). Accompanied by the sounds of Hitler addressing a Nazi rally, the dove dies, books tumble from shelves and are burned, and what appears to be a gas chamber filled with struggling beings in bags is emptied into a burial pit.[81] The sounds of explosions signal revolt and change. The video ends with books flying back onto the stacks accompanied by a cheering crowd: a new cycle has begun.

The most ambitious of Qiu's early videos is *New Classic of Mountains and Seas I*, completed in 2006 (FIG. 95).[82] The title and content are inspired by *Classic of Mountains and Seas*

(*Shanhaijing*), an ancient encyclopedic cosmography "encompassing religion, mythology, geography, flora, fauna, minerals, and medicine," as well as many strange imaginary creatures.[83] In his video, Qiu conjures up nothing less than a vision of the birth and death of civilization. A pristine world surrounded by a vast sea is gradually altered by farms, dwellings, a walled town, and the Great Wall. In the early stages of this evolution, Qiu includes references to a number of classical Chinese paintings that further identify this landscape as China.[84] When a Pandora's box is dropped into this premodern world, a strand of DNA is released, initiating change. Explosive urbanization chokes the landscape until it is abandoned and overgrown. In subsequent scenes, Qiu portrays the ruthless exploitation of natural resources as the greatest threat to civilization. A desert inhabited by camels and chador-clad women is transformed into a vast oil field that feeds an array of mutant beasts — the machines of modern life. War prompts the creatures to devastate the oil fields, but out of the ruined land emerge figures draped in black. Two of them fly to a city where a pair of towering buildings is destroyed. Shortly thereafter, a mushroom cloud leaves only a wasteland with a lone figure as witness to a postapocalyptic world.[85]

In 2008 Qiu followed the creation of his *New Classic* bestiary with a series of prints that simulate a traditional woodblock-printed text with accompanying illustrations. Each image bears a title with the creature's name — a thinly veiled phonetic equivalent of its name in English — and an enumeration of its salient characteristics. The "aotuo," for example, is an automobile-like creature that has on its back "a glass-like shell, eyes as big as torches, and feet that run like a whirlwind. It does not eat, but drinks oil and can travel a thousand *li* in one day" (FIG. 96). Commenting on these strange beasts, Qiu explains, "I have been upset by the chaotic situations of the world today and found it difficult to reconcile what is happening around me. As satire, I have set eyes on modern life's ingenious inventions and clever stratagems as though I was a naïve observer, and looked upon them as exotic monsters."[86]

Although this postmodern morality tale has resonance in both China and the West, Qiu focuses his critique on contemporary China, where misconceptions about East and West, new and old, still abound. In his preface to the series, Qiu addresses the issue directly: "While China actively sought modernization, it simultaneously became critical of tradition, going so far as to completely repudiate it. China's modernization was based on a superficial misreading of Western culture. In its overzealous and unlimited appropriation of all things Western, it buried this fundamental fallacy for future

Fig. 93. Qiu Anxiong (b. 1972). Stills from *In the Sky*,
2005. Single-channel animated video with sound;
8 min. 17 sec. Collection of the artist [Exhib.]

Fig. 94. Qiu Anxiong (b. 1972). Stills from *Flying
South*, 2006. Single-channel animated video
with sound; 9 min. 18 sec. Collection of the artist
[Exhib.]

Fig. 95. Qiu Anxiong (b. 1972). Stills from *New Classic of Mountains and Seas I*, 2006. Three-channel animated video with sound; 30 min. Collection of the artist [Exhib.]

日行千里勝於駿馬。今世人皆馭之。其名曰敖駝叉名奇轍。

阿美利坎洲始有獸。頭扁腹空背甲似琉璃眼大如炬足蹬風輪。不食而飲油。

《敖駝》

Fig. 96. Qiu Anxiong (b. 1972). *Aotuo,* from the portfolio *New Classic of Mountains and Seas I,* 2008. One of twelve woodblock prints; ink on paper, 19 ¾ × 16 ½ in. (50 × 42.1 cm). The Metropolitan Museum of Art, New York, Purchase, Friends of Asian Art Gifts, 2013 [Exhib.]. The "autuo" also appears in Qiu's animated video *New Classic of Mountains and Seas I;* see fig. 95.

Fig. 97. Qiu Anxiong (b. 1972). Stills from *Temptation of the Land,* 2009. Three-channel animated video with sound; 13 min. 25 sec. Collection of the artist [Exhib.]

generations. Modern China now faces all manner of crises bereft of traditional roots, especially cultural, spiritual and religious." Like the figure left stranded on a parched and cracked plain at the end of the work, "An individual facing this kind of world can only feel an overwhelming kind of nothingness."[87]

In 2009 Qiu stepped back from this nihilist fable to make *Temptation of the Land,* an examination of three stages in recent Chinese history (FIG. 97). After a preamble of images celebrating China's ancient landscape — the Three Gorges, West Lake, Mount Huang, and the Great Wall — the first section treats nearly a century of continual warfare, starting with the destruction of the Old Summer Palace in 1860 by French and British troops during the Second Opium War and ending with Chairman Mao's proclamation of the founding of the People's Republic in 1949. The middle section alludes to the failures of the Maoist era — the disastrous Great Leap Forward, when people melted down their iron implements in an attempt to create backyard foundries, and the persecutions of the Cultural Revolution — ending with Mao's death in 1976. The final section highlights the technological advances and material prosperity of the post-Maoist era — oil refineries, modern cities, and the creation of the "Bird's Nest" Olympic stadium, a symbol of the New China. But the very last image emphasizes the human cost of modernization: the "Chongqing nail house," a lone structure perched on a nail-like pedestal of earth amid a giant excavation site from which an elderly couple refused to move to make way for a new development. Thus the work acknowledges China's progress after decades of unimaginable suffering while warning against the dangers of absolute power — whether political or commercial — that continue to haunt China today.

The work was commissioned for "The China Dream," a special issue of the magazine *Modern Weekly,* and was distributed with each copy.[88] As such, it challenged the traditional

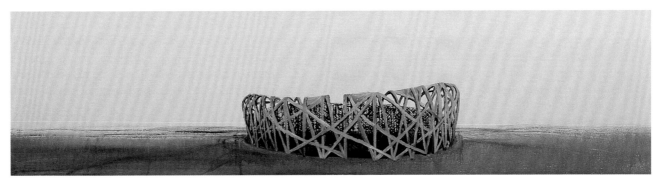

mechanisms for the display and censorship of films by entering rapidly into wide circulation, with Qiu prioritizing dissemination over profit or copyright protection.[89]

In contrast to Qiu's somber allegorical visions of a world threatened by the follies of humankind, the short animations of Chen Shaoxiong (b. 1962) offer keenly observed commentaries on modern life. Chen's animations, while evocative of traditional brush and ink painting, are done in a Western realist manner based directly on photographs.

Born in Shantou, Guangdong Province, Chen was a 1984 graduate from the department of printmaking at the Guangzhou Academy of Fine Arts. His interdisciplinary practice, which includes performance, installation, and photography, has benefited from the fact that this region, encompassing Shenzhen, Hong Kong, and Macau, has enjoyed a special status with relatively greater economic, social, and cultural openness.[90]

In 2005 Chen embarked on a laborious animation process by which he makes hundreds of ink sketches based either on his own photographs or those found through the Internet.[91] He then scans the drawings and assembles them digitally into an animated video. Commenting on his method, he explains, "A photograph presents an opportunity, but does not necessarily call up a memory. In the process of copying the images by hand even more opportunities come forth. The photograph is 'raw,' and the painting is 'cooked.' It's best to give the audience something cooked to look at — the artist should be a chef."[92]

Ink City (2005), a striking statement on the interchangeability of urban settings and experiences, follows the artist on a daylong odyssey through a variety of cities, including Guangzhou and Shanghai (FIG. 98).[93] The video, made from some three hundred painted images and accompanied by a soundtrack of typical city noises, presents a succession of public and private spaces in rapidly alternating wide-angle city views and close-ups of people's faces. It is impossible for the viewer to linger on any of the sights that flash by, but one cannot fail to appreciate the artist's facility in capturing facial expressions or the quality of light that models his forms. As night falls and the video abruptly ends, one is left with a vivid sense of the fragmentary nature of the urban experience in which the pace of life and plethora of activities can lead to sensory overload. The message is similar in *Ink Things* (2007), which speaks to the proliferation of possessions that both facilitate and encumber our existence (FIG. 99).[94] The torrent of images suggests that, in a society driven by materialism, we are ultimately products of our own unbridled consumerism, allowing it to define who we are, what we want, and what we believe.

The juxtaposition of imagery in *Ink Diary* (2006) is more jarring, and the work unfolds at an even more frenetic pace, with changes in the urban environment conveyed by a cityscape that evolves with each stroke of the artist's brush (FIG. 100).[95] Punctuating this vision of feverish urban growth are rapid-fire sequences documenting Chen's family — including outings to the beach and to the Great Wall — a naked couple in varied sexual positions, and a stream of images taken from world news reports. Chen's video emphasizes how the ubiquity of modern media has made it increasingly difficult to separate our daily lives from events occurring around the globe, the transience of which is underscored by the concluding image: Chen's invented cityscape obliterated as quickly as it was built by a flight of jet planes and a rain of black marks (bombs?), followed by the word *ai* 爱 (love), sketched swiftly like the city itself. It remains unclear whether this final sequence of images is merely the artist's playful graffiti or a vision of terrorist destruction.

The absence of an overarching narrative or obvious sequential logic in all these works emulates the way in which the subconscious stitches together seemingly unrelated memories to illuminate revealing details of our identity, and offers a telling portrait of our fragmentary modern condition.[96] *Ink History*, by contrast, completed in 2010 — a year after Qiu Anxiong's *Temptation of the Land* — manifests a radically different intent (FIG. 101).[97] The animation employs Chen's familiar technique of juxtaposing places with people, but the apparent randomness of his selections conceals a compelling narrative that mixes patriotic tributes to China's achievements with incidents that have been censored from China's officially condoned history.[98] Rather than document the artist's personal encounters with his environment, this video surveys historical events of the past century. Accompanied by a soundtrack of propaganda songs, historical speeches, and a ticking clock, the video chronicles China's emergence as a modern state, starting with Sun Yat-sen's (1866–1925) nationalist revolution, which toppled the last imperial dynasty in 1911, and ending with the 2008 Beijing Olympics. Challenging these heroic scenes are startling glimpses of repression and suffering — the military occupation of Tibet, public executions, the victimization of intellectuals and Buddhist monks during the Cultural Revolution, and a lone man preventing a column of tanks from proceeding to Tiananmen Square. Such images, excised from official narratives, are forceful reminders of China's unwillingness to confront its recent past. In a country where pictures have been repeatedly repainted to rewrite history, Chen's seemingly casual style of repainting photographic images conveys a powerful sense of indelible truth.

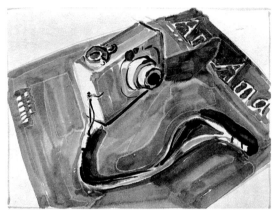

Fig. 98. Chen Shaoxiong (b. 1962). Stills from *Ink City*, 2005. Single-channel animated video with sound; 3 min. Collection of the artist [Exhib.]

Fig. 99. Chen Shaoxiong (b. 1962). Stills from *Ink Things*, 2007. Single-channel animated video with sound; 3 min. Collection of the artist [Exhib.]

Fig. 100. Chen Shaoxiong (b. 1962). Stills from *Ink Diary*, 2006. Single-channel animated video with sound; 3 min. Collection of the artist [Exhib.]

Fig. 101. Chen Shaoxiong (b. 1962). Stills from *Ink History*, 2010. Single-channel animated video with sound; 3 min. Collection of the artist [Exhib.]

One of the youngest and most prolific video artists active in China today is Sun Xun (b. 1980). Born in Liaoning Province, Sun attended the high school of the China Academy of Art in Hangzhou, and in 2001 was accepted into the academy to study printmaking. At the time, academy director Zhang Peili (b. 1957), China's foremost video-art pioneer, was establishing a new-media department, which enabled Sun to experiment with animated videos while still in school. He graduated in 2005 and the next year established Pi Animation Studio, from which he has produced a steady stream of hand-drawn animated videos with a growing team of assistants. He also has created a number of large-scale painted installations.[99]

In his 2005 graduation piece, *Lie of Magician*, Sun uses his face and body as a canvas to suggest that history is a lie that may be manipulated either by an artist or by a government. For Sun, the magician is "the only legal liar" because "magicians by trade deceive people for their amusement."[100] Three subsequent works — *Mythos*, *Shock of Time*, and *Lie*, all completed in 2006, expand upon this concept. All are pointedly political videos inspired by the socially engaged works of William Kentridge, whose influence is particularly apparent in *Shock of Time*, in which Sun's black silhouetted figures drawn on old newspapers recall a similar use of materials in Kentridge's work.[101]

In 2011 Sun undertook an even more demanding form of animation. In a clear homage to the coarse style and strident revolutionary content of the New Woodcut Movement, Sun's *Some Actions Which Haven't Been Defined Yet in the Revolution* (2011) is composed entirely of images created from more than five thousand woodblock prints (**FIG. 102**).[102] The New Woodcut Movement, championed by Lu Xun (1881–1936) and active from the 1920s through the 1940s, used the "low-tech" medium of woodblock printing to create high-contrast, forceful images that advocated for social justice on behalf of the proletariat. Woodcuts were easy to produce, and their visual language was intended to be read just as easily. Here, Sun turns this formula upside down, employing woodcut as one part of a laborious and technically demanding animation process that only an artist with extensive training could accomplish. Further, though his images share the same angular, rough-hewn quality of the New Woodcut Movement, their message is darker and less inspiring, a dystopian vision of rootlessness and confusion.

The video roughly follows one day in the life of a modern city dweller. As he gets out of bed, an alarm clock rings until the hour reaches twelve o'clock, but whether it is noon or midnight remains uncertain, as the black-and-white scenes could

be interpreted as either day or night. The mundanity of the man's daily routine is interrupted by sexual and violent visions from his subconscious, but none, no matter how disturbing, sways him from his course or wakes him from his boredom. An exploding bomb brings the day to its conclusion, and a ticking clock again advances to either noon or midnight, signaling the start of another, seemingly interchangeable cycle. Such a bleak vision of the anomie that pervades contemporary urban existence reveals Sun's deep skepticism about the agendas governing modern society and the perception, shared by a growing number of Chinese artists, that the resulting environment is becoming increasingly antithetical to human life.

A similar notion of malaise that afflicts the contemporary condition finds expression in the work of Fang Lijun (b. 1963), one of a group of Chinese artists whose sardonic takes on the style and imagery of Socialist Realist painting have been labeled Cynical Realism (*Wanshi xianshi zhuyi*).[103] Fang grew up in Handan, an industrial city south of Beijing, where his father worked for the railroad.[104] Classified as "rich peasants," the family suffered discrimination during the Cultural Revolution when they were labeled "class enemies." To avoid prejudicial treatment in school, Fang was educated at home for several years and was encouraged to entertain himself by drawing. He would later drop out of high school to enroll in a vocational school, where he received training in ceramics production. After graduating in 1983, Fang took a job making billboards for an advertising company. Dissatisfied with his long-term prospects, he resigned after one year and tried his hand as an entrepreneur, first by selling garments in the free market and then by opening a railway advertising company. But the oppressive inertia of state-run institutions thwarted Fang's enterprising spirit. He concluded that the only way to achieve the independence and self-improvement he sought was to pursue advanced training in the arts. With the encouragement of Li Xianting, an art critic from Handan, Fang applied to China's premier arts institution, the Central Academy of Fine Arts. To improve his chances, he traveled to Beijing to meet with professors, including Xu Bing, and in 1985 gained acceptance into the department of printmaking. He continued also to practice drawing and painting in the realist manner that was then the academic norm.

Fang had once shaven his head in a teenage act of rebellion and did so for a second time in 1988, after which his works began to feature bareheaded peasants whose blank expressions reflected the dual consequences of poverty and the Cultural Revolution: a lack of education and lowered economic prospects.[105] Fang also valued the anonymity conferred on his

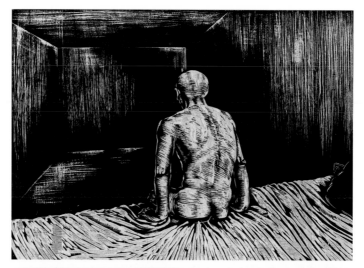

Fig. 102. Sun Xun (b. 1980). Stills from *Some Actions Which Haven't Been Defined Yet in the Revolution*, 2011. Single-channel woodblock-animation video with sound; 12 min. 22 sec. Collection of the artist [Exhib.]

figures by their shaved heads: "The first bald-headed paintings appeared when I was a senior in college. . . . I discovered first that they were extremely powerful, visually speaking. This power had a way of rubbing out the individuality of each subject and this visual effect fit precisely with my understanding of the place of the individual in this society. Finally, the image of the bald-headed man is ambiguous. It is unclear exactly what kind of person he is or what kind of position he occupies."[106]

Fang faced a similarly uncertain future when his graduation from the academy was disrupted by the suppression of democracy demonstrations in Tiananmen Square, which left him and his classmates disillusioned about their opportunities for free expression. Characteristically, he turned down an assigned job that would have guaranteed a good salary and Beijing residency papers and instead chose to live in a farming village not far from the overgrown ruins of the Old Summer Palace (Yuanmingyuan); left with few options, becoming "rogue" seemed the best solution.[107] Soon, more than one hundred aspiring artists moved to what became known as Yuanmingyuan Artist Village, for as Fang himself put it, "We'd rather be lost, bored, crisis-ridden misguided punks than be cheated again."[108] By the time the authorities razed the community in 1994, Fang had already relocated to Songzhuang, a rural area on the northeast fringes of Beijing that has since become popular among artists.

Fang's prospects improved dramatically in late 1993, when one of his paintings featuring a yawning or screaming, bald-headed figure appeared on the cover of *The New York Times Magazine* (FIG. 103). Fang's figures, possibly self-portraits, thereafter became emblems of the ennui and helplessness felt by Fang's generation as a consequence of the government crackdown on political freedom.

For Fang, water — one of the paradigmatic elements in Chinese landscape painting — has served as a major context for visualizing these enigmatic figures. Within his oeuvre is a well-known group of images in which a single figure is surrounded by a boundless expanse of water.[109] He began painting variations on the theme in 1993, and starting in 1995, he expanded his repertoire to include large-scale woodblock prints made with sheets of plywood, among them the billboard-size, seven-panel *2003.3.1* (FIG. 104). Owing to the difficulty of working at this scale with traditional gravures and knives, Fang uses electric routers and jigsaws.[110] In contrast to the subtle rendering of facial features seen in his paintings, in the woodblock medium Fang defines his forms with calligraphic white lines and planes of black or gray pigment that

Fig. 103. Fang Lijun (b. 1963). *Series 2, No. 2,* 1991–92. Oil on canvas, 78 ¾ × 90 ½ in. (200 × 230 cm). Museum Ludwig, Cologne

both model and animate the subject. His austere palette, limited to shades of ink, reinforces the starkness of the imagery and pointedly recalls the monochrome tonalities of traditional ink painting.

In *2003.3.1* Fang confronts his audience with an image of a man, his bare head barely protruding above the waves, mouth open as if gasping for air. The agitation of the surrounding waves and the man's closed eyes and furrowed brow suggest distress, but it is unclear whether he is swimming or drowning. The work's immense scale further dramatizes the scene by underscoring both the vastness of the body of water and the isolation of the figure in its midst. Fang sees water as a fitting vehicle through which to express his generation's experience of China: "People are above all social animals; they cannot leave society, but they are often drowned by this society, by the damage it inflicts, or they are lost in society. That is a relation similar to the one between man and water."[111]

Fang's image has historical resonance. On May 31, 1956, Mao Zedong swam across the Yangzi River, in part to demonstrate his desire to tame the river with human structures (FIG. 105).[112] In 1958 the widely publicized image of Mao with his head above water was painted by Fu Baoshi (1904–1965; FIG. 106). Fang was certainly aware of this well-known propaganda photo, and his print might comment on the fate of the "Great Helmsman," who was no more able to restrain the Yangzi

Fig. 104. Fang Lijun (b. 1963). *2003.3.1*, 2003.
Seven-panel woodblock print; ink on paper, each
panel 13 ft. 1 ½ in. × 48 in. (400 × 121.7 cm);
overall 13 ft. 1 ½ in. × 27 ft. 11 ½ in. (400 × 852 cm).
Private collection, Hong Kong [Exhib.]

Fig. 105. Mao Zedong swimming in the Yangzi River at Wuhan, 1956. Photograph by Hou Bo (b. 1924).

Fig. 106. Fu Baoshi (1904–1965). *After Mao Zedong's Poem "Swimming,"* 1958. Album leaf; ink on paper, 14 3/16 × 19 11/16 in. (36 × 50 cm). Nanjing Museum

Fig. 107. Liu Wei (b. 1965). *Untitled No. 6 "Flower,"* 2003. Accordion album of twenty-four leaves with silk brocade cover; pencil, acrylic, ink, and watercolor on paper, each leaf 9 ⅝ × 6 ½ in. (24.5 × 16.5 cm). Private collection, New York [Exhib.]

River's current than he was the flow of history, or the Chinese people's surging desire for freedom.

An equally unorthodox use of traditional landscape motifs is a striking feature of a select body of works created by Liu Wei (b. 1965), who, like Fang Lijun, is more widely known as a figure painter in the Cynical Realist style. Liu grew up in a special residential compound for military families in Beijing because both his parents worked in missile research for the People's Liberation Army.[113] An early interest in art led him to study printmaking at the Central Academy of Fine Arts from 1985 to 1989, when Fang Lijun and Hong Hao were also at the academy. Deeply affected by the suppression of the democracy demonstrations in Tiananmen Square, Liu, in spite of his privileged and sheltered background, has since expressed his sense of disillusionment by consistently challenging the boundaries of social and political convention.

In the decade after he graduated, Liu ignored his training in printmaking and took up oil painting, and he was among the first wave of independent artists to establish a studio in the Songzhuang Artist Village in the eastern suburbs of Beijing. During this period, Liu gained prominence as a Cynical Realist figure painter. Later, he worked in a more abstract, impressionistic manner that incorporated landscape imagery, nudes, and writing.[114] All of these themes came together in a series of ten works executed between 2003 and 2004, each titled *Flower* (in Chinese, a homophone for "painting"), that in medium, format, and scale marked a dramatic departure from his earlier paintings.[115] In the series Liu reintroduced ink and paper into his repertoire and adopted the traditional format of an accordion-style album. In addition to its intimate size, the format allows the contents to be viewed either sequentially as one turns the pages or continuously by opening the album into a single horizontal composition.

Untitled No. 6 "Flower," dated 2003, is an excellent example of the frenzied complexity of Liu's fecund imagination at work on what he has referred to as his "messy sex diaries" (**FIG. 107**).[116] The album has a traditional brocade cover and vertical title strip, but Liu immediately challenges convention by inelegantly inscribing his title in both Chinese (*huaer* 花儿) and English (Flower) at the top, then signing it "Baba hua" (Painted by Papa) in a childish scrawl at the bottom. Even more heterodox is his decision to repeat the title directly on top of the brocade cover by first painting out a part of the textile pattern, then using white pigment to reinscribe the bilingual title.

Upon opening the album, one confronts illogical shifts in scale and a dense layering of disparate media, subjects, and

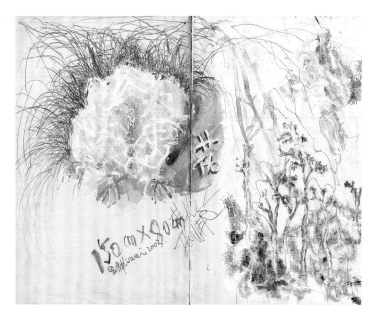

Fig. 108. Detail of *Untitled No. 6 "Flower"*

Fig. 109. Detail of *Untitled No. 6 "Flower"*

styles; there are recurring themes, but no clear narrative emerges. Frequent amendments or additions that necessitate overpainting earlier elements — including underlying vignettes of monochrome landscapes that resemble those by the celebrated scholar-artist Dong Qichang (1555–1636) — frankly contradict the spontaneous brushwork and absence of reworking that are hallmarks of literati painting.[117] Further subverting the literati tradition, Liu eschews the calligraphic outlines of this earlier master and defines the contours of mountains and boulders with hairlike fringes that enhance their anthropomorphic nature.

Painted over the landscape scenes in semiopaque colors are large-scale pink flowers that resemble female genitalia; the phallic forms of a carrot, banana, and tiger; and grotesque naked figures with exaggerated or distorted genitals. Additional naked figures, again drawn with "hairy" modeling lines, serve to frame the landscapes. Finally, Liu has inserted crudely written words — in English and Chinese — as gratuitous captions or comments alongside his imagery together with squiggles and doodles done with either a ballpoint pen or a brush (FIG. 108).

In two instances, Liu has given added prominence to his figures by setting them against a darkly painted background. One of these is a portrait of Qi Baishi (1864–1957), one of the most celebrated modern masters of traditional Chinese painting (FIG. 109).[118] In a reversal of the traditional ink-to-paper relationship, the elderly Qi with his long wispy beard is drawn in white pigment on a black ground. Written on his chest is *dashi*, or "great master," but immediately below this Liu has written "250%," which when read in Chinese (*erbaiwu*) is a slang expression for "stupid." Two more characters above the figure's head appear to read *chongqu*, or "insects [are] interesting," a reference to Qi's area of specialization. But if Qi represents an ideal Chinese scholar-gentleman, then Liu's sexually charged imagery suggests that the cerebral world of literati painting concealed a darker realm of carnal passions that only contemporary art has been able to confront.

Landscape imagery in China has long been read as emblematic of human values and moral standards, and the above selection of artworks demonstrates that this view of nature continues to resonate among contemporary artists. As Liu Wei's anthropomorphized mountains and Huang Yan's *Tattoo* suggest, landscape in China is still deeply connected to individual cultural identity.

A number of the artists considered here have drawn inspiration from earlier masterpieces that invite viewers to enter vicariously into an idealized world. But in these artists' reinterpretations of antique models, the role of landscape as a spiritual sanctuary has been subverted, and the promise of refuge within the natural environment has become remote or unattainable. Ren Jian, Liu Dan, Shao Fan, and Qiu Shihua each present visions of a cosmic, primordial world that is constantly in flux and devoid of human life. A similar emptiness broods over Shi Guorui's eerily still image of Shanghai and Yang Yongliang's artificially composed mountainscape. In Yang Jiechang's sumptuous "blue-and-green" images, industrial and political edifices appear threatened and vulnerable; Duan Jianyu paints iconic Chinese vistas on disposable cardboard; and the pristine Song and Yuan dynasty landscapes that inspired Qiu Anxiong are gradually overwhelmed in his videos by humankind's interventions: cities and their trash heaps, the exploitation of natural resources, the devastation of war. Even water ceases to be a refreshing or neutral element: Yang Yongliang ends his long scroll with a tsunami-like tidal bore that threatens to engulf the shore; Qiu Zhijie juxtaposes the illusory safety of the Nanjing Bridge with the eternal flow of the Yangzi River; Fang Lijun isolates a lone figure in an expanse of agitated waves; and Yang Fudong sets his protagonists adrift in a dreamlike waterscape.

Reacting to the inexorable transformation of the urban landscape, Hong Hao demonstrates how the normal bustle of city life, celebrated in a twelfth-century handscroll, has become chaotic in present-day Beijing, while Chen Shaoxiong mimics the frenetic pace of modern life in his headlong rush through seemingly interchangeable cityscapes. Ai Weiwei emphasizes the destruction and desolation that accompany development; Xing Danwen explores the hollow promise of happiness behind flashy new building complexes; and Sun Xun suggests the oppressive impact of an impersonal urban environment and a suffocating political atmosphere on the human psyche.

Underlying all these works is a sense of disillusionment with the notion that economic development brings with it a better life. Viewed in the context of recent history as chronicled by Qiu Anxiong and Chen Shaoxiong, China has emerged from a century of foreign oppression and political turmoil, but the human values and natural rhythms of life, embodied in the Chinese landscape, now appear more vulnerable than ever.

While purely nonrepresentational art did not exist in China prior to the late twentieth century, Chinese painters have been pushing up against the boundaries of abstraction since at least the late eighth century, when several artists were labeled "untrammeled" (*yipin*) because their styles so departed from orthodox techniques that they were otherwise unclassifiable. Zhu Jingxuan (active early 9th century) described the method of one of these painters, Wang Mo ("Ink Wang," active late 8th century), as follows: "Whenever he wanted to paint a picture, he would first drink wine, and when he was sufficiently drunk, would spatter ink on the painting surface. Then, laughing and singing all the while, he would stamp on it with his feet and smear it with his hands, besides swashing and sweeping it with the brush."[1] Later, in the eleventh century, scholar-amateur artists pointedly rejected the representational goals of painting in favor of calligraphic self-expression, and this disavowal became a fundamental characteristic of literati painting after the thirteenth century, with the brush mark regarded as an extension of the artist's hand.[2]

In addition to serving as a vehicle by which Chinese artists manifest expressions of personal creativity, calligraphy possesses an intrinsically graphic nature that exists independently of its lexical function. Indeed, Western artists from Franz Kline (1910–1962) and Robert Motherwell (1915–1991) to Brice Marden (b. 1938) have derived inspiration from the nonfigurative forms and gestural dynamism inherent in East Asian calligraphy.[3] While calligraphy carries semantic meaning, individual ideographs are neither pictographs nor phonemes, and their execution lends them formal qualities that may be analyzed in terms of composition, figure-ground relationships, gesture, and kinesthetic movement — all qualities that have formed part of the discourse surrounding nonrepresentational art.

Following on such well-established traditions of exploiting the abstract expressive potential of painting and writing, the step toward pure abstraction was a very short one for contemporary Chinese artists to make. And as it has done for centuries, ink has remained a fundamental medium for Chinese artists working in this mode, along with a more recent use of oil and acrylic. Often, Western modernist abstractions serve as points of departure for hybrid works in which the traditional medium of brush and ink on paper is used to create works of imposing scale and visual drama, but the premise behind these abstract compositions is typically quite different in China from that in the West. Presented here are works that focus on four different aspects of abstraction — gesture, process, materiality, and nonfigurative imagery — that are equally informed by qualities inherent to the Chinese pictorial tradition.

The classically trained calligrapher Wang Dongling (b. 1945) exemplifies those artists who have used their command of traditional techniques to create large-scale abstractions that emphasize the dynamic gestural qualities of calligraphy while divorcing the work from any suggestion of semantic signification. A native of Rudong, Jiangsu Province, Wang studied fine art at Nanjing Teachers' College until 1966, when the school was closed and Wang was assigned the task of writing political slogans in big-character posters. The experience liberated him from the strictures of his academic training and gave him his first taste of artistic freedom.[4] His commitment to calligraphy deepened in 1968 when he joined a group studying under the master Lin Sanzhi (1898–1989). It was Lin who taught Wang that the patient mastery of classical models would give him the deeply ingrained brush habits that would allow him to work spontaneously, whether he chose to extend or depart from calligraphy's traditional canon.[5]

After the Cultural Revolution, Wang furthered his study of calligraphy at the progressive Zhejiang Academy (1979–81), afterward becoming an academy instructor.[6] He taught at the school until 1988 and during this time became increasingly involved in China's avant-garde movement (in 1985 he shared a studio with Gu Wenda). While his years at the academy exposed him to modern Western art and concepts, it was as a visiting professor at the University of Minnesota and the University of California, Santa Cruz, from 1989 to 1991 that he was first able to study Western paintings firsthand. These encounters inspired him to uncouple his calligraphic training from the task of transcribing texts and to experiment with the abstract potential of calligraphic forms. Today, Wang works in three distinct modes: traditional, pictorial, and abstract. His transcriptions in cursive script of poems and other classical texts demonstrate his commitment to tradition and command of established styles (**FIG. 110**); a second mode isolates seal-script characters and sets them against a shaded ground, lending them a painterly appearance (**FIG. 111**); finally, he creates monumental compositions whose abstract structures have an almost sculptural presence (**FIGS. 112–114**).

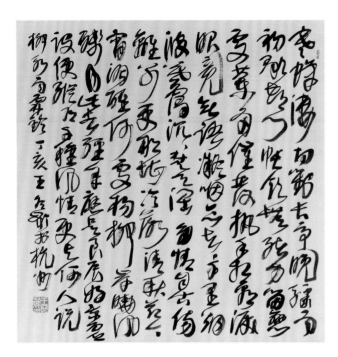

Fig. 110. Wang Dongling (b. 1945). *Poem to the Tune of "The Rain-Soaked Bell,"* 2007. Ink on paper, 26 ½ × 26 ¼ in. (67.3 × 66.7 cm). The Metropolitan Museum of Art, New York, Purchase, Friends of Asian Art Gifts, 2012 (2012.321)

Fig. 111. Wang Dongling (b. 1945). *Canon*, 1991. Ink on paper, 39 ½ × 26 ⅞ in. (100.3 × 68.3 cm). The Metropolitan Museum of Art, New York, Purchase, Friends of Asian Art Gifts, 2012 (2012.320)

Canon, dated 1991, a large-scale, broadly brushed interpretation of the character for that word (法), is an imposing example of Wang's exploration of the expressive qualities of archaic calligraphic forms **(FIG. 111)**.[7] Wang first applied ink wash along the upper and lower borders of the paper, leaving an uninked horizontal band at the center. The varied density of the spontaneously applied wash gives these passages a rich atmospheric quality that, according to the artist, is meant to evoke the separation of the sky from the earth, as well as periodic autumn floods, as described in the classic Daoist text

Zhuangzi (ca. 300 B.C.).[8] Only after the ink-washed areas were dry did Wang execute the character, using the archaic seal-script form and wielding a large brush. But while seal script, which evolved from inscriptions carved in stone or cast in bronze, generally is composed of lines of uniform width, Wang's brushstrokes are variable and imprecise, reasserting the immediacy of the artist's touch. Additionally, Wang rearranged the character's usual configuration to achieve greater graphic equilibrium, tilting its elements inward so that they appear to pivot around the central void, exactly where Wang has placed his seal,

"Wang Dongling yin" (Seal of Wang Dongling). Through this reinterpretation, Wang suggests the primacy of the composition over adherence to calligraphic precedents.

By the late 1990s Wang began to untether his compositions from any text, creating a series of monumental abstractions that may be appreciated purely as gestural art. His powerful brushwork, executed with a mop-size brush (thus engaging his entire body), calls to mind Action Painting. But Wang's emphasis on balancing spontaneous, energized strokes with the surrounding white space is equally informed by years of calligraphic practice, particularly of cursive script, a tenet of which asserts that the interaction of ink and ground — especially the spatters and streaks that communicate the impact and momentum of the brush — is crucial to an appreciation of the figure. In this way, Wang's composition resonates with both the formal calligraphic traditions of China and the radically reimagined spatial conventions that are fundamental to Western abstraction: the white paper is not simply the absence of ink, it is the "space" into which Wang's ink structure is thrust.

Untitled, dated 1999, evolves from Wang's earlier images of single, isolated characters. It uses a traditional hanging-scroll format but explores the expressive potential of brush, ink, and paper without reference to any recognizable character form (**FIG. 112**). Large areas of the composition are saturated with black ink, which has been allowed to seep outward, creating uneven edges. Several bold brushstrokes intersect these areas, and what little white space is left has been spattered with ink dots, blurring the usual figure-ground relationship of ink and paper and infusing the work with dynamic tension.

Being Open and Empty and *Dark (Heaven) and Yellow (Earth)*, both dated 2005, exemplify the artist's most recent monumental abstractions (**FIGS. 113, 114**).[9] Their powerfully inked lines convey a vivid sense of the artist's physical engagement with the works so that it is possible to reexperience the act of creation. Wang borrowed the phrase "being open and empty" (*shou bai*) from the *Zhuangzi,* in which it refers to a state of enlightenment achieved by ridding one's mind of mundane trifles. Its literal meaning, however, "protect the white," may also reflect Wang's awareness of the uninked paper as a significant component of the whole. The title of *Dark (Heaven) and Yellow (Earth)* echoes the work's grand scale in its reference to the colors of the sky and the earth at the beginning of creation, as described in the ancient *Book of Changes* (*Yi jing*).

While Wang's move toward pure abstraction evolved gradually with time, Li Huasheng (b. 1944) radically transformed the nature of his art almost from one day to the next. After a long career as a New Literati painter of landscapes and figures, in October 1998 Li began to paint compositions consisting entirely of lined grids, drawing emphasis to his process. These works are not merely the product of some sudden enlightenment but are grounded in the basic skills derived "from Li's long practice of modern landscape painting. In his 'Line Grid' series, Li Huasheng has reduced . . . the traditional ink applying technique to the minimum, and changed center-tip brushstrokes into thin center-tipped lines. Using enormous willpower, he takes great pains in drawing crossed lines. This is indeed a kind of Buddhist practice."[10] Li's own explanation is more elusive. He has described his state of mind as "experimenting wholeheartedly with emptiness with an empty mind."[11]

Li's abrupt renunciation — at the age of fifty-four — of narrative content, subject matter, and autographic brushwork, as well as any wish to explain his artistic motivation, bespeaks an independent, even defiant personality in keeping with his career up to that point.[12] Born near Chongqing, Sichuan Province, into a family of modest means — his father was a barge worker on the Yangzi River — Li's determination to become a landscape painter led him to enroll in a technical school attached to the Yangzi River Shipping Administration so that he could gain easy passage through the Yangzi Gorges and study their dramatic scenery. During the Cultural Revolution, Li practiced painting in secret, but in 1973 he sought out Chen Zizhuang (1913–1976), another self-taught painter from a similarly humble background. After initially being rebuffed, Li eventually became Chen's student. It was undoubtedly Chen, whose attraction to the mystical teachings of Zhuangzi (traditional dates ca. 369–286 B.C.) led him to take the reverse of the philosopher's name for his sobriquet, who inculcated Daoist thought and values in Li.[13]

During the 1980s, Li's dual landscape styles — playful, colored depictions of rural scenery and darker, more somber images of rain-soaked villages and mountains (**FIG. 115**)— earned him notoriety, particularly after his works were included in a group exhibition that traveled to eight American museums between 1984 and 1985.[14] In 1987 Li visited America; it was his first opportunity to travel outside China and his first exposure to Western art and artistic practices.[15] This encounter gradually led him to modify his painting style. During the early 1990s Li still took landscape as his subject matter, but his compositions became increasingly dense, dark, and abstract.[16] His discovery of the ubiquitous presence of grids in the wood structure and brick pavement of his traditional courtyard house, combined with growing frustration with his place within the official arts hierarchy, led to his dramatic break with traditional subject matter and his shift to abstract compositions based on the disciplined execution of linear grids.

Fig. 112. Wang Dongling (b. 1945). *Untitled*, **1999.**
Hanging scroll; ink on paper, 96 ¾ × 57 ½ in.
(245.7 × 146.1 cm). Private collection, New York
[Exhib.]

Fig. 113. Wang Dongling (b. 1945). *Being Open and Empty,* 2005. Hanging scroll; ink on paper, 87 ¼ × 57 in. (221.6 × 144.8 cm). The Metropolitan Museum of Art, New York, Gift of the artist (2013.188.2) [Exhib.]

Fig. 114. Wang Dongling (b. 1945). *Dark (Heaven) and Yellow (Earth)*, 2005. Horizontal scroll; ink on paper, 57 in. × 12 ft. ⅝ in. (144.8 × 367.3 cm). The Metropolitan Museum of Art, New York, Gift of the artist, 2013 (2013.188.3) [Exhib.]

Fig. 115. Li Huasheng (b. 1944). *Coming through the Gorges*, 1986. Hanging scroll; ink on paper, 20 ¼ × 38 ¾ in. (51.4 × 98.4 cm). The Metropolitan Museum of Art, New York, Gift of Jerome Silbergeld and Michelle DeKlyen, 2010 (2010.474)

Fig. 116. Li Huasheng (b. 1944). *0669*, 2005. Four hanging scrolls; ink on paper, each 9 ft. × 48 in. (274.3 × 121.9 cm). Collection of the artist [Exhib.]

Deceptively simple, Li's compositions vary primarily in the width of the lines and the scale of the grid. The paper left exposed between lines is more or less blank. Where the lines intersect or where Li has reinked his brush, concentrations of pigment create nodes of darkness that offer a counterpoint to the regularity of the grid. Li draws his lines freehand, and to execute such long straight lines of consistent thickness demands extraordinary brush control and concentration. Li sees this painstaking process as an embodiment of his time, like visual records of a meditative state in which he has emptied himself of all emotions and has achieved a mind-set equivalent to a monk reciting a scripture or repeatedly intoning a mantra: "I once visited Lhasa, and listened to the Lamas chanting their sutras, and I felt that my painting was a bit like chanting sutras . . . *om mani padme hum*, just six syllables, but they keep on chanting it, year after year. . . . My subject matter is the time I spend painting. People's lives are measured by time, and my life is being used up in this way."[17]

Li's *0669*, four huge vertical scrolls densely filled with thin vertical and horizontal lines, is a tour de force of sustained focus (FIGS. 116, 117). He completed the work in 2005, after two years of work. Li has described his method as follows: "Each brushstroke must accord with principle; it can't deviate, it can't change in thickness, it can't tremble. One day, two days, three days. . . . I continue to paint, I really can't stop, but when I take a break, then again continue, my mind-set before and after must be consistent, my emotions during this period can have no distractions, my energy and spirit must be settled and still."[18] Li's intense involvement with the process of creation, in a manner similar to that of his contemporaries

Fig. 117. Detail of *0669* showing gridwork

Ding Yi (b. 1962), Lu Qing (b. 1964), and Chen Guangwu (b. 1967), draws emphasis away from the abstract qualities of line and ground and refocuses it on the hand and mind of the creator — the performance.[19] As with traditional Chinese painting, Li's compositions are ultimately embodiments of his physical and mental state — they are about self-expression and the presentation of the artist.[20]

A similar sense of focused repetition and the marking of time plays a key role in *100 Layers of Ink*, a series created between 1989 and 1998 by Yang Jiechang. As with the abstract works of Wang Dongling and Li Huasheng, this series may be read as an outgrowth of Yang's engagement with Daoist and Chan philosophy, particularly during the period from 1984 to 1986, when he studied with Master Huangtao at Mount Luofu, in Guangdong Province.[21] For Yang, however, the end result focuses not on the process of creation or on the hand of the artist but on the materiality of ink as a medium.

Yang began the series in 1989, when he was invited to participate in the exhibition "Magiciens de la terre" at the Centre Georges Pompidou in Paris. Yang noted that "the space the curator had chosen for my works was situated in the middle of some very well-known artists of the period: [Anselm] Kiefer, Sigmar Polke, On Kawara, [Ilya] Kabakov, Sarkis, Nam Jun-Paik, [Alighiero] Boetti. I thought if I went ahead with the work I did in China a dialogue with these artists would be impossible. . . . I therefore returned to the basic elements I had distilled during my process of deconstruction in China: the process of applying ink, water, ink and paper itself."[22] Over the next two months, Yang applied a fresh layer of ink to the same square sheets of paper every day. The result was more sculptural than pictorial: "I felt that these were not flat two-dimensional paintings but actual three-dimensional spaces."[23]

In *100 Layers of Ink, Nos. 1, 2, and 3,* a trio of paintings created in 1994, color and pictorial form are eliminated (FIGS. 118–120). Instead, sheets of paper that have been saturated with ink are at once black and luminous — a quality that recalls the yin-yang dualism of Daoism.[24] Yang's process not only subverts traditional technique, subject matter, and the autographic "hand" of the artist, but it also resembles "the process of self-sublimation in meditation."[25] But the large scale of these pieces; the sculptural quality of their wrinkled surfaces, with their almost metallic reflectivity; and their thick rectilinear frames give them an imposing physicality that recalls works of Western abstract art. This ambiguity is intentional. As one of the first Chinese contemporary artists to settle abroad, Yang is conscious of standing "in between" East and West, and cultural identity has been a central concern of his life and work.[26]

Consequently, Yang's method has been to embrace the cultural complexity that comes with globalization and to explore the tensions, discontinuities, and new possibilities that arise when different traditions or points of view come together.

Zhang Yu (b. 1959), since the early 1990s one of the leading theorists and practitioners of "experimental ink painting" (*shiyan shuimo*), has also been concerned with defining a new creative space that exists between East and West, traditional and contemporary. While retaining the use of brush, ink, and paper, Zhang, like other artists in the experimental ink movement, has disavowed the importance of brushwork (*bimo*), the fundamental identifier of the "hand" of the Chinese literati artist, creating abstract compositions inspired by Western modernism though not directly derived from Western proto-types.[27] Through his participation in and organization of numerous exhibitions, symposia, and publications, Zhang has had a transformative effect on the discourse surrounding what he believes to be a new form of painting that is neither Chinese nor Western.[28]

Born in Tianjin into a middle-class family, Zhang and his parents suffered greatly during the Cultural Revolution when their home was ransacked by the Red Guard and they were sent to the countryside.[29] During this time Zhang developed a passion for sketching that led him at the age of sixteen to Ma Da (1903–1978), a famous printmaker who had been sent to the same village to be reeducated. In 1979, shortly after finishing middle school, Zhang began to work in the woodcut studio of the Yangliuqing Painting Institute, famous for its traditional New Year prints.[30] During this period he also worked as a copyist of traditional paintings, as an apprentice preparing paste in the painting mounting studio, and, starting in 1985, as a designer of book covers. This last job led to his participation in planning a new series of publications, *World of Traditional Chinese Painting* (*Guohua shijie*); by 1986, he was named chief editor, publishing four volumes before the series came to an end in 1991. But this initial foray into art publishing led Zhang to a far more ambitious series of publications that, along with exhibitions he curated and articles he authored, became important vehicles for advancing his theories on experimental ink painting.[31] All the while his art evolved from figurative works in the fan and album formats to increasingly abstract and conceptual works, particularly after a five-month visit to the former Soviet Union in 1992, when he viewed Western paintings for the first time in Saint Petersburg and Moscow.

Zhang's breakthrough came when he began to experiment with schematic signs, or what he calls "non-figurative schemata," in his *Divine Light* (*Lingguang*) series.[32] Developed

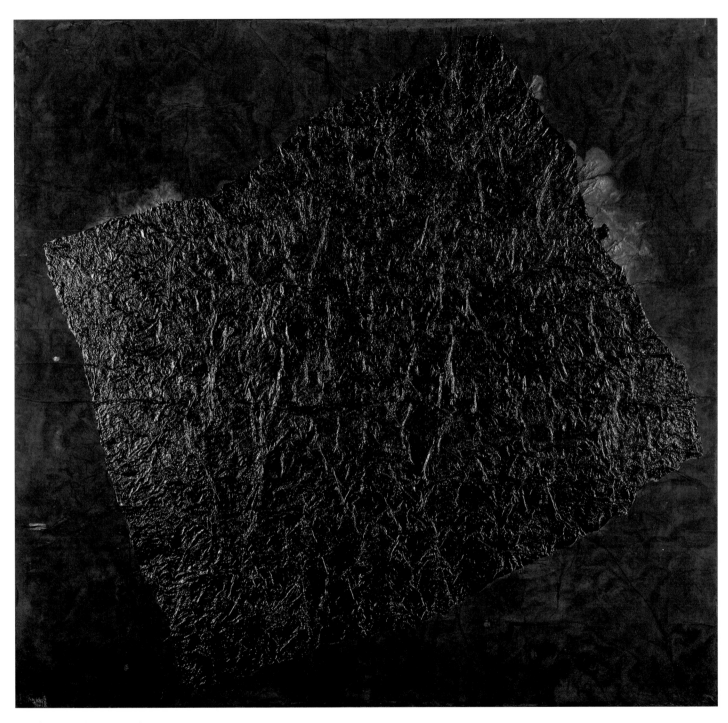

Fig. 118. Yang Jiechang (b. 1956). *100 Layers of Ink, No. 1*, 1994. Ink and acrylic on paper laid down on canvas, 67 × 73 ¼ in. (170 × 186 cm). Private collection, Hong Kong [Exhib.]

Fig. 119. Yang Jiechang (b. 1956). *100 Layers of Ink, No. 2*, 1994. Ink and acrylic on paper laid down on canvas, 69 × 73 ¼ in. (175.5 × 186 cm). Private collection, Hong Kong [Exhib.]

between 1994 and 2003, this series features spherical or rectilinear forms that evoke cosmic events — an exploding star or a planet coalescing from a sphere of gaseous elements — that are at once beautiful and terrifying. According to the artist, these images are also deeply psychological: "Incomplete circles, broken squares, and fragments in motion appear to revolve and float in the universe against a black background shrouded by sound and light. In their floating state, fissures

develop . . . and fragments break off, colliding with the soul and creating fear and disquiet. The collisions, fission, floating and alternation articulate the complexity and pain, anxiety and uneasiness in the deep recesses of the human soul."[33]

One may also see in these nonfigurative images a melding of divergent philosophies that ultimately transcends definition as either Eastern or Western: "The paper, left an untouched white, takes on the elemental role of light as a

Fig. 120. Yang Jiechang (b. 1956). *100 Layers of Ink, No. 3*, 1994. Ink and acrylic on paper laid down on canvas, 69 × 73 ¼ in. (175.5 × 186 cm). Private collection, Hong Kong [Exhib.]

symbol of life, of knowledge, of a pure philosophical vision. The fathomless darkness of ink suggests the rich depths of the unknowable, and acts as a foil for the white — in a universally recognized duality known in China as Yin and Yang."[34]

Divine Light Series No. 59: The Floating Incomplete Circle (FIG. 121), dated 1998, is one of the largest works in the series. Suspended in a dark "sky" spangled with starlike dots of uninked paper is a giant circle surrounded by a radiant halo.

Variations in ink tonality suggest a three-dimensional sphere composed of fragmentary concentric layers that allow one to peer into the dark heart of the globe — as if one were staring into a cosmic eye whose darkly veined iris and jagged edges make it unclear whether the oculus is opening or closing, coalescing or crumbling. In the darkness above the sphere, the artist has impressed a single small seal that reads "Shiyu bi" (Brush of Shiyu) — Shiyu, or "stone rain," being Zhang's

Fig. 121. Zhang Yu (b. 1959). *Divine Light Series No. 59: The Floating Incomplete Circle*, 1998. Hanging scroll; ink on paper, 9 ft. 7 ⅜ in. × 70 ⅞ in. (293 × 180 cm). Private collection, Hong Kong [Exhib.]

sobriquet. Dwarfed by the scale of the sphere, the red seal nonetheless declares man's presence within this vast firmament — the artist as creator.

Zhang began by sketching the general contours of his abstract forms with light grayish ink and a dry brush. Next, water and ink were applied in sprays or with brushes of varying sizes to produce dramatic graphic and tonal variations, followed by dry-brushed ink and washes, although the areas that were first saturated with water resisted the ink, leaving numerous white spots. As a final step, Zhang obliterated most traces of his brushwork with layers of wash; only at the margins of the composition can one see brush marks. The result is a sense of three-dimensionality that radiates light within a dark, immeasurable space.

If *Divine Light Series No. 59* appears like a sphere floating in space, then *Divine Light 2000–8*, created two years later, resembles a cross section of a sedimentary rock that is undergoing metamorphosis (**FIG. 122**). The work stands out within the series for its tall, narrow format and the complex geometry of its composition.[35] Measuring more than thirteen feet in height, this monumental image is composed of fragmented rectilinear fields interwoven with irregular horizontal bands in starkly contrasting shades of ink. The picture surface is further animated by webs of delicate crackles and clusters of water drops, creating a sparkling, vibrating visual effect. This painting is a masterful embodiment of the artist's goal to create a work of ink and wash that is neither strictly Chinese nor strictly Western but a bridging of both traditions.

This notion of bridging is key to understanding much of China's contemporary art. In particular, abstraction in China, while sharing qualities that traditionally have defined Western abstraction, has emerged naturally from indigenous pictorial precedents that remain indelible to the works themselves. The result is a complex form of nonobjective imagery that exists quite easily in both worlds.

Fig. 122. Zhang Yu (b. 1959). *Divine Light 2000–8*, 2000. Hanging scroll; ink on paper, 13 ft. 1 ½ in. × 39 ⅜ in. (400 × 100 cm). The Metropolitan Museum of Art, New York, Gift of Chung Ching-hsin, 2011 (2011.121) [Exhib.]

In the foregoing discussion, I have divided works of art not by media or format but by theme: words, landscapes, abstractions. These thematic divisions are elastic, able to encompass photography — including records of installations and performance pieces — animation, film, and woodblock prints together with works in ink, watercolor, oil, and acrylic. In each case, these works derive part of their core meaning from references to earlier ink art traditions, for example, subject matter, symbolism, mood, or self-expressive brushwork. The works that follow do not fit neatly into any of the above three thematic categories. None derives its primary identity from traditional forms of ink art, yet all exhibit what might be termed an ink art aesthetic through their rich associations with Chinese literati pastimes or patronage. Furthermore, the manner in which they revive and transform past models adheres to a pattern of Chinese archaistic revival that has a history of more than one thousand years. Their inclusion in this survey is therefore appropriate to the extent that the artists are cognizant of China's cultural past and use it to inform and enrich their creations.

Two artists who have excelled at appropriating distinctive elements of Chinese material culture — divination implements, herbal medicines, and gunpowder — and transforming them into new mediums of artistic expression are Huang Yongping (b. 1954) and Cai Guo-Qiang (b. 1957). Each has lived abroad since the late 1980s and has been the subject of major retrospectives.[1] In spite of their residency outside China and their engagement with the international art scene, they have continued to explore themes and to mine historical references that reveal an ongoing identification with their Chinese heritage.[2] And while their works are primarily installations or performance pieces, it is significant that both these artists have continued to make use of traditional media and formats to document their time-based, often ephemeral creations.

Huang Yongping was among the first wave of students to enter college after the Cultural Revolution. In 1977 he was admitted to the department of oil painting at the Zhejiang Academy and upon graduation was assigned to teach art in a secondary school in his hometown of Xiamen, a port city in the southeastern province of Fujian. In spite of Xiamen's geographic isolation on the periphery of the contemporary art scene, in 1986 Huang caused a national sensation when he led a group of ten artists in the creation of an exhibition entitled "Xiamen Dada."[3] As this title implies, Huang's merging of Eastern and Western concepts was aimed at further problematizing the historical expectations of what constituted art. In his accompanying manifesto, "Xiamen Dada: Postmodern?,"[4] Huang noted that China's encounter with "Modern Art" in the early 1980s had "turned the art establishment upside down and contributed to a new generation." The resulting confusion, Huang mused, was "very 'Dada,'" but he also saw distinct parallels among some Western art concepts and Daoist and Chan Buddhist philosophies, declaring, "Chan is Dada, Dada is Chan. Postmodernism is the modern renaissance of Chan Buddhism." In the same document he also stated: "[Robert] Rauschenberg's use of whatever elements he came across and his juxtaposing of diverse objects in his painting are very much in tune with Daoism's ideas of the equality, sameness, and coexistence of everything." In Huang's view, "A work by Robert Rauschenberg can exist over a long or short time period, be made of any material, in any place, for any purpose, and have any outcome. This corresponds closely to the ubiquity of Dao, which is found in an ant, in weeds, in a potsherd, and in urine (Zhuangzi)."[5] By advocating parallels between Daoist and Chan Buddhist thought on the one hand and the works of Rauschenberg, Marcel Duchamp, John Cage, and Joseph Beuys on the other, Huang playfully characterized the works in Xiamen Dada as a logical outgrowth of Chinese concepts.[6]

Ultimately, the works of art were far less significant than his manifesto, which asserted the need for a clear break from the older generation's ideas about what constituted modern art. Huang saw "non-art as the beginning of a new art."[7]

To underscore their commitment to a fresh start, at the conclusion of the exhibition, having no place to store their works, the group orchestrated a public burning of the exhibits, again accompanied by a statement by Huang that declared, "It is good that China does not have art collections. This way, artists can arbitrarily choose how to deal with their works and need not be overly careful. An artist's attitude toward his own works is emblematic of the degree to which he has liberated himself."[8] Shortly thereafter, in December 1986, the group held another exhibition at the Fujian Art Museum. Instead of

Cai Guo-Qiang (b. 1957). *Project to Extend the Great Wall of China by 10,000 Meters*, 1993 (fig. 127, detail)

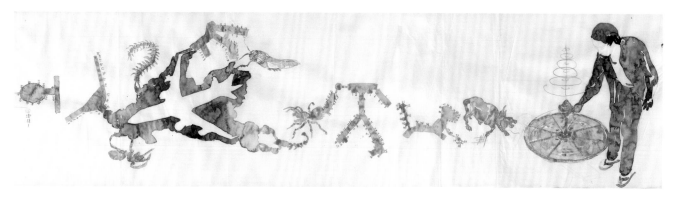

Fig. 123. Huang Yongping (b. 1954). Two sections of *Long Scroll*, 2001. Handscroll; watercolor, pencil, colored pencil, and ink on paper, overall 13 ¼ in. × 50 ft. 3 in. (33.7 × 1531.6 cm). The Museum of Modern Art, New York [Exhib.]

showing the works included in the approved exhibition proposal, they simply moved in construction materials from a neighboring lot, proclaiming, "What is being attacked here is not the audience, but their opinions on 'art.' Likewise, it is not the art museum itself that is under attack, but the art museum as an example of the art system."[9]

Huang has continued to challenge notions of art, globalization, and the viability of cultural interchange through his installations and performances, many of which are documented in his *Long Scroll*, a remarkable visual record of his artistic output from 1985 to 2001 (FIG. 123). Adopting the traditional handscroll format, the painted portion of the scroll, an area that according to the artist's inscription measures 1,320 centimeters (more than 43 feet) in length, consists of images drawn in pencil and tinted with a simple palette of orange and blue watercolors on "cicada-wing" *xuan* paper (*chanyi xuan*).[10] Some are augmented with penciled notes. The sequence of images is not chronological; rather, Huang has juxtaposed works in which he sees subtle visual or conceptual relationships.

The scroll opens with a depiction of *Clinic* (1997), a Y-shaped structure through which viewers are invited to pass into Huang's world. The illustrations that follow record installations in which Huang employed fortune-telling devices to guide his execution of "Non-Expressive" paintings — works in which the artist's decision making was ceded to chance.[11] He returns to this theme later in the scroll, where he has traced a photograph of himself turning what he called a "roulette wheel" — his first effort, in 1985, to automate the process of painting.[12] Nearby, a series of diagrammatic airport plans is interspersed with drawings of insects, the whole clustered around a jet plane silhouetted in blue. The insects refer to Huang's *World Theater* of 1993 in which he caged a selection of insects and reptiles — some natural enemies — and left them to struggle for survival, while the jet refers to the American spy plane that collided with a Chinese fighter jet on April 1, 2001, about fifty miles southeast of China's Hainan Island — a

cultural collision of a different sort — that inspired Huang's famous *Bat Project* (2001–5).[13]

Farther along in the scroll is an illustration of Huang's 1987 masterpiece, *The History of Chinese Painting and A Concise History of Modern Painting Washed in the Washing Machine for Two Minutes* (FIG. 126). To create this work, Huang ran through his washing machine the two most prominent introductory texts to Chinese and Western art history in China, Wang Bomin's *History of Chinese Painting* and the Chinese translation of Herbert Read's *A Concise History of Modern Painting*.[14] He piled the resulting pulp onto a broken sheet of glass set atop a wood crate. The act was reminiscent of the Chan injunction to destroy Buddhist texts and images as a way of transcending them; for Huang, it also acknowledged that it is only through such messy collisions of traditions, time, and geography that new possibilities emerge.[15]

The image of the work appears adjacent to a rendering of *Reptiles,* Huang's contribution to "Magiciens de la terre" (FIG. 124). In it, he used pulped books, newspapers, and photographs to re-create the forms of Chinese tombs. These three-dimensional pieces were described as resembling "a species of animal that creeps slowly forward (like a tortoise, a symbol of longevity in China). Culture is like a tomb, but it remains alive, it always crawls, it is slow like a tortoise. Wash newspapers: wash culture. 'The conception of "culture" must constantly be washed and dried.'"[16]

Both the challenge and the potential of cultural interchange is epitomized in a final juxtaposition of Dada and Buddhist imagery that appears toward the end of the scroll. There, drawings of French bottle-drying racks of the type made famous by Marcel Duchamp are compared with an image of a Buddhist savior, the Thousand-armed Guanyin (FIG. 125). This recalls Huang's 1997 installation in which he indicated how a utilitarian object from the West might call to mind an Asian deity whose many arms manifest its supernatural power to succor countless individuals at once.[17]

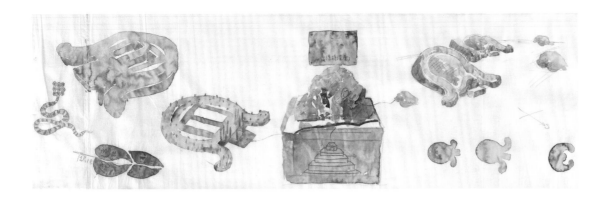

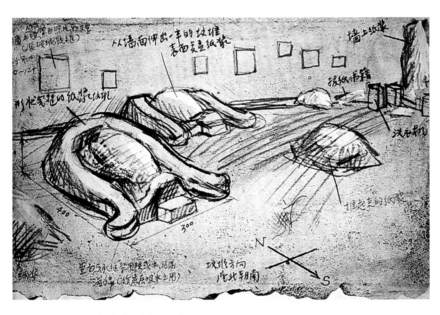

Fig. 124. Huang Yongping's sketch for *Reptiles*, 1989

Fig. 126. Huang Yongping (b. 1954). *The History of Chinese Painting and A Concise History of Modern Painting Washed in the Washing Machine for Two Minutes*, 1987. Installation with glass, wood case, paper, and book pulp, dimensions variable. Destroyed

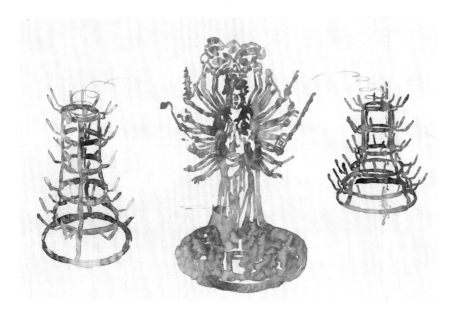

Fig. 125. Detail of *Long Scroll*

Since 1989 Huang has lived and worked in Paris, but as his *Long Scroll* demonstrates, while living as a cultural outsider in the West, he has increasingly sought to explore themes from his Chinese heritage.[18] Huang's work also suggests that artistic inspiration may arise out of cultural appropriations even when what is being appropriated is not entirely understood: "I never [thought] that it is a problem that I cannot really understand Duchamp. . . . What is important is not discovering the real face of Duchamp, but what I actually get out of him. I always benefit from all sorts of 'misunderstandings' and 'distortions.'"[19]

Like Huang Yongping, Cai Guo-Qiang has derived much of his inspiration from Chinese traditional sources, even though he has chosen to live outside China.[20] Born and raised in the southeastern coastal city of Quanzhou, Fujian Province, Cai benefited from his father's position as manager of the local New China (*Xinhua*) Bookstore, which gave him access to foreign publications and to the local cultural community.[21] He remained in Quanzhou during the Cultural Revolution, generating propaganda for the municipal authorities, and in the early 1980s studied with the Quanzhou Municipal Gaojia Opera Troupe and in the department of stage design at the Shanghai Drama Institute, where he was also exposed to the academic craft of oil painting. In 1986 Cai obtained a visa to study in Japan, where he became a studio assistant to Kawaguchi Tatsuo (b. 1940), a Conceptual sculptor whose work was shown in "Magiciens de la terre."[22] The Tiananmen Square incident later that year prompted Cai and his wife to remain abroad, and a number of commissions and residencies enabled him to spend time in Germany, France, and New York, where the artist and his family have lived since 1995.

In Japan, where traditional and modern art have shared a strong indigenous identity, Cai felt liberated from the historical opposition he encountered in China, where Western art was seen as modern and traditional Chinese ink painting as premodern.[23] His projects began to reflect a desire to transcend the boundaries of culturally specific artistic traditions: "I was thinking, 'Would there be a way to go beyond the very narrow East and West comparison? Was there an even larger context or a broader approach?'"[24] Inspired by Stephen Hawking's *A Brief History of Time* (1988) and the Big Bang theory of creation, Cai began to employ the metaphor of communicating with other beings in the universe.

Cai described his *Project to Extend the Great Wall of China by 10,000 Meters: Project for Extraterrestrials No. 10* (FIG. 127) as a "cultural activity, supported by people from various countries, including China, [that] took place at the Great Wall of China, which was built and repeatedly rebuilt . . . to separate nations. [This] cooperative effort to extend the wall finally invalidated its original practice and ideological function."[25] To realize the project, the artist appropriated the Great Wall as a work of Land Art, revitalizing one of China's most ancient and enduring cultural icons by tapping into its perceived cosmic energy (*qi*).[26] He and a team of volunteers laid a ten-kilometer fuse across the barren ridges of the Gobi Desert, starting at the westernmost end of the Ming dynasty wall at Jiayuguan, Gansu Province.[27] Small charges were placed along the line at three-meter intervals, while a larger charge was set at every kilometer.

The fuse was ignited at dusk on February 27, 1993. The initial explosion, moving at more than ten meters per second and punctuated at intervals by the exploding charges, took fifteen minutes to travel the entire length of the line and was seen by forty thousand residents and tourists. Through the fire, explosions, and billowing smoke, Cai sought to animate the "dragon meridians" (*longmai*) of the landscape in a conscious evocation of this auspicious Chinese mythological creature — a visualization of *qi* that is itself never entirely visible as it weaves in and out of the clouds.[28]

Integral to Cai's process at this time was the documentation of his ideas and methods in a series of Chinese-style folding albums, each a compact, accordion-bound notebook with a cloth cover and title strip that opens into a long horizontal composition and is read from right to left.[29] Notes and sketches are rendered in both ink and gunpowder in a blurring of Chinese artistic traditions and Cai's contemporary practice. For Cai, such albums are not just preparatory sketches but an essential part of his oeuvre as a painter: "People ask me why I do these sketches. The answer is simple: it is a desire to paint, the idea of becoming a painter, passed on from master to disciple, from generation to generation. It is in painting that my personal culture appears most naturally."[30]

One such album, created in 1990 (more than two years before Cai realized his *Project to Extend the Great Wall*), reveals the artist's motivations and aims for the project. In it, an eight-foot-long gestural rendering of the entire wall in bold brushstrokes of ink meets with a writhing, gunpowder-singed trail that evokes the anticipated path of the actual event (FIG. 128). The album opens with a sweeping curve indicating the shoreline of the East China Sea (labeled "sea" in dilute ink). This stroke intersects with an equally robust line meant to suggest the undulating path of the Great Wall. The point of intersection is labeled Shanhaiguan ("Pass between the sea and mountains"), the starting point of the Ming-era wall. In lighter ink above is a crenellated line also labeled Shanhaiguan, with an

Fig. 127. Cai Guo-Qiang (b. 1957). *Project to Extend the Great Wall of China by 10,000 Meters: Project for Extraterrestrials No. 10*. Realized in the Gobi Desert, west of the Great Wall, Jiayuguan, Gansu Province, February 27, 1993

extension of the wall going northeastward to the Yalu River. Other sites along the length of the wall are similarly identified: a small square below the bold line is labeled Beijing, while a nearby segment of the wall is labeled Juyongguan, the Yuan dynasty gateway just outside the city. Along the lower margin of the album is the project's title, in English and Chinese, as well as a small sketch of the Great Wall and Cai's proposed "extension."

The remainder of the album maps the course of the Great Wall to its endpoint at Jiayuguan. To either side of the inked line, Cai has added cursive inscriptions that offer his musings on the project and its significance: "The only man-made edifice visible from satellites is the 10,000 *li* Great Wall; wouldn't an additional 10,000 meters make it visible from remote planets?" Considering the symbolic power of the Great

Wall, he wonders, "From the Han dynasty to the present day, an endless cycle of days and months has passed, but the Great Wall majestically has survived for over two thousand years, so isn't it a manifestation either of China's enduring spirit through space and time or of the human spirit that pervades the globe?" He does not fail to consider the human cost of the wall — "The enormous labor of countless people symbolizes an unyielding spirit, just as the 'silvery serpent' [of falling snow] never ceases to claw itself forward"[31] — or to question its ability to limit people's movements: "It would seem that a long wall could help avert trouble, but the result is quite the opposite! It cuts in two an originally unified landmass. 'Give back my rivers and mountains!'[32] To whom should I direct this demand? Day after day building the wall while the mountains

Fig. 128. Cai Guo-Qiang (b. 1957). *Project to Extend the Great Wall of China by 10,000 Meters: Project for Extraterrestrials No. 10*, 1990. Accordion album of twenty-four leaves; ink and gunpowder burn marks on paper, each leaf 13 ¼ × 4 ¾ in. (33.7 × 12 cm). Private collection, New York [Exhib.]

and rivers gradually disappear. Take this blue planet and don't distinguish between east, west, south, north, and center; don't add, subtract, multiply or divide it." In his final comment, Cai proclaims his project a transformation of the wall into a work of art with lasting resonance: "Endless construction! The 10,000 *li* Great Wall is the only man-made edifice visible from space, yet this great project can never end. [Now,] by extending it by 10,000 meters, [the light created] may extend to other planets and even to the entire universe?!"

Cai's *Project to Extend the Great Wall*, a profound meditation on transience and the hubris of human monuments,[33] considers China's place within the larger world and the

mutability of imposed boundaries — questions also at the heart of Hong Hao's *Selected Scriptures* (FIG. 129).[34] In this series of thirty-seven prints, created between 1992 and 2000, Hong sought "to compile a 'new encyclopaedia' to put forward my own understanding of this ever-changing world. I would like to reshuffle various aspects of culture, to effectively dissolve boundaries and meanings, just like a computer virus. I would also like to make my works appear as 'respectable' as the ancient classics. Thus the title: *Selected Scriptures* [*Cang jing*]."[35]

Selected Scriptures encompasses five general themes: maps, martial strategy according to Sunzi, words, sacred cave temples, and the human body, including acupoints and face

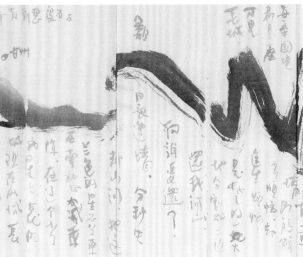

reading. But the largest category is world maps, about which Hong has observed, "I have long been interested in maps, especially historical maps, because they are capable of inspiring ideas on what we take as common knowledge. They are also the most direct and the most economical way to know the world."[36]

The prints are conceived as two-page spreads from a traditional woodblock-printed book, the edges of its pages stained and yellowed and its title and folio number written in Chinese along the outer margins.[37] But the scriptural reliability of Hong's images is subverted with titles and subtitles intentionally printed in different orientations and mismatched typefaces and type sizes, and with spelling errors. Often, Hong's maps

resemble collages of random images and words that recall prints by Robert Rauschenberg, an exhibition of whose work Hong visited in 1985 at Beijing's National Art Museum of China.[38]

The earliest maps in the series show the continents in a standard projection but with varying narrative content. In *New Political World* (1995), Hong has rearranged both the locations and shapes of countries and cities: China has been relocated to North America, while the United States has been reduced to a chain of small islands off the coast of what was once China (**FIG. 129A**). Much of Central Europe has been turned into a pig-shaped nation labeled Mozambique; Bosnia and Herzegovena occupy a tree-shaped country in West Africa; and Brazil and Monaco appear like a goblet and a wine bottle in Central Asia. *World Defense Layout Map* (1995) correctly identifies the continents but fills these landmasses with weaponry, armed figures, and victims of torture and rape (**FIG. 129B**). Submarines and a battleship ply the seas, and red and blue arrows indicate lines of attack or retreat. In *Latest Practical World Map* (1995), continents have been renamed "Crisis," "Hope," "Change," and "Desire"; the oceans are labeled "Be satisfied," "The lonely," "Be careful," and "Don't believe"; and cities bear names such as "Recently," "Brain Drain," "New Age," "Never Mind," and "Confusion" (**FIG. 129C**).

Toward the end of 1995, Hong began to reorder the world's topography in more radical ways. In *New World Survey Map*, for example, he presents countries according to their international status and influence: "The rich and powerful countries occupy vast areas on the map, while the rest is almost invisible" (**FIG. 129D**).[39] In *New World Geomorphic Map* (1996), the continents have been enlarged relative to the oceans, and the artist "makes extensive use of yellow to underline a certain idea of glory and richness" (**FIG. 129E**).[40] Ubiquitous emblems of consumerism — phones, computers, cars — compete for space with traditional motifs — a tree with gibbons, birds and flowers, craggy mountains. The computer screens provide tongue-in-cheek advice: "Be careful," "Control, gain, own, exploit," and "名利双收 Fame and fortune, you can have them both." In *Physical World* (1999), Hong transposes sea and land (**FIG. 129F**).[41]

Hong's maps represent the triumph of Western conceptions of mapmaking, which favor the accurate measurement of the distance between two points, in contrast to traditional Chinese maps, which are governed not by mathematical principles but by narrative and pictorial objectives.[42] But in each, scale and content are subverted in ways that undermine the viewer's expectations and suggest alternative readings. Hong's approach recalls Chinese literati painting in which depictions of landscape are understood to be reflections of the artist's

Fig. 129. Hong Hao (b. 1965). *Selected Scriptures*, 1992–2000. Six prints from a set of thirty-seven; silkscreened ink and color on paper, each 12 ⅛ × 23 ⅛ in. (30.8 × 58.7 cm). Private collection, New York [Exhib.]

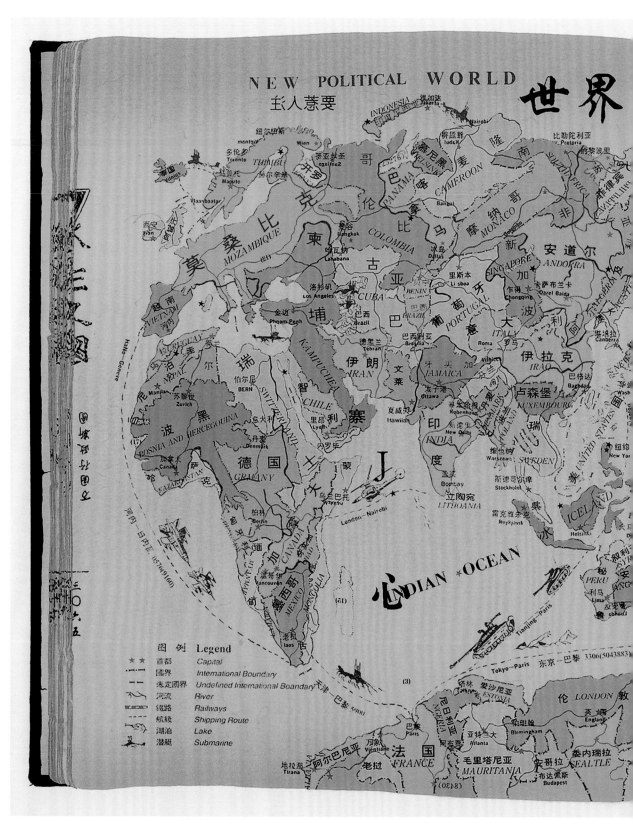

Fig. 129a. *Selected Scriptures: New Political World*, 1995

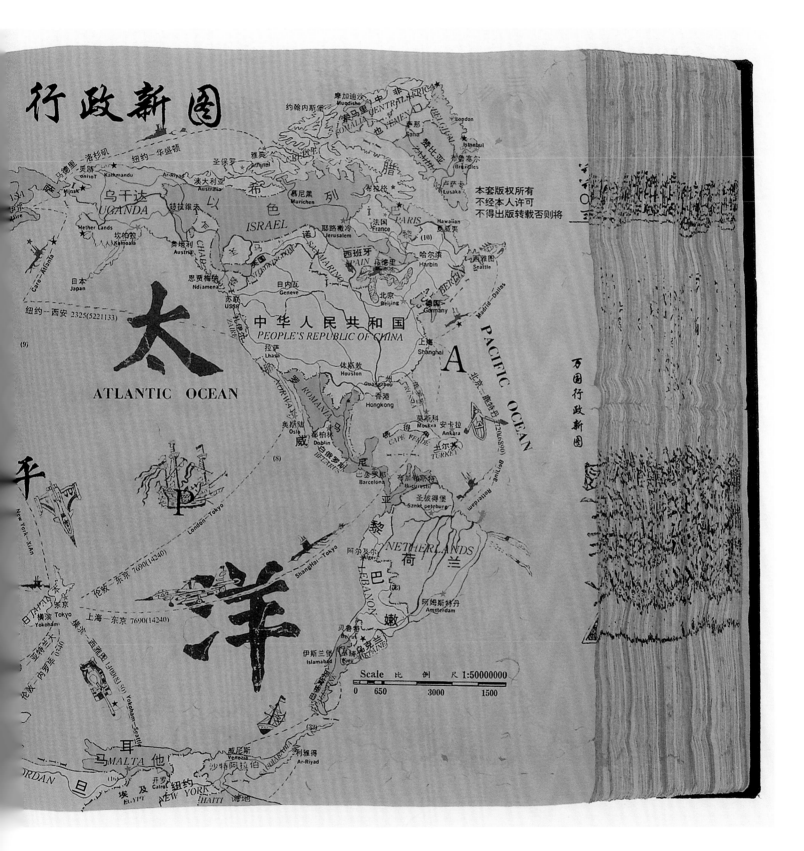

行政新图

万国行政新图

ATLANTIC OCEAN
太

平

洋

PACIFIC OCEAN

中华人民共和国
PEOPLE'S REPUBLIC OF CHINA

Scale 比 例 尺 1:50000000
0   650   3000   1500

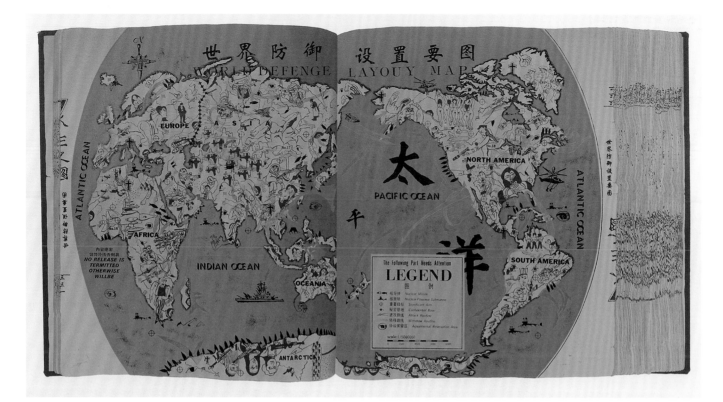

Fig. 129b. *Selected Scriptures:*
World Defense Layout Map, 1995

Fig. 129c. *Selected Scriptures:*
Latest Practical World Map, 1995

Fig. 129d. *Selected Scriptures:*
New World Survey Map, 1995

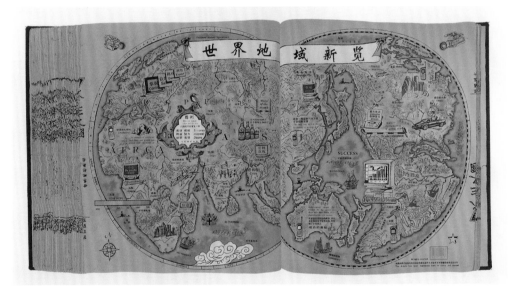

Fig. 129e. *Selected Scriptures:*
New World Geomorphic Map, 1996

Fig. 129f. *Selected Scriptures:*
Physical World, 1999

Fig. 130. Ai Weiwei (b. 1957). *Map of China*, 2006.
Ironwood (*Tieli mu*) from dismantled Qing dynasty
(1644–1911) temples, 31 ½ × 63 in. (80 × 160 cm).
Stockamp Tsai Collection [Exhib.]

state of mind. Here, maps are manipulated to reveal the diverse and subjective ways in which the world is visualized and understood. The images do not equate with topographic reality; rather, they become trenchant commentaries on concepts of nationalism, power, and the shifting nature of global awareness.

Ai Weiwei's *Map of China* not only replicates China's official cartographic identity, including the island of Taiwan, it also embodies something of China's history and cultural heritage (**FIG. 130**).[43] According to the artist, the interlocking wood elements from which the map is constructed were salvaged from dismantled Qing dynasty temples. Thus, Ai's *Map* becomes a poignant assertion that modern China is a mosaic of fragments from its past. It also makes the map a reliquary — a memento mori of the vast proportion of China's physical history that has been lost. The richness and complexity of that past are suggested by *Map's* fine wood tones and polished finish as well as the intriguing manner in which it was fabricated. Each interlocking element was carved using traditional tongue-and-groove joinery, starting with the outer layer of blocks (which are more than thirty inches tall) and working inward, with each piece uniquely shaped to fit precisely with those adjacent (**FIG. 131**). The entire process required an enormous amount of labor and nearly a year to complete. The result, a jigsaw-puzzle-like configuration of heterogeneous pieces, may be read as a symbol of China's cultural and ethnic diversity, asserting that while China remains distinctly singular, it is a fusion of countless individuals.[44] Its height, moreover, is an apt metaphor for both China's longevity as a coherent political and cultural entity and the amount of human labor required to shape and sustain that entity over time. When compared to Europe's political diversity, China's monolithic identity is astonishing. Ai's *Map* challenges our ability to imagine how such a complex state came into existence, how it has managed to survive for so long, and whether or not it can be maintained. The complex iconography and layers of historical reference that are embedded in *Map* reflect a sensibility that is akin to literati painting, which also transmutes natural imagery into a potent vehicle for expressing human values.

Map belongs to a category of contemporary artworks inspired not by ink painting or calligraphy but by objects associated with the literatus, ascribing them in spirit, if not in form or medium, to the ink art aesthetic. Repurposing familiar images or recontextualizing traditional iconography to insinuate new layers of meaning was a tactic favored by both literati artists and craftsmen, and Ai has been particularly adept in following this strategy in his own work. One telling example is his reinterpretation of a *ruyi* (wish fulfillment) scepter, an emblem

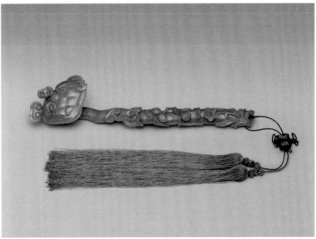

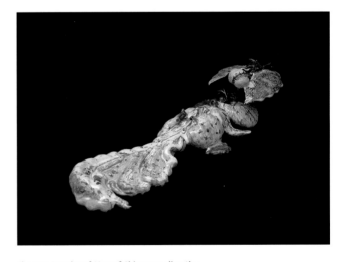

Fig. 131. Interior of *Map of China* revealing the tongue-and-groove joinery technique

Fig. 132. Scepter *(ruyi)* with longevity fungus, peaches, and narcissus. Qing dynasty (1644–1911), 18th century. Jadeite, 14 × 3 ⅛ × 1 ⅛ in. (35.5 × 8 × 2.9 cm). The Metropolitan Museum of Art, New York, Gift of Heber R. Bishop, 1902 (02.18.491)

Fig. 133. Ai Weiwei (b. 1957). *Ruyi,* 2006. Glazed ceramic, 6 × 30 ¼ × 9 in. (15 × 77 × 23 cm). M+ Sigg Collection, Hong Kong [Exhib.]

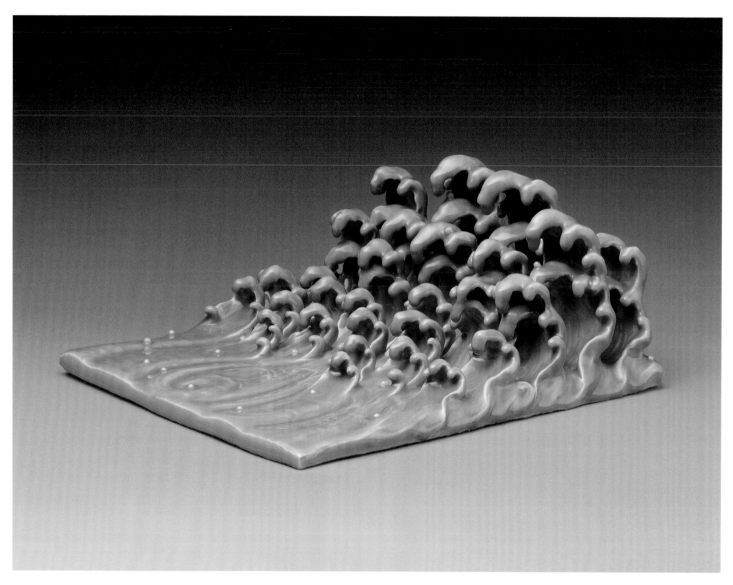

Fig. 134. Ai Weiwei (b. 1957). *The Wave*, 2005.
Glazed ceramic, 6 ⅛ × 16 ⅞ × 14 ¾ in. (15.7 × 42.9 ×
37.6 cm). Private collection, New York [Exhib.]

Fig. 135. Ma Yuan (ca. 1160/65–1225). *The Yellow River Reaches Its Course*, from the album *Twelve Scenes of Water*. Southern Song dynasty (1127–1279), dated 1222. Album leaf mounted as a handscroll; ink and light color on silk, 10 ½ × 16 ⅜ in. (26.8 × 41.6 cm). The Palace Museum, Beijing

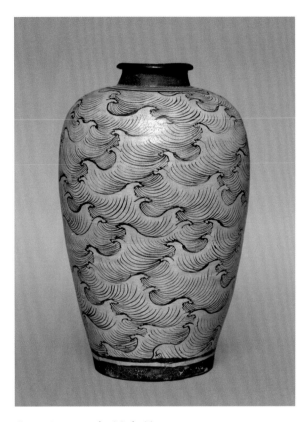

Fig. 137. Prunus vase (*meiping*) with waves. Jiangxi Province, Yonghezhen kilns. Southern Song (1127–1279)–Yuan dynasty (1271–1368), 13th–14th century. Glazed stoneware with slip-painted decoration (Jizhou ware), 10 ⁵⁄₁₆ × 6 ⁹⁄₁₆ in. (26.3 × 16.7 cm). Cleveland Museum of Art

Fig. 136. Katsushika Hokusai (1760–1849). *Under the Wave off Kanagawa (The Great Wave)*, from the series *Thirty-six Views of Mount Fuji*, Edo period (1615–1868), ca. 1830–32. Polychrome woodblock print; ink and color on paper, 9 ⅝ × 14 ⅟₁₆ in. (24.4 × 35.7 cm). The Metropolitan Museum of Art, New York, Rogers Fund, 1914 (JP10)

Fig. 138. Ai Weiwei (b. 1957). *Stool*, ca. 2007. Wood, 43 × 34 ¾ × 48 in. (109.2 × 88.3 × 122 cm). Private collection, Hong Kong [Exhib.]

Fig. 139. Ai Weiwei (b. 1957). *Table with Two Legs*, 2004. Wood, 51 ⅛ × 44 ⅛ × 39 ⅜ in. (130 × 112 × 100 cm). Private collection, New York [Exhib.]

Fig. 140. Ai Weiwei (b. 1957). *Han Dynasty Urn with Coca-Cola Logo*, 1994; urn, Western Han dynasty (206 B.C.–A.D. 9). Earthenware and paint, 9 ⅞ × 11 × 11 in. (25 × 28 × 28 cm). M+ Sigg Collection, Hong Kong [Exhib.]

of longevity and good fortune (**FIG. 132**). The form is derived from *lingzhicao*, a mushroom-shaped fungus that for more than two millennia was thought to confer immortality. Today, it is still believed to have curative powers as an anticarcinogen. Ai's scepter riffs on this belief by making its health-granting properties anatomically specific: richly embellished with colored glazes, it is composed of ceramic human organs (**FIG. 133**). Gruesome in appearance, these body parts are at odds with their intended meaning, serving not to herald long life but to call to mind humankind's physical frailty and vulnerability.

Ceramic is a medium that Ai has found to be a rich area for artistic exploration. Some of his earliest works were iconoclastic interventions with ancient Chinese ceramics: dropping a Han dynasty jar, overpainting another with the Coca-Cola logo (**FIG. 140**).[45] He subsequently began to create ceramics that mimicked earlier styles. One particularly striking reinterpretation of an earlier pictorial form is his *Wave* of 2005 (**FIG. 134**). Ai produced a number of variants on this theme with the assistance of craftsmen at Jingdezhen, in Jiangxi Province, China's center for fine porcelain production. This example

Fig. 141. Shao Fan (b. 1964). *Round-backed Armchair*, 2000. Stainless steel, 35 ½ × 24 ½ × 24 ½ in. (90 × 62 × 62 cm). The Metropolitan Museum of Art, New York, Gift of Pearl Lam, 2010 (2010.476.1) [Exhib.]

Fig. 142. Shao Fan (b. 1964). *Shadow*, 2009. Rosewood, 35 × 40 ¾ × 40 ¾ in. (89 × 103.5 × 103.5 cm). The Metropolitan Museum of Art, New York, Gift of Pearl Lam, 2010 (2010.476.3) [Exhib.]

evokes associations with the arts of the Southern Song dynasty. Its celadon-glazed body recalls vessels produced by the Longquan kilns located outside the Southern Song capital of Hangzhou, while its form may have been inspired by a depiction of waves by the Southern Song court painter Ma Yuan (ca. 1160/65−1225; **FIG. 135**) as well as the Japanese woodblock print *Under the Wave off Kanagawa* by Katsushika Hokusai (1760−1849; **FIG. 136**).[46] Even the square configuration of *The Wave* recalls the square album format of Ma's painting. The work also quotes Southern Song ceramics decorated with an overall pattern of waves (**FIG. 137**), demonstrating that Ma's vision was part of a broader interest in related motifs that extended across different media. Ai has succeeded in conveying an image of a roiling sea with a dynamism comparable to Ma's naturalistic renderings, prompting the question of whether one has greater aesthetic merit than the other. Bearing in mind the absence of Ai's hand from the actual fabrication of the piece, a task dear to the literatus but here conferred on anonymous workshop assistants, complicates this consideration still further.

Many of Ai's three-dimensional works — vessels, light fixtures, furniture — similarly reflect an interest in the anonymous mass production that generates the ready-made objects of daily life while subverting the functionality of such objects. This is most evident in his deconstruction and reconfiguration of traditional pieces of furniture in ways that render them inoperative (**FIGS. 138, 139**). The works question the ways in which modernization has made China's past inaccessible and whether, in seeking to perpetuate tradition by adapting inherited forms, one instead distorts it irrevocably. Shao Fan's transformation of Ming-style chairs into modern hybrids using contemporary forms, techniques, and materials refutes both implications, demonstrating how China's past can both adapt to and coexist with its rapidly changing and increasingly globalized present (**FIGS. 141, 142**).

Dream of China (2008), by the Beijing artist Wang Jin (b. 1962), poses similar questions about the present's relationship to the past (**FIG. 143**). The work, part of a series begun in 1997, appropriates the form of a Qing dynasty dragon robe and re-creates it in polyvinyl chloride (PVC), a consumer plastic the

Fig. 143. Wang Jin (b. 1962). *Dream of China*, 2008.
Polyvinyl chloride robe with vinyl filament and
iron chain and hook, 64 ½ × 85 ¾ × 11 ¾ in. (164 ×
218 × 30 cm). The Metropolitan Museum of Art,
New York, Purchase, Friends of Asian Art Gifts, 2012
(2012.145) [Exhib.]

Fig. 144. Zhang Jianjun (b. 1955). *Scholar Rock
(The Mirage Garden)*, 2008. Silicone rubber, 86 ⅝ ×
59 × 33 ½ in. (220 × 150 × 85 cm). Sigg Collection
[Exhib.]

artist sees as a perfect representation of contemporary society.[47] Wang, a graduate of the Zhejiang Academy whose earlier performances focused on social issues arising from contradictions between traditional Chinese values and global consumer culture, did not make the robe himself.[48] Instead, he engaged peasant women from a rural Hebei village known for their fine needlework to embroider the robe. Using nylon filament, they sewed intricate patterns of stylized waves, clouds, and dragons in imitation of the original silk garment that served as a model.[49] Despite the heft and stiffness of the PVC, the translucent robe appears weightless and ethereal, a ghostly memory of China's imperial past from which all prestige and power have been eviscerated, transforming the robe into an empty emblem of a dynasty that was unable to shield China from foreign incursions. As the title of the work implies, China's traditional identity is again challenged by a new wave of consumerism and industrialization that threatens to transform China's past into an equally inert vestige.

Both Zhang Jianjun (b. 1955) and Zhan Wang (b. 1962) also comment on China's struggle to fuse tradition and globalization by transmuting a revered art form — Chinese scholars' rocks — through the use of industrial materials. Born in Shanghai and inspired by a father who practiced calligraphy every day, Zhang Jianjun studied *guohua* in his youth and for one semester at the Shanghai Drama Institute before switching to oil painting. After graduating in 1978, Zhang served first as an artist in residence and later as a curator and administrator at the Shanghai Art Gallery while continuing to create abstract, mixed-media paintings that in the early 1980s were criticized as "Western bourgeois art."[50] In 1989 Zhang immigrated to America, where he gradually rediscovered ink as a medium, using it in a number of installations, including his 2002 *Ink Garden of Re-Creation*, which featured ornamental garden rocks made of hardened ink (SEE FIG. 21).[51] In 1997 Zhang began teaching art at New York University, and since 2007 he has alternated between NYU's campuses in New York and Shanghai. In coming to terms with his dual identity, Zhang realized "that I was actually a bridge between two lands and two cultures, and that I could see through both experiences. Combining these two cultures, I could see the differences, and play with it in my artwork."[52]

Zhang's *Scholar Rock (The Mirage Garden)* of 2008, a re-creation of a garden rock in purple silicone, playfully demonstrates how Chinese traditions may evolve within a new global context (FIG. 144). According to the artist, the work comments on the sometimes incongruous collision of cultures that is modern China: "I chose the scholar's rock, a symbol charged

with traditional cultural specificity, cast in [silicone], a post-industrial material, with fashionable colors added in, to construct a societal landscape specific to our time."[53]

Beijing artist Zhan Wang learned traditional painting from his grandfather before studying sculpture at the Beijing Industrial Arts School (1978–81; now the College of Arts and Design, Beijing Technology University) and the Central Academy of Fine Arts (1983–88). In the early 1990s Zhan left his traditional training behind to experiment with diverse media and haunting installations inspired by the demolition of many Beijing neighborhoods to make way for new high-rise structures.

In 1995, responding to the incongruous sight of modern buildings with Chinese-style roofs or traditional rockeries at their entrances, Zhan proposed creating garden rocks fabricated from a material that would both reflect and harmonize with a modern architectural environment: "Placed in a traditional courtyard, [rockeries (*jiashan*)] satisfied people's desire to return to Nature by offering them stone fragments from Nature. But huge changes in the world have made this traditional ideal increasingly out of date. I have thus used stainless steel to duplicate and transform natural [rockeries] into manufactured forms. The material's glittering surface, ostentatious glamour, and illusory appearance make it an ideal medium to convey new dreams [in contemporary China]."[54]

Artificial Rock #10 is based on a type of limestone with unusually erosive properties long prized by Chinese literati as a tangible embodiment of the creative forces of nature (FIG. 145).[55] Zhan first made a mold from one such rock, then cast a replica in iron. Next, workmen hammered thin sheets of steel onto the iron model, guided by lines drawn on its surface. Once removed from the model, the sheets were welded together and burnished to a mirrorlike finish, leaving no hint of how the piece had been fabricated.[56] Zhan's wish to eliminate any trace of human intervention is the same goal traditional craftsmen sought to achieve with scholars' rocks, which were almost always enhanced by sculpting. And like Zhan, traditional artisans frequently created imitations of naturally eroded limestone in materials including wood, ceramic, metal, and hardstones. By evoking a traditional form in a radically modern medium, however, *Artificial Rock #10* encourages a reexamination of the traditional qualities of surface texture, leanness, interior perforations, and instability that define a good rock.

Untitled, a bronze sculpture dated 2009 by Zeng Fanzhi (b. 1964), presents another kind of transmutation of a traditional literati art form — from a two-dimensional painting to a three-dimensional bronze (FIG. 146). A prolific and highly successful oil painter with an oeuvre characterized by expressive

Fig. 145. Zhan Wang (b. 1962). *Artificial Rock #10*, 2001. Stainless steel, 29 ½ × 17 ¾ × 7 ½ in. (75 × 45 × 19 cm). The Metropolitan Museum of Art, New York, Purchase, Friends of Asian Art Gifts, 2006 (2006.244a–c) [Exhib.]

Fig. 146. Zeng Fanzhi (b. 1964). *Untitled*, 2009. Bronze, 46 × 24 × 16 ½ in. (117 × 61 × 42 cm). The Metropolitan Museum of Art, New York, Gift of Thomas Yaping Ou, 2011 (2011.378a, b) [Exhib.]

brushwork and rich symbolism, Zeng grew up in the city of Wuhan, Hubei Province, and studied oil painting at the Hubei Institute of Fine Arts (1987–91), where he was first exposed to non-Chinese art: "In the 1980s, we only wanted to learn Western things. For the whole decade, we wanted to learn philosophies, arts, everything from the West."[57] Zeng rejected the Soviet Socialist Realism being taught in his classes in favor of German Expressionism, which strongly colored his own developing style of figure painting.[58] For his graduation work, Zeng chose to paint disturbing images of doctors and patients, a response to the scenes he encountered daily growing up next to a hospital: "I decided to paint the things around me, the things I experienced and saw day in and day out, the things that moved me and made me feel."[59] This series was followed by one featuring images of butchered carcasses (*Meat*, 1992–93) and another in which figures' faces are covered with masks (*Masks*, 1994–2001). In all these works, Zeng explores a sense of alienation prompted by the increasingly impersonal interactions of modern life.

A similarly tortured sensibility is evoked by *Untitled*, Zeng's first sculpture.[60] Possibly inspired by a wisteria vine, it suggests the gnarled texture and convoluted form of a blasted tree trunk that continues to send forth new shoots.[61] The twisted and bent "trunk," scarred with knotholes and cracks, is seemingly a product of a harsh environment and punishing forces, but the upward-reaching "branches" convey a sense of resilience reminiscent of traditional paintings of ancient plum trees — a powerful symbol of survival, renewal, and moral purity. The sculpture's form may also reference a recurring motif in Zeng's contemporaneous paintings: skyward-reaching tree branches in the foreground that partially screen the view of what lies behind — lone animals, desolate receding paths, or recognizable figures from pop culture or the arts.[62] Set on a tall, narrow pedestal, the work's contorted silhouette juxtaposed against the rectilinear base is a strikingly austere reinterpretation of a traditional emblem of hope.

•   •   •

The underlying contention of this volume is that the past remains very much present in Chinese contemporary art, but as exemplified by the works discussed above, the invocation of Chinese artistic traditions goes far beyond the use of a single medium, and sources of inspiration have exceeded the boundaries of space and time defined by China's cultural heritage. While China has been exposed to outside influences throughout its history, the explosive influx of foreign concepts and values that has occurred since 1980 has brought with it unequivocally seismic change — in politics, economics, society, and in the arts. This study has sought to demonstrate that, having gone through a collective period of self-examination and struggle with the past, artists in China have with growing self-confidence begun to explore the diverse sources of their own heritage, freely learning from and adapting both ancient and more recent models — including the visual legacy of the Cultural Revolution — as well as earlier twentieth-century traditions of cinema, graphic design, and oil painting. And at the same time that artists have become conversant with the discourse on global contemporary art, they have increasingly asserted their own cultural identity and a willingness to acknowledge the significance of their past.[63]

The continued viability of ink, both as a medium and as a wellspring of inspiration, is very much a consequence of Chinese artists' interest in examining and sustaining a tradition that for more than two millennia has been the preeminent mode of artistic expression in China. Indeed, it is the primacy of ink and the extent to which the principles of ink art have seeped into the broader artistic consciousness of China that I have chosen it as the unifying rubric by which to examine works of such disparate media and formats. Historically, one of the challenges facing each generation of artists has been how to innovate a tradition with such extraordinary longevity. At the same time, it has become impossible to ignore artistic trends that have evolved outside China. Since the 1980s, there has been a concerted effort on the part of many artists to transcend the perceived divisions between East and West. For instance, some artists have interpreted Western movements and artworks through references to Daoism and Chan Buddhism. Thus can Huang Yongping draw parallels between Dada and Buddhism, and see in Robert Rauschenberg's work an embodiment of Daoist principles. Others reject as unproductive the perceived dichotomy between East and West, embracing a new eclecticism in their sources of inspiration and exploring new genres and materials. At the same time, some artists have asserted the relevance of their artistic heritage at a global level, acknowledging that their traditions can resonate just as powerfully with artists and audiences outside China.

Regardless of whether they utilize ink or other media, the artists treated here have all challenged and been challenged by precedents from China's past, and they have exploited the friction between tradition and their individual visions to create works of great diversity and originality. Underlying all these efforts and informing the identity of both artist and artwork is a distinctively Chinese aesthetic consciousness rooted in a recognition of China's cultural heritage — a contemporary ink aesthetic in which references to time-honored pictorial, calligraphic, and cultural concepts remain a defining feature of an artist's vision without limiting that artist's formal solutions. To appreciate China's art today, therefore, one must never lose sight of its past.

艾未未　可口可乐罐子
AI WEIWEI (B. 1957)
Han Dynasty Urn with Coca-Cola Logo, 1994; urn, Western Han dynasty (206 B.C.–A.D. 9)
Earthenware and paint
9 ⅞ × 11 × 11 in. (25 × 28 × 28 cm)
M+ Sigg Collection, Hong Kong
Fig. 140

艾未未　暂时的风景
AI WEIWEI (B. 1957)
Provisional Landscapes, 2002–8
Nine chromogenic prints from a series
Each 38 ⅛ × 48 in. (97 × 122 cm)
M+ Sigg Collection, Hong Kong
Fig. 86

艾未未　桌
AI WEIWEI (B. 1957)
Table with Two Legs, 2004
Wood
43 × 34 ¾ × 48 in.
(109.2 × 88.3 × 122 cm)
Private collection, New York
Fig. 139

艾未未　浪
AI WEIWEI (B. 1957)
The Wave, 2005
Glazed ceramic
6 ⅛ × 16 ⅞ × 14 ¾ in.
(15.7 × 42.9 × 37.6 cm)
Private collection, New York
Fig. 134

艾未未　中国地图
AI WEIWEI (B. 1957)
Map of China, 2006
Ironwood (*Tieli mu*) from dismantled Qing dynasty (1644–1911) temples
31 ½ × 63 in. (80 × 160 cm)
Stockamp Tsai Collection
Fig. 130

艾未未　如意
AI WEIWEI (B. 1957)
Ruyi, 2006
Glazed ceramic
6 × 30 ¼ × 9 in. (15 × 77 × 23 cm)
M+ Sigg Collection, Hong Kong
Fig. 133

艾未未　椅子
AI WEIWEI (B. 1957)
Stool, ca. 2007
Wood
20 ½ × 26 ¾ × 17 ⅜ in.
(52 × 68 × 44 cm)
Private collection, Hong Kong
Fig. 138

蔡国强　将万里长城延长一万米
CAI GUO-QIANG (B. 1957)
Project to Extend the Great Wall of China by 10,000 Meters: Project for Extraterrestrials No. 10, 1990
Accordion album of twenty-four leaves; ink and gunpowder burn marks on paper
Each leaf 13 ¼ × 4 ¾ in.
(33.7 × 12 cm)
Private collection, New York
Fig. 128

蔡国强　将万里长城延长一万米
CAI GUO-QIANG (B. 1957)
Videography by Araki Takahisa
Project to Extend the Great Wall of China by 10,000 Meters: Project for Extraterrestrials No. 10, 1994
Three-channel color video with sound; 9 min. 29 sec.
Collection of the artist
Fig. 127

陈劭雄　墨水城市
CHEN SHAOXIONG (B. 1962)
Ink City, 2005
Single-channel animated video with sound; 3 min.
Collection of the artist
Fig. 98

陈劭雄　墨水日记
CHEN SHAOXIONG (B. 1962)
Ink Diary, 2006
Single-channel animated video with sound; 3 min.
Collection of the artist
Fig. 100

陈劭雄　墨水东西
CHEN SHAOXIONG (B. 1962)
Ink Things, 2007
Single-channel animated video with sound; 3 min.
Collection of the artist
Fig. 99

陈劭雄　墨水历史
CHEN SHAOXIONG (B. 1962)
Ink History, 2010
Single-channel animated video with sound; 3 min.
Collection of the artist
Fig. 101

段建宇　美丽的梦 2
DUAN JIANYU (B. 1970)
Beautiful Dream 2, 2008
Ink on cardboard
10 ¼ × 19 ¾ in. (26 × 50 cm)
Sigg Collection
Fig. 76

段建宇　美丽的梦 3
DUAN JIANYU (B. 1970)
Beautiful Dream 3, 2008
Ink on cardboard
15 ⅜ × 21 ¼ in. (39 × 54 cm)
Sigg Collection
Fig. 73

段建宇　美丽的梦 4
DUAN JIANYU (B. 1970)
Beautiful Dream 4, 2008
Ink on cardboard
17 ¼ × 13 in. (44 × 33 cm)
Sigg Collection
Fig. 74

段建宇　美丽的梦 7
DUAN JIANYU (B. 1970)
Beautiful Dream 7, 2008
Ink on cardboard
11 ½ × 17 ¼ in. (29 × 44 cm)
Sigg Collection
Fig. 75

方力钧　2003.3.1
FANG LIJUN (B. 1963)
2003.3.1, 2003
Seven-panel woodblock print
Each panel 13 ft. 1 ½ in. × 48 in.
(400 × 121.7 cm); overall
13 ft. 1 ½ in. × 27 ft. 11 ½ in.
(400 × 852 cm)
Private collection, Hong Kong
Fig. 104

冯明秋　心经
FUNG MINGCHIP (B. 1951)
Heart Sutra, 2001
Pair of hanging scrolls; ink on paper
Each 26 ⅝ × 27 ½ in. (67.6 × 69.8 cm)
The Metropolitan Museum of Art, New York, Gift of Susan L. Beningson and Steve Arons, in memory of Renée Beningson, 2011 (2011.527.2a, b)
Fig. 42

谷文达　遗失的王朝系列—静观的世界 (太朴图.文字的构成.文字的综合)
GU WENDA (B. 1955)
Mythos of Lost Dynasties Series— Tranquility Comes from Meditation (Primitive World, Composition of Words, Synthesized Words), 1985
Three hanging scrolls from original set of five; ink on paper
Scroll 1: 9 ft. ¾ in. x 69 ⅛ in.
(276.2 × 175.6 cm);
scroll 2: 9 ft. ½ in. x 69 ⅜ in.
(275.6 × 176.2 cm);
scroll 3: 9 ft. ½ in. x 69 in.
(275.6 × 175.3 cm)
Collection of Guo Zhen
Figs. 24, 25

谷文达　遗失的王朝系列—我批阅
三男三女书写的静字
GU WENDA (B. 1955)
Mythos of Lost Dynasties Series—
I Evaluate Characters Written by
Three Men and Three Women, 1985
Hanging scroll; ink on paper
9 ft. 4 ¼ in. × 70 in. (285 × 178 cm)
Private collection, Hong Kong
Fig. 40

谷文达　遗失的王朝系列—正反的
字
GU WENDA (B. 1955)
Mythos of Lost Dynasties Series—
Negative and Positive Characters,
1984–85
Three hanging scrolls; ink on paper
Each 9 ft. 4 ⅝ in. × 68 ½ in.
(286 × 174 cm)
Private collection, Hong Kong
Fig. 41

洪浩　藏经　（世界行政新图，世
界防御设置要图，最新实用世界地
图，世界测绘新图，世界地域新览，
世界地形图）
HONG HAO (B. 1965)
Selected Scriptures, 1992–2000
(New Political World, 1995; *World*
Defense Layout Map, 1995; *Latest*
Practical World Map, 1995; *New*
World Survey Map, 1995; *New World*
Geomorphic Map, 1996; *Physical*
World, 1999)
Six prints from a set of thirty-seven;
silkscreened ink and color on paper
Each 12 ⅛ × 23 ⅛ in. (30.8 × 58.7 cm)
Private collection, New York
Fig. 129

洪浩　清明上河图
HONG HAO (B. 1965)
Spring Festival along the River, 2000
Accordion album of thirty-four
leaves; chromogenic print
Each leaf 14 ¼ × 12 ¼ in.
(36.2 × 31.1 cm)
Collection of David Solo
Fig. 84

黄岩　中国山水纹身
HUANG YAN (B. 1966)
Chinese Landscape Tattoo No. 2
and No. 4, 1999
Two chromogenic prints
Each 20 × 24 in. (50.8 × 61 cm)
Private collection, New York
Fig. 77

黄永砯　长卷
HUANG YONGPING (B. 1954)
Long Scroll, 2001
Handscroll; watercolor, pencil,
colored pencil, and ink on paper
Overall 13 ¼ in. × 50 ft. 3 in.
(33.7 × 1531.6 cm)
The Museum of Modern Art,
New York
Figs. 123, 125

李华生　0669
LI HUASHENG (B. 1944)
0669, 2005
Four hanging scrolls; ink on paper
Each 9 ft. × 48 in. (274.3 × 121.9 cm)
Collection of the artist
Fig. 116

刘丹　水墨画卷　（铅笔稿）
LIU DAN (B. 1953)
Study for *Ink Handscroll,* 1990
Pencil on paper
3 ½ × 65 ¾ in. (9 × 167 cm)
Collection of Alexandra Munroe
Fig. 53

刘丹　水墨画卷
LIU DAN (B. 1953)
Ink Handscroll, 1990
Handscroll; ink and color on paper
37 ¾ in. × 58 ft. 4 in. (95.6 × 1780 cm)
The San Diego Museum of Art,
Museum purchase (1998.1)
Fig. 52

刘丹　字典
LIU DAN (B. 1953)
Dictionary, 1991
Ink and watercolor on paper
81 ⅛ in. × 10 ft. (206 × 304.8 cm)
Collection of Akiko Yamazaki and
Jerry Yang
Fig. 47

刘炜　花儿
LIU WEI (B. 1965)
Untitled No. 6 "Flower," 2003
Accordion album of twenty-four
leaves with silk brocade cover; pencil,
acrylic, ink, and watercolor on paper
Each leaf 9 ⅝ × 6 ½ in.
(24.5 × 16.5 cm)
Private collection, New York
Fig. 107

邱黯雄　在空中
QIU ANXIONG (B. 1972)
In the Sky, 2005
Single-channel animated video
with sound; 8 min. 17 sec.
Collection of the artist
Fig. 93

邱黯雄　雁南
QIU ANXIONG (B. 1972)
Flying South, 2006
Single-channel animated video
with sound; 9 min. 18 sec.
Collection of the artist
Fig. 94

邱黯雄　新山海经一
QIU ANXIONG (B. 1972)
New Classic of Mountains and
Seas I, 2006
Three-channel animated video
with sound; 30 min.
Collection of the artist
Fig. 95

邱黯雄　新山海经一
QIU ANXIONG (B. 1972)
New Classic of Mountains and
Seas I, 2008
Portfolio of twelve woodblock prints;
ink on paper
Each print 19 ¾ × 16 ½ in.
(50 × 42.1 cm)
The Metropolitan Museum of Art,
New York, Purchase, Friends of
Asian Art Gifts, 2013
Fig. 96

邱黯雄　山河梦影
QIU ANXIONG (B. 1972)
Temptation of the Land, 2009
Three-channel animated video
with sound; 13 min. 25 sec.
Collection of the artist
Fig. 97

邱世华　无题
QIU SHIHUA (B. 1940)
Untitled, 1996
Oil on canvas
45 ¼ × 71 ⅝ in. (115 × 182 cm)
Sigg Collection
Fig. 62

邱世华　无题
QIU SHIHUA (B. 1940)
Untitled, 2001?
Oil on canvas
36 ¼ × 66 ¹⁵⁄₁₆ in. (92 × 170 cm)
M+ Sigg Collection, Hong Kong
Fig. 63

邱世华　无题
QIU SHIHUA (B. 1940)
Untitled, 2002
Mixed media on canvas
31 ⅞ × 68 ½ in. (81 × 174 cm)
M+ Sigg Collection, Hong Kong
Fig. 64

邱志杰　书写兰亭序一千遍
QIU ZHIJIE (B. 1969)
Writing the "Orchid Pavilion Preface"
One Thousand Times, 1990–95
Five chromogenic prints
Each 19 ¼ × 39 in. (49 × 99 cm)
M+ Sigg Collection, Hong Kong
Fig. 36

邱志杰　给邱家瓦的三十封信
QIU ZHIJIE (B. 1969)
30 Letters to Qiu Jiawa, 2009
Three hanging scrolls from a set
of thirty; ink on paper
Each 16 ft. 4 ⅞ in. × 74 ⅞ in.
(500 × 190 cm)
Private collection, New York
Fig. 70

任戬　元化
REN JIAN (B. 1955)
Primeval Chaos, 1987–88
Handscroll; ink on polyester
59 in. × 98 ft. 5 in. (150 × 3000 cm)
Hong Kong Museum of Art, donated
by Ms. Wong Ying-Kay, Ada
Fig. 50

少番　不锈钢圈椅
SHAO FAN (B. 1964)
Pair of Round-backed Armchairs,
2000
Stainless steel
Each 35 ½ × 24 ½ × 24 ½ in.
(90 × 62 × 62 cm)
The Metropolitan Museum of Art,
New York, Gift of Pearl Lam, 2010
(2010.476.1, .2)
Fig. 141

少番　山水
SHAO FAN (B. 1964)
Landscape, 2009
Pencil on paper
62 ¼ × 62 ¼ in. (158 × 158 cm)
The Metropolitan Museum of Art,
New York, Gift of Frank Kong Siu
Ming, 2011 (2011.100)
Fig. 58

少番　影
SHAO FAN (B. 1964)
Shadow, 2009
Rosewood
35 × 40 ¾ × 40 ¾ in.
(89 × 103.5 × 103.5 cm)
The Metropolitan Museum of Art,
New York, Gift of Pearl Lam, 2010
(2010.476.3)
Fig. 142

史国瑞　上海
SHI GUORUI (B. 1964)
Shanghai, China, 15–16 October
2004, 2004
Unique camera obscura gelatin
silver print
50 ¾ in. × 14 ft. 1 ¼ in. (129 × 430 cm)
M+ Sigg Collection, Hong Kong
Fig. 78

宋冬　印水
SONG DONG (B. 1966)
Printing on Water (Performance in
the Lhasa River, Tibet, 1996), 1996
Thirty-six chromogenic prints
Each 23 ¾ × 15 ¾ in. (60.5 × 39.9 cm)
The Metropolitan Museum of Art,
New York, Promised Gift of
Cynthia Hazen Polsky (L.2011.70.6)
Fig. 45

孙逊　一场革命中还未来得及定义的行为
SUN XUN (B. 1980)
Some Actions Which Haven't Been Defined Yet in the Revolution, 2011
Single-channel woodblock-animation video with sound; 12 min. 22 sec.
Collection of the artist
Fig. 102

王冬龄　无题
WANG DONGLING (B. 1945)
Untitled, 1999
Hanging scroll; ink on paper
96 ¾ × 57 ½ in. (245.7 × 146.1 cm)
Private collection, New York
Fig. 112

王冬龄　守白
WANG DONGLING (B. 1945)
Being Open and Empty, 2005
Hanging scroll; ink on paper
87 ¼ × 57 in. (221.6 × 144.8 cm)
The Metropolitan Museum of Art, New York, Gift of the artist, 2013 (2013.188.2)
Fig. 113

王冬龄　玄黄
WANG DONGLING (B. 1945)
Dark (Heaven) and Yellow (Earth), 2005
Horizontal scroll; ink on paper
57 in. × 12 ft. ⅝ in. (144.8 × 367.3 cm)
The Metropolitan Museum of Art, New York, Gift of the artist, 2013 (2013.188.3)
Fig. 114

王晋　中国之梦
WANG JIN (B. 1962)
Dream of China, 2008
Polyvinyl chloride robe with vinyl filament and iron chain and hook
64 ½ × 85 ¾ × 11 ¾ in. (164 × 218 × 30 cm)
The Metropolitan Museum of Art, New York, Purchase, Friends of Asian Art Gifts, 2012 (2012.145)
Fig. 143

王天德　数码 No. 02HP01–03
WANG TIANDE (B. 1960)
Digital No. 02HP01–03, 2002
Three pairs of unmounted sheets; ink and burn marks on paper
Each sheet 8 ft. 8 ¾ in. × 26 ¾ in. (266.1 × 67.9 cm)
Private collection, New York
Fig. 43

吴山专　字象的黑体
WU SHANZHUAN (B. 1960)
Character Image of Black Character Font, 1989
Six unmounted sheets; ink and color on paper
Each 33 × 26 ⅜ in. (84 × 67 cm)
Private collection, Hong Kong
Fig. 39

邢丹文　长卷 A1
XING DANWEN (B. 1967)
Scroll A1, 1999–2000
Chromogenic print
9 in. × 9 ft. 3 ⅞ in. (22.8 × 284 cm)
Private collection, New York
Fig. 87

邢丹文　长卷 B2
XING DANWEN (B. 1967)
Scroll B2, 1999–2000
Chromogenic print
4 ⅝ × 62 ⅞ in. (11.8 × 159.7 cm)
Collection of Christopher Phillips
Fig. 88

邢丹文　都市演绎
XING DANWEN (B. 1967)
Urban Fiction No. 13, 2005
Digitally manipulated chromogenic print
67 × 86 ⅜ in. (170 × 219.5 cm)
M+ Sigg Collection, Hong Kong
Fig. 89

徐冰　天书
XU BING (B. 1955)
Book from the Sky, ca. 1987–91
Installation of hand-printed books and ceiling and wall scrolls printed from wood letterpress type; ink on paper
Each book, open, 18 ⅛ × 20 in. (46 × 51 cm); three ceiling scrolls, each 38 in. × approx. 115 ft. (96.5 × approx. 3500 cm); each wall scroll 9 ft. 2 ¼ in. × 39 ⅜ in. (280 × 100 cm)
Collection of the artist
Figs. 26, 27

徐冰　天书
XU BING (B. 1955)
Carved type for *Book from the Sky*, ca. 1987–91
Pearwood
Single frontispiece block 12 ½ × 8 ½ × ½ in. (31.8 × 21.6 × 1.3 cm); racked type 17 × 20 × 1 ½ in. (43.2 × 50.8 × 3.8 cm); small type block ¼ × ¼ × ¾ in. (.6 × .6 × 1.9 cm); large type block ¾ × ¾ × ¾ in. (1.9 × 1.9 × 1.9 cm)
Collection of the artist
Fig. 28

徐冰　新英文书法说明
XU BING (B. 1955)
An Introduction to Square Word Calligraphy, 1994–96
Handscroll; ink on paper
19 in. × 17 ft. (48.3 × 518.2 cm)
Private collection, New York
Fig. 35

徐冰　英文方块字叶慈诗一首
XU BING (B. 1955)
The Song of Wandering Aengus by William Butler Yeats, 1999
Pair of hanging scrolls; ink on paper
Each 63 ¼ × 51 ½ in. (160.5 × 130.8 cm)
Private collection, New York
Fig. 32

杨福东　留兰
YANG FUDONG (B. 1971)
Liu Lan, 2003
Single-channel video, 35 mm black-and-white film transferred to DVD, with sound; 14 min.
Courtesy Marian Goodman Gallery, New York
Fig. 91

杨诘苍　千层墨
YANG JIECHANG (B. 1956)
100 Layers of Ink, No. 1, 1994
Ink and acrylic on paper laid down on canvas
67 × 73 ¼ in. (170 × 186 cm)
Private collection, Hong Kong
Fig. 118

杨诘苍　千层墨
YANG JIECHANG (B. 1956)
100 Layers of Ink, No. 2, 1994
Ink and acrylic on paper laid down on canvas
69 × 73 ¼ in. (175.5 × 186 cm)
Private collection, Hong Kong
Fig. 119

杨诘苍　千层墨
YANG JIECHANG (B. 1956)
100 Layers of Ink, No. 3, 1994
Ink and acrylic on paper laid down on canvas
69 × 73 ¼ in. (175.5 × 186 cm)
Private collection, Hong Kong
Fig. 120

杨诘苍　会叫的风景
YANG JIECHANG (B. 1956)
Crying Landscape, 2002
Set of five triptychs; ink and color on paper
Each triptych 9 ft. 10 ⅛ in. × 16 ft. 4 ⅞ in. (300 × 500 cm)
Private collection, New York
Fig. 66

杨泳梁　蜃市山水
YANG YONGLIANG (B. 1980)
View of Tide, 2008
Inkjet print
17 ¾ in. × 32 ft. 9 ¾ in. (45 × 1000 cm)
M+ Sigg Collection, Hong Kong
Fig. 79

曾梵志　无题
ZENG FANZHI (B. 1964)
Untitled, 2009
Bronze
46 × 24 × 16 ½ in. (117 × 61 × 42 cm)
The Metropolitan Museum of Art, New York, Gift of Thomas Yaping Ou, 2011 (2011.378a, b)
Fig. 146

展望　假山石
ZHAN WANG (B. 1962)
Artificial Rock #10, 2001
Stainless steel
29 ½ × 17 ¾ × 7 ½ in. (75 × 45 × 19 cm)
The Metropolitan Museum of Art, New York, Purchase, Friends of Asian Art Gifts, 2006 (2006.244a–c)
Fig. 145

张洹　家谱
ZHANG HUAN (B. 1965)
Family Tree, 2001
Nine chromogenic prints
Each 21 × 16 ½ in. (53.3 × 41.9 cm)
Yale University Art Gallery, New Haven, Leonard C. Hanna, Jr., Class of 1913, Fund
Fig. 46

张健君　假山石（幻园）
ZHANG JIANJUN (B. 1955)
Scholar Rock (The Mirage Garden), 2008
Silicone rubber
86 ⅝ × 59 × 33 ½ in. (220 × 150 × 85 cm)
Sigg Collection
Fig. 144

张羽　灵光59号：漂浮的残圆
ZHANG YU (B. 1959)
Divine Light Series No. 59: The Floating Incomplete Circle, 1998
Hanging scroll; ink on paper
9 ft. 7 ⅜ in. × 70 ⅞ in. (293 × 180 cm)
Private collection, Hong Kong
Fig. 121

张羽　2000–8
ZHANG YU (B. 1959)
Divine Light 2000–8, 2000
Hanging scroll; ink on paper
13 ft. 1 ½ in. × 39 ⅜ in. (400 × 100 cm)
The Metropolitan Museum of Art, New York, Gift of Chung Ching-hsin, 2011 (2011.121)
Fig. 122

INK ART: AN INTRODUCTION

1   For an overview of the discussion surrounding *guohua* versus *xihua*, see Mayching Kao, "Reforms in Education and the Beginning of the Western-Style Painting Movement in China," in *A Century in Crisis: Modernity and Tradition in the Art of Twentieth-Century China*, ed. Julia F. Andrews and Kuiyi Shen, exh. cat. (New York: Solomon R. Guggenheim Museum, 1998), pp. 146–61. See also Kuiyi Shen, "A Debate on the Reform of Chinese Painting in Early Republican China," *Qing hua xuebao Tsing Hua/Journal of Chinese Studies*, n.s., 26, no. 4 (December 1996), pp. 447–69.

2   For a general overview of the art scene in China since the 1970s, see Wu Hung, ed., *Contemporary Chinese Art: Primary Documents* (New York: The Museum of Modern Art, 2010).

3   Zhang has identified this aesthetic as "Oriental culture spirit." See Zhang Yu, "Ink and Wash Is a Kind of Spirit," in *Zhang Yu: A Case Study on a Contemporary Artist, 1984–2008*, ed. Yin Shuangxi (Changsha: Hunan Fine Arts Publishing House, 2008), p. 30.

4   Cai Guo-Qiang and Fei Dawei, "To Dare to Accomplish Nothing," in *Cai Guo-Qiang* (New York: Thames & Hudson, 2000), p. 117.

5   See Leng Lin, "Yong shenti qu ganshou he biaoxian" [To feel and express with the body], in Leng Lin, *Shi wo* [It's me] (Beijing: Zhonggou wenlian chubanshe, 2000), p. 142; also excerpted and translated in Zhang Huan, "A Piece of Nothing," in *Zhang Huan: Altered States*, ed. Melissa Chiu, exh. cat. (New York: Asia Society; Milan: Charta, 2007), p. 74.

6   Ibid.

7   As Miwon Kwon has observed, contemporary art history sits at a crossroads between very different formations of knowledge and traditions as it designates a temporal bracketing—coming *after* the modern—but also encompassing a new geographic identity that extends beyond the Euro-American sphere to include the Americas, Africa, and Asia. See Miwon Kwon, in "Questionnaire on 'The Contemporary,'" *October* 130 (Fall 2009), p. 13.

8   According to Chang Tsong-Zung, Chinese avant-garde artists were featured at the Venice Biennale for the first time in 1993. Among the fourteen contemporary Chinese artists who showed work in Venice that year were Xu Bing, Fang Lijun, and Liu Wei. See Chang Tsong-Zung, "Beyond the Middle Kingdom: An Insider's View," in *Inside Out: New Chinese Art*, ed. Gao Minglu, exh. cat. (San Francisco: San Francisco Museum of Modern Art; New York: Asia Society Galleries, 1998), p. 71.

TRANSCENDING THE EAST / WEST DICHOTOMY

1   Art academies in the People's Republic of China typically include a *guohua xi*—department of Chinese painting—separate from the departments of oil painting, sculpture, graphic art, and, more recently, design and new-media art.

2   Made from elm, mulberry, and bamboo fiber, *xuan* paper has been the preferred support for ink painting and calligraphy for more than one thousand years, owing to the way it reveals both the flow and crispness of an artist's brushwork.

3   Julia F. Andrews's exhaustive discussion of art policy, criticism, and education in the PRC provides a background to these issues; see her *Painters and Politics in the People's Republic of China, 1949–1979* (Berkeley and Los Angeles: University of California Press, 1994).

4   Other terms include "modern ink painting" (*xiandai shuimo*), "conceptual ink painting" (*guannian shuimo*), and simply "new Chinese-style painting" (*xin guohua*). Two main exhibitions on the history and achievement of experimental ink painting were "China: 20 Years of Ink Experiment," curated by Pi Daojian and held at the Guangdong Museum of Art, 2001; and "A Retrospective of Experimental Ink and Wash 1985–2000" at the Shenzhen Fine Art Institute, 2005.

5   For an introduction to the '85 Art New Wave, see Lü Peng, *A History of Art in 20th-Century China*, trans. Bruce Gordon Doar (Milan: Charta, 2010), pp. 793–888.

6   Wu Guanzhong, "Huihua de xingshi mei" [Formalist aesthetics in painting], *Meishu* [Fine arts], no. 5 (1979), pp. 33–35, 44; Wu Guanzhong, "Guanyu chouxiang mei" [About abstract beauty], *Meishu* [Fine arts], no. 10 (1980), pp. 37–39. The 1979 essay is partially translated in Wu Hung, ed., *Contemporary Chinese Art: Primary Documents* (New York: The Museum of Modern Art, 2010), pp. 14–17.

7   Li Xiaoshan, "Dangdai Zhongguohua zhi wojian" [My view of today's Chinese-style painting], *Jiangsu huakan* [Jiangsu pictorial], no. 7 (1985), pp. 2–3.

8   Li cited the modern painters Liu Haisu (1896–1994), Lin Fengmian (1900–1991), Zhu Qizhan (1892–1996), and Shi Lu (1919–1982) and the four influential *guohua* artists as Pan Tianshou (1897–1971), Fu Baoshi (1904–1965), Li Keran (1907–1989), and Li Kuchan (1899–1983). Ibid., p. 3.

9   Ibid., p. 2.

10   Li Xiaoshan, "Zhongguohua yi daole qiongtu mori de shike" [Chinese-style painting has reached the end of its days], *Zhongguo meishu bao* [Chinese fine arts weekly], no. 14 (October 26, 1985), p. 1.

11   Entitled "Young Art of Progressive China," this exhibition was held in the Gallery of the Artist Association in Xi'an, Shaanxi Province.

12   Guo Yaxi, "Zhongguo shiyan shuimo fazhan kaocha baogao" [An investigative report on the development of Chinese experimental ink painting], in *Shiyan shuimo huigu, 1985–2000* [A retrospective of experimental ink and wash, 1985–2000], ed. Dong Xiaoming, exh. cat., Shenzhen Fine Art Institute (Changsha: Hunan Fine Arts Publishing House, 2005), pp. 235–36.

13   For example, in 1987, Wang Gongyi exhibited her *Time and Space*, which combined ink painting and installation, in Paris. It was also quite common for an adventurous ink painter to try out unconventional materials and methods.

14   As stated in the interview "Ren Jian: Zai yangchun baixue yu xiali baren zhijian" [Ren Jian: Between elite and ordinary art], *Dongfang yishu: Dajia* [Oriental art: Master], no. 241 (November 2011).

15   See Shi Jian, "Gu Wenda fangtan" [An interview with Gu Wenda], in *'85 Xinchao Dang'an, I* [Archives of the '85 New Wave, I] ed. Fei Dawei, exh. cat. (Shanghai: Shanghai renmin chubanshe, 2007), pp. 19, 31.

16   For example, Liu Zijian graduated from the department of Chinese-style painting of the Hubei Art Academy in 1983 and began to experiment with abstract ink painting from the mid-1980s. He and several other local artists formed the J. L. Group in November 1986 and participated in the Hubei Youth Art Festival under the group's collective identity.

17   The exhibition opened in February 1989 at the National Art Gallery in Beijing. Ink painters in the exhibition included Shen Qin, Wang

Gongyi, Song Gang (b. 1960), Yang Jiechang, Wang Chuan, and Liu Zijian.

18   This exhibition took place November 21–31, 1985, at the Wuhan Museum in Hubei Province.

19   Li Xianting, "Chuncui chouxiang shi Zhongguo shuimohua de heli fazhan" [Pure abstraction is the logical development of Chinese ink painting], *Meishu* [Fine arts], no. 1 (1986), p. 1.

20   Wu Guanzhong, "Bimo dengyu ling" [*Bimo* counts for nothing], *Mingbao yuekan* [Mingbao monthly], no. 4 (1992).

21   Wan Qingli, "Wubi wumo dengyu ling" [There is nothing left without *bimo*: On Ming-Qing paintings in the collection of the Xubai Studio], in Xu Liping, *Mingjia hanmo* [Works by famous artists] (Hong Kong and Taipei: Hanmo xuan, 1992).

22   Zhang Yu, ed., *Zhongguo xiandai shuimohua* [Modern Chinese ink painting] (Tianjin: Yangliuqing chubanshe, 1991). Among these artists are Gu Wenda, Shi Hu, Liu Zijian, Yan Binghui, Wang Chuan, Li Jin, Zhang Yu, Zhuo Hejun, Chen Xiangxun, Zhang Jin, Huang Yihan, Tian Liming, Li Xiaoxuan, Wang Yanping, Liu Jin'an, and Zou Jianping.

23   *Ershi shiji mo Zhongguo xiandai shuimo yishu zoushi* [Tendencies of Chinese modern ink art at the end of the twentieth century], ed. Zhang Yu (Tianjin: Tianjin yangliuqing huashe, 1993). The first volume of the series, published in 1993, introduced nine artists and included seven theoretical essays. The following volumes, published in 1994, 1995, 1997, and 2000, adopted the same format and accumulated a rich collection of artists' works and writings, critical analyses, and accounts of activities related to experimental ink painting.

24   Huang Zhuan and Wang Huangsheng, eds., special issue of *Guangdong meishujia* [Guangdong artists], no. 2 (1993).

25   See note 4 above.

26   Zhang Yu, for example, expresses this view in "Zhendui guoji xuezhe dui Zhongguo xiandai shiyan shuimo fazhan de wudu" [On the misreading of modern Chinese experimental ink painting by international scholars], *Shijie yishu* [World art], no. 112 (April–May 2012), p. 34. Significantly, artists who hold this view often reject calling their works "abstract," a designation that they believe refers to an established genre in Western modern art and is not applicable to their ink works.

27   This English title is translated from the Chinese (重返家园：中国当代实验水墨联展). It is interesting to note that when the exhibition was held in San Francisco, its English title—"Homecoming: Chinese Contemporary Ink and Wash Group Exhibition"—omitted the word "experimental." It is possible that this word has a specific meaning in Western art history and is thus uncalled for. This exhibition was sponsored by the Gallery on the Rim and the World Journal Gallery in San Francisco.

28   Two other overseas exhibitions of experimental ink painting were "Ink and Light: An Exhibition of Contemporary Chinese Abstract Painting," curated by Zhang Yu and held in November 1995 at the Flanders Expo in Ghent, Belgium; and "New Ink Art: A Traveling Exhibition of Works by Three Chinese Artists," held in three cities in Germany in 1996. The three artists in the second exhibition were Zhang Yu, Li Jin, and Yan Binghui.

29   The conference received twenty papers, eleven of which were presented and discussed. Nine artists also participated in the conference and exhibited their works. Selected papers and artworks were then published in the third volume of *Ershi shiji mo Zhongguo xiandai shuimo yishu zoushi* [Tendencies of Chinese modern ink art at the end of the twentieth century] (Tianjin: Tianjin yangliuqing huashe, 1997).

30   Huang Zhuan, "Jinru jiushi niandai de Zhongguo shiyan shuimohua" [Experimental Chinese ink painting at the beginning of the 1990s], *Xiongshi meishu* [Lion fine arts], no. 271 (1996).

31   For a basic bibliography of these Chinese writings, see Dong, *Shiyan shuimo huigu* [Retrospective of experimental ink and wash], pp. 298–305.

32   *Jiushiniandai Zhongguo shiyan shuimo* [1990s Chinese experimental ink painting] (Hong Kong: Shijie huaren yishu chubanshe, 1998).

33   Yin Shuangxi, "Kaifang yu yanshen: Shiyan shuimo de lishi yiyi" [Opening up and extension: The historical significance of experimental ink painting], in *Kaifang de Zhongguo shiyan shuimo* [The open field of experimental Chinese ink painting] (Hong Kong: Yinhe chubanshe, 2002). Reprinted in Dong, *Shiyan shuimo huigu* [Retrospective of experimental ink and wash], p. 224.

34   For reproductions of representative works, see Pi Daojian and Wang Huangsheng, eds., *Zhongguo shuimo shiyan ershi nian* [China: 20 years of ink experiment] (Harbin: Heilongjiang meishu chubanshe, 2001), and Dong, *Shiyan shuimo huigu* [Retrospective of experimental ink and wash].

35   Bingyi Huang, "From Chu to Western Han: Re-reading *Mawangdui*" (Ph.D. diss., Yale University, New Haven, 2005).

36   From an email interview conducted by Peggy Wang in 2006; cited in Wu Hung, ed., *Shu: Reinventing Books in Contemporary Chinese Art* (New York: China Institute Gallery, 2006), p. 90.

PAST AS PRESENT IN CONTEMPORARY CHINESE ART

1   Inspired by observations made by Helen Molesworth, in "Questionnaire on 'The Contemporary,'" *October* 130 (Fall 2009), p. 113.

THE WRITTEN WORD

1   For an introduction to the principles and history of Chinese calligraphy, see Ouyang Zhongshi et al., *Chinese Calligraphy* (New Haven and London: Yale University Press; Beijing: Foreign Languages Press, 2008).

2   Although a small number of Chinese characters may retain their pictographic forms, the majority of characters might better be referred to as "ideographs," as their forms have lexigraphic significance, but they are not pictographs. See Ernest Fenollosa, *The Chinese Written Character as a Medium for Poetry*, ed. Ezra Pound (1936; reprint San Francisco: City Lights Books, 1968).

3   Chang Tsong-zung, "Power of the Word," in *Power of the Word*, exh. cat. (New York: Independent Curators International, 2001), pp. 6–7.

4   For a discussion of these changes, the reader may consult *A Conversion Table of Simplified Chinese Characters/Jianhuazi zong biao jianzi*, Far Eastern Publications, Mirror Series C, no. 16 (New Haven: Far Eastern Publications, Yale University, [1970]).

5   I am indebted to Gan Xu for this observation; see his "Neo-Hexagram: Early Work," in *Wenda Gu: Art from Middle Kingdom to Biological Millennium*, ed. Mark H. C. Bessire, exh. cat. (Cambridge, Mass.: MIT Press, 2003), pp. 196–97.

6   Gu's father, a Communist party member, was the son of the noted dramatist and calligrapher Gu Jianchen (1897–1976) and himself wrote poetry and practiced calligraphy, having studied with the Buddhist monk-artist Hongyi Fashi (Li Shutong, 1880–1942). Biographical information on Gu Wenda is derived from Gu Wenda, "Wo de shuimo licheng" [A personal history with ink], in *Shuimo lianjinshu: Gu Wenda de shiyan shuimo/Ink Alchemy: The Experimental Ink of Gu Wenda*, ed. Huang Zhuan, exh. cat. (Guangzhou: Lingnan Art Publishing House, 2010), pp. 62–99, and from an interview conducted by Jane DeBevoise on November 4, 2009, for the Asia Art Archive; see www.china1980s.org/en/interview_detail.aspx?interview_id=39. Additional information is taken from Gu Wenda's website, www.wendagu.com/noflash.html.

7   Gu, "Wo de shuimo licheng" [A personal history with ink], p. 64.

8   For examples of Li Keran's work, see Mei Mosheng, *Li Keran* (Shijiazhuang City: Hebei jiaoyu chubanshe, 2000).

9   Gu's tutor, Cao Jianlou, was a teacher at the Shanghai School of Arts and Crafts. Gu had been unable to take Cao's classes while enrolled in school, since he was assigned to the woodworking department. See Gu, "Wo de shuimo licheng" [A personal history with ink], p. 66. For examples of Wu Changshuo's work, see Mei Mosheng, *Wu Changshuo* (Shijiazhuang City: Hebei jiaoyu chubanshe, 2002).

10   For images of Lu Yanshao's work from the late 1970s and early 1980s, see Lu Yanshao and Hong Zaixin, *Lu Yanshao zuopin jingcui/Masterpieces of Lu Yanshao* (Hangzhou: Xiling yinshe chubanshe, 1994).

11   For Gu Wenda's descriptions of this exhibition, see Gu, "Wo de shuimo licheng" [A personal history with ink], p. 75.

12   *Shuimo lianjinshu/Ink Alchemy*, p. 211.

13   For Gu's acknowledgment of Freud's influence on his work, see the DeBevoise interview, 2009, cited in note 6 above. A photograph from a 1985 performance piece shows Gu, grinning broadly, lying in front of this painting with his legs spread; see *Shuimo lianjinshu/Ink Alchemy*, p. 277.

14   See Gu Wenda, "Fei chenshu de wenzi" [Non-expressive characters], *Meishu sichao* [Art trends], no. 6 (1986), pp. 32–36, fully reprinted in Fei Dawei, ed., *'85 Xinchao Dang'an, I* [Archives of the '85 New Wave, I] (Shanghai: Shanghai renmin chubanshe, 2007), pp. 81–85.

See also Melissa Chiu, *Breakout: Chinese Art Outside China* (Milan: Charta, 2006), p. 74.

15   From the 2009 DeBevoise interview; see note 6 above.

16   Interview by Melissa Chiu, January 4, 2002, New York, accessed from Gu Wenda's website, www .wendagu.com/noflash.html.

17   In a 2002 interview conducted by David Cateforis, Gu remarked, "I had a little bit of difficulty getting into the Red Guard organization, but finally I got in because I had some skill in doing the big character posters. So I was always hired to do the propaganda posters." He goes on: "What I wanted to do was just differ from the tradition, and there wasn't much of a political implication. It was about language, about how to renew the tradition." See David Cateforis, "Interview with Wenda Gu," in Bessire, *Wenda Gu: Art*, pp. 144, 146.

18   See Fei Dawei, "Xiang xiandaipai tiaozhan, fang huajia Gu Wenda" [Challenging modernity, an interview with the painter Gu Wenda], *Meishu* [Fine arts], no. 7 (1986), pp. 53–56, 63 (reprinted in *Shuimo lianjinshu/ Ink Alchemy*, pp. 119–23), in which Gu asserts that the main task of contemporary artists is to overcome both Chinese and Western traditions.

19   Xu Bing, "The Living Word," trans. Ann L. Huss, in Britta Erickson, *The Art of Xu Bing: Words without Meaning, Meaning without Words*, exh. cat. (Washington, D.C.: Arthur M. Sackler Gallery, 2001), p. 14.

20   "I decided to create four thousand invented characters because there are approximately four thousand real characters in common usage"; Xu Bing, "The Making of *Book from the Sky*," trans. Drew Hammond, in *Tianshu: Passages in the Making of a Book*, ed. Katherine Spears, exh. cat. (London: Bernard Quaritch Ltd., 2009), p. 55. Various numbers have been assigned to the actual number of characters Xu Bing invented, depending on how they are counted. If one counts the number carved (many characters were carved at multiple sizes) rather than the number invented, one can easily reach four thousand. Britta Erickson has asserted that the number of characters invented is more than a thousand. See Erickson, *Art of Xu Bing*, p. 33.

21   According to the artist, "This typeface was not devised by a single person, but evolved from the Song period through the Ming. As such,

you could say that it was 'made in heaven.'" See Xu, "Making of *Book from the Sky*," p. 52.

22   Ibid., p. 60.

23   Ibid.

24   This translation of Xu's title is from John Cayley, "Extended Bibliographic Description of *Tianshu*," in *Tianshu: Passages in the Making of a Book*, p. 99, n. 1.

25   Erickson suggests that this title was coined in response to the 1988 exhibition, specifically referring to the texts hanging from the ceiling, and that "Xu Bing acquiesced as it came into general usage." See Erickson, *Art of Xu Bing*, p. 39.

26   Xu Bing, *Jichu sumiao jiaoxue biji* [Teaching notes for basic drawing] ([Beijing], 1981), serialized in the journal *Meishu xiangdao* [Fine arts guide], 1985–87. "Wohua ziji ai de dongxi" [I picture what I love], *Meishu* [Fine arts], May 1981, pp. 18–19; excerpted in Xu Bing, *Chun hui: Xu Bing banhua zuopin* [Spring sun: Xu Bing's prints] (Beijing: China Renmin University Press, 1986).

27   Erickson, *Art of Xu Bing*, p. 36, quoting Xu Bing's artist's statement in "Jing tiandi, qi guishen/To Frighten Heaven and Earth and Make the Spirits Cry," in Shinoda Takatoshi, *Baberu no toshokan: Moji, shomotsu, media/The Library of Babel: Characters, Books, Media*, exh. cat. (Tokyo: NTT Shuppan, 1998), p. 69.

28   According to Erickson, the texts on the wall panels and hanging sheets exhibited in 1991 and afterward were reproduced mechanically; only the bound books were printed with hand-carved blocks. Erickson, *Art of Xu Bing*, pp. 37, 41. For Xu Bing's own detailed account of the making of *Book from the Sky*, see Xu, "Making of *Book from the Sky*."

29   For this groundbreaking exhibition of New Wave art curated by Gao Minglu and Li Xianting, see *Zhongguo xiandai yishu zhan* [China avant-garde] (Nanning: Guangxi renmin chubanshe, 1989).

30   Erickson, *Art of Xu Bing*, p. 41, quoting Yang Chengyin, "'Xinchao' meishu lungang" [A discussion of the main principles of the "New Wave" of fine arts], *Wenyi bao* [Literature and art newspaper], June 2, 1990, p. 5.

31   The content of this scroll comes from the first of two instruction manuals that Xu Bing created to teach his new form of writing. For a discussion of these manuals, see Erickson, *Art of Xu Bing*, pp. 56–57.

32   Jerome Silbergeld and Dora C. Y. Ching, eds., *Persistence-Transformation:*

Text as Image in the Art of Xu Bing (Princeton: P. Y. and Kinmay W. Tang Center for East Asian Art, Princeton University, 2006), p. 114.

33   Comments from Qiu Zhijie, "All We See Can Only Disappear," in Jérôme Sans, *China Talks: Interviews with 32 Contemporary Artists by Jérôme Sans*, ed. Chen Yun and Michelle Woo; trans. Chen Yun and Philip Tinari (Hong Kong: Timezone 8, 2009), p. 55.

34   Qiu Zhijie, "The Boundary of Freedom: A Personal Statement on *Assignment No. 1* (*Zuoye yihao*) (1994/2003)," trans. Kristen Loring, in Wu, *Contemporary Chinese Art*, p. 188.

35   For a discussion of the significance of Wang Xizhi and his "Orchid Pavilion Preface," see Wang Yuchi, "Striving for Perfection amid Social Upheavals: Calligraphy during the Wei, Jin, Southern and Northern Dynasties," in Ouyang et al., *Chinese Calligraphy*, pp. 157–59.

36   Qiu, "Boundary of Freedom," p. 188. Qiu has described his process as akin to peeling an onion, to "gradually remove the insubstantial elements of traditional calligraphy." He continued: "The first item to eliminate was the literary nature of calligraphy in order to return calligraphy to its original activity of modeling or, specifically, composing ink traces, to arrive at pure visual abstraction. The second step was to return writing to the original act of writing itself without producing the formal traces of the brush. . . . Repetitive writing on an ink background strictly observes the classical standards of Chinese calligraphy and strengthens its innate meaning as a form of 'written meditation.'"

37   Qiu Zhijie, "Wu's Question or the Questioning of Wu," in *Wu Shanzhuan: Guoji hongse youmo/ Red Humour International* (Hong Kong: Asia Art Archive, 2005), pp. 24–25.

38   Gao Minglu translated many of the expressions in this installation; see Gao Minglu, *Total Modernity and the Avant-Garde in Twentieth-Century Chinese Art* (Cambridge, Mass.: MIT Press, 2011), p. 223. See also Wu Hung, "Ruins, Fragmentation, and the Chinese Modern/Postmodern," in *Inside Out: New Chinese Art*, ed. Gao Minglu, exh. cat. (San Francisco: San Francisco Museum of Modern Art; New York: Asia Society Galleries, 1998), pp. 61–62.

39   Interpretation by Gao Minglu; see Gao, *Total Modernity and the Avant-Garde*, p. 221.

40   The title is not Wu's. Rather, the term "word image" was given to Wu's works by the Zhejiang professor Fan Jingzhong. See Gao Minglu, *Zhongguo dangdai meishu shi 1985–1986* [A History of contemporary Chinese art] (Shanghai: Shanghai renmin chubanshe, 1991), p. 193.

41   An effort has been made to read meaning into Wu's images using a group of five works from this series, including three of these images. See *Wu Shanzhuan: Guoji hongse youmo/Red Humour International*, p. 37.

42   Qiu, "Wu's Question," in ibid., p. 26. Paraphrasing Karl Popper, he continues, "We should consider any of our interpretations of a thing to be no more than a process of trial and error."

43   "[Our painting] is a form of 'new' pure art that extends artistic language. Artistic language always plays a crucial role in the fate of art history, and as such the value of the artist lies in his creation and discovery of an artistic language (that's why Kandinsky and Duchamp have been so inspirational to us)." Ibid.

44   Wu Shanzhuan, "Guanyu women de huihua" [On our painting], in *Meishu sichao* [Art trends], 1987, p. 1, as cited and translated in "Artists' Writings 7," an insert opposite p. 52 in *Wu Shanzhuan: Guoji hongse youmo/Red Humour International*.

45   Ibid.

46   Wu Shanzhuan, "On Cultural Revolution Art," an unpublished manuscript dated 1987 as cited and translated in "Artists' Writings 9," an insert opposite p. 52 in *Wu Shanzhuan: Guoji hongse youmo/ Red Humour International*. Qiu Zhijie, who has known Wu Shanzhuan for more than twenty years, sees Wu's simplified and miswritten characters, big-character posters, and use of the color red as deriving from his visual memories of the Cultural Revolution. See Qiu, "Wu's Question," in ibid., p. 24.

47   Despite the closing of this exhibition, Gu has insisted that his main motivation was not political: "The Stars Group was more politically oriented and I wasn't. I was just more interested in playing with language [and] had no intention of trying to break taboo [or] break any barriers"; DeBevoise interview, 2009, cited in note 6 above. The Stars Group, which held its first exhibition in 1979, was one of China's earliest unofficial collectives to be completely independent of the state's art system. See Kuiyi Shen and Julia F. Andrews,

Blooming in the Shadows: Unofficial Chinese Art, 1974–1985, exh. cat. (New York: China Institute Gallery, 2011). Gu's conceptual works attracted attention from artists and critics alike; discussions of the exhibited pieces appeared in several important art publications—including *Meishu* [Fine arts] and *Zhongguo meishu bao* [Fine arts in China]—the following year. See Gu Wenda, "Wo de shuimo licheng" [A personal history with ink], pp. 77–79.

48 As a Red Guard, Gu had crossed out the name of his elementary school teacher in this fashion; see DeBevoise interview, 2009, cited in note 6 above.

49 See *Shuimo lianjinshu/Ink Alchemy*, p. 226, for Gu's description of how this work was made. He asserts that the six students all wrote their version of "quiet" on the same large sheet of paper, but a close examination of the painting reveals that the six characters were written on separate sheets that were subsequently mounted together. The newsprint on the upper right sheet is the result of Gu's using newspaper to absorb the water that he poured over the written surface to achieve a blurred effect. Email communication with Guo Zhen, Gu's ex-wife, who participated in the production of this work, August 1, 2013.

50 In reference to another work, a tapestry installation also created in 1986 in which Gu combined the miswritten characters for "he" and "she," DeBevoise has written that Gu's "doubled and disjointed characters referred to homosexuality. Having recently discovered the theories of Freud, he relished the opportunity to expose this social taboo." She quotes Gu as remarking: "I was fearless. I wanted to make a splash." From Jane DeBevoise, "Between State and Market: Chinese Contemporary Art in the Post-Mao Era," ms., July 24, 2012.

51 Fung Mingchip, "Calligraphy Journey," Hanart TZ Gallery website, www.hanart.com/artist_detail .php?l=1&id=47&s=3.

52 Fung Mingchip, "Muse from Within," Hanart TZ Gallery website, www.hanart.com/artist_detail .php?l=1&id=47&s=3#.

53 To maintain the square sixty-four-character grid, Fung removed the three occurrences of "and" (*yi* 亦) from the body of the text and wrote them at a smaller scale between the columns.

54 "The Heart of Prajna Paramita Sutra," 1997, Buddhist Text Translation

Society, www.drba.org/dharma /heartsutra.asp. See also Red Pine, *The Heart Sutra: The Womb of Buddhas* (Washington, D.C.: Shoemaker & Hoard, 2004). According to Fung, he edited the text from about two hundred to sixty-seven characters, primarily by excising passages from the beginning and end of the sutra (conversation with the artist, January 22, 2013).

55 Wang has explored novel ways of integrating ink painting into daily life by transforming familiar utilitarian forms—oversized oval fans and traditional robes—into abstract patterns of inked paper. He also created a full-scale installation featuring a round banquet table complete with chairs, dishes, serving utensils, bottles, and plates all wrapped in paper and daubed with ink; see p. 28, fig. 15, in the present volume.

56 According to DeBevoise (personal communication, January 15, 2013), Wang Tiande said he was one of the six students who collaborated with Gu Wenda in the creation of *I Evaluate Characters Written by Three Men and Three Women* of 1985.

57 Wu Hung, *Variations of Ink: A Dialogue with Zhang Yanyuan* (New York: Chambers Fine Art, 2002), p. 20.

58 See Julie Walsh, "Song Dong—the Diary Keeper," in Song Dong and Yin Xiuzhen, *Song Dong: Kuaizi/ Chopsticks*, exh. cat. (New York: Chambers Fine Arts, 2002), pp. 12–15.

59 For biographical information on Song Dong, see Sans, *China Talks*, pp. 64–71. For an overview of Song's work, see Shen Qibin, ed., *Song Dong*, exh. cat. (Shanghai: Shanghai Zendai Museum of Modern Art, 2008).

60 Another work that took water as its medium is *Catching Moonbeams in Water* (2001). Commenting on the work, Song noted: "Catching moonbeams in water is a set phrase [in Chinese] . . . that means to try and do something that is fundamentally impossible." See Leng Lin, "Catching Moonbeams in Water" (written 2004), in Shen, *Song Dong*, p. 15.

61 These observations and those that follow are from notes transcribed from a conversation between Song Dong, Yin Xiuzhen, Maxwell K. Hearn, and Malcolm Daniel at The Metropolitan Museum of Art on February 19, 2010 (see object file, Department of Photography, Metropolitan Museum). In that interview Song reported that the photographs for *Printing on Water*

were printed in a commercial Beijing lab and that he was present in the darkroom. Song regards the accidental variations in the color of the prints as a desirable indication of the hands-on production process, and he chose color rather than black and white because he feels color is more connected to the reality of daily life.

62 According to Song, "if we accept the notion that all people are Buddhas, we could also say 'I am a man, but I also have a Buddha-like presence.'" Ibid.

63 As Philippe Vergne has noted, "Whatever topic Song Dong approaches, his critique always manages to walk the thin line between the politic and the poetic. Like many artists of his generation, his political awareness is free of any didacticism, and provides a gentle, if not absurd sense of subversion." Philippe Vergne, "Song Dong," in Shen, *Song Dong*, p. 42.

64 Conversation with Sarah J. S. Suzuki, June 25, 2009, from *Art Salon: Song Dong; the Culture of Contemporary Chinese Art*, DVD produced by China Institute in America, New York.

65 For an overview of Zhang's career in his own words, see Zhang Huan, "A Piece of Nothing," in *Zhang Huan: Altered States*, ed. Melissa Chiu, exh. cat. (New York: Asia Society; Milan: Charta, 2007), pp. 51–97.

66 This quotation is taken from an interview in Chinese between Zhang and Leng Lin but has been modified based on Zhang's subsequent account in English, which derives from the earlier interview. See Leng Lin, "Yong shenti qu ganshou he biaoxian" [To feel and express with the body], in Leng Lin, *Shi wo* [It's me] (Beijing: Zhongguo wenlian chubanshe, 2000), pp. 143–45; see also Zhang, "Piece of Nothing," p. 74.

67 The characters read "Master Yu moves the mountain" (*Yu gong yi shan* 愚公移山). This is the title of a well-known story of an old man who sets his family to work moving a mountain knowing that, as his descendants multiply, eventually they will succeed. For Zhang, the moral of this story is that "as long as you have determination, nothing is beyond reach. Your dreams will come true." Zhang, "Piece of Nothing," p. 87.

68 Ibid.

69 Biographical information on Liu Dan is drawn from the following sources: Hugh Moss, *Ink: The Art of Liu Dan* (Hong Kong: Umbrella,

1993); Alexandra Munroe, *Alternative Visions*, [vol. 3], *Liu Dan* ([Tokyo]: Takashimaya Co., Ltd., 1993); Jerome Silbergeld, "What Realism, Which Beauty?," in Jerome Silbergeld et al., *Outside In: Chinese x American x Contemporary Art*, exh. cat. (Princeton: Princeton University Art Museum; P. Y. and Kinmay W. Tang Center for East Asian Art, Princeton University, 2009), pp. 239–46; and "Conversation with Jerome Silbergeld," in *ARTiculations: Undefining Chinese Contemporary Art*, ed. Jerome Silbergeld and Dora C. Y. Ching (Princeton: P. Y. and Kinmay W. Tang Center for East Asian Art, Princeton University, 2010), pp. 94–111.

70 Liu's pencil sketch after a drawing by Ingres—one of Liu's favorite artists—done in 1972 at the age of nineteen, reveals that he continued to find ways to study Western art on his own. See Silbergeld, "What Realism, Which Beauty?," p. 239.

71 For Ya Ming, see *Ya Ming huaji* [Ya Ming's paintings] (Nanjing: Jinling shuhua she, 1982).

72 For this painting, *Aceldama*, 1987–88, see Munroe, *Alternative Visions: Liu Dan*, pp. 11–12, fig. 1.

73 Ibid.

74 For an illustration of this preparatory drawing, see Silbergeld et al., *Outside In*, pl. 28.

75 As Wu Hung has observed, "By depicting the dictionary with a painstaking, photorealistic style, [Liu] stresses its vulnerability to time and to human touch: the book's yellowish paper and worn pages arouse nostalgia, testifying probably to a life-long intimate relationship with a human subject." Wu Hung, *Shu: Reinventing Books in Contemporary Chinese Art*, exh. cat. (New York: China Institute Gallery, 2006), p. 11. Another interpretation of *Dictionary* was offered by Liu Dan's friend Chen Danqing (b. 1953), who told him that what he was painting was "a vagina." See Silbergeld, "What Realism, Which Beauty?," p. 242.

76 This discussion is based on "Liu Dan in Conversation with Jane DeBevoise and Colleagues" (March 25, 2010) as transcribed by Ali Van; see www.aaa-a.org/2010/06 /04/conversation-with-liu-dan/, accessed November 30, 2012.

NEW LANDSCAPES

1 Shu Qun and Wang Guangyi, "Beifang yishu qunti" [Northern Art Group], *Zhongguo meishu bao* [Fine arts in China], no. 18 (November 23, 1985), cited in "Northern Art Group," in *U-turn: 30 Years of Contemporary Art in China (1983–1987)*, ed. Philip Tinari (New York: AW Asia and Office for Discourse Engineering, 2007), vol. 2.4. See also Gao Minglu, "From Elite to Small Man," in *Inside Out: New Chinese Art*, ed. Gao Minglu, exh. cat. (San Francisco: San Francisco Museum of Modern Art; New York: Asia Society Galleries, 1998), pp. 151–53.

2   Zhou Yan, "Beifang yishu qunti" [Northern Art Group], in *'85 Meishu yundong/The '85 Movement* (Guilin: Guangxi Normal University Press, 2008), vol. 2, p. 165.

3   Ren has acknowledged in an email to Xin Wang, Research Assistant, Department of Asian Art, The Metropolitan Museum of Art (dated December 17, 2012), that he painted this scroll from left to right: "Modern Chinese already write from left to right; the same shift from tradition to modernity is also taking place in the making of images. It's also a kind of reaction."

4   Alexandra Munroe, "Why Ink? The Art of Liu Dan," in *Liu Dan: Alternative Visions* ([Japan]: Takashimaya, 1993), p. 12. As Hugh Moss describes it, the painting was done in response to two previous large handscrolls painted for Moss by Liu Kuo-sung and Ho Huai-shuo. See Hugh Moss, *Ink: The Art of Liu Dan* (Hong Kong: Umbrella, 1993), pp. 22–23.

5   Britta Erickson, "Liu Dan: To Paint the Unmeasurable," *Orientations* 43, no. 2 (March 2012), p. 139.

6   The description of Liu's working method and his quotation are from Moss, *Ink: Art of Liu Dan*, p. 30.

7   Quoted in Jerome Silbergeld, "What Realism, Which Beauty?," in Jerome Silbergeld et al., *Outside In: Chinese x American x Contemporary Art*, exh. cat. (Princeton: Princeton University Art Museum; P. Y. and Kinmay W. Tang Center for East Asian Art, Princeton University, 2009), p. 243.

8   Liu Dan, "Artist's Statement," in Silbergeld et al., *Outside In*, p. 237.

9   For biographical information on Shao Fan, see Pan Zhen, "Shao Fan: 'Bawan' Zhongguo gudian yuansu" [Shao Fan: "Play with" China's traditional elements], *Da Meishu* [All], no. 9 (2005), p. 27; Chris Moss, "Shao Fan at Chelsea: Fertile Ground," *Telegraph.co.uk*, April 26, 2008, www .telegraph.co.uk/gardening/3347809 /Shao-Fan-at-Chelsea-fertile-ground .html; Volker Fischer and Stephan

von der Schulenburg, *Sit in China: Ein Streifzug durch 500 Jahre Kultur des Sitzens/An Excursion through 500 Years of the Culture of Sitting* (Fellbach, Ger.: Edition Axel Menges, 2009), p. 95; and www.artnet.com /artists/shao+fan/biography-links. For Shao Fan's mother, Shao Jingkun (b. 1923), who studied with Xu Beihong (1895–1953) and Dong Xiwen (1914–1973), see www .artlinkart.com/cn/artist/overview /ee0euAr. For Shao Fan's father, Zhao Yu (1926–1980), who joined the revolutionary army at the age of thirteen and trained at the Lu Xun Academy of Fine Arts in Yan'an, becoming a leading artist after the founding of the PRC in 1949, see Wang Min'an, "Jubilancy from Graft: Emptiness, History and Competition," 2009, Galerie Urs Meile, Beijing and Lucerne, www.galerieursmeile.com/ fileadmin/images/Artists/SHAO _FAN/Shao_Fan_Texts/WangMinan _ShaoFan_2009_E.pdf.

10   Moss, "Shao Fan at Chelsea," *Telegraph.co.uk*, April 26, 2008.

11   Email correspondence on January 14, 2013, between the artist and Xin Wang.

12   Dong Qichang, *Hua zhi* [Aim of painting] (Hangzhou: Xiling yin she, 2008), pp. 26–28.

13   Details of the painting's creation were learned in personal conversations with the artist in 2010.

14   Volker Fischer has commented about other of Shao's works: "In a metaphoric way, the artist is capable of simultaneously alluding to harmony and violence, the dialectics of tradition and modernism, the relationship between orient and occident, past and present, an emblematic dialectic that altogether characterizes China today." Volker Fischer, "Shao Fan: The Ming Deconstructivist," in Fischer and von der Schulenburg, *Sit in China*, p. 37.

15   As Chang Tsong-zung has observed, "By taking us to the outer reaches of visibility, [Qiu] trans- forms both painting and viewing into a spiritual exercise." Chang Tsong-zung, "Painting at the Edge of Visibility: The Art of Qiu Shi-hua," in *Qiu Shihua: Niansan jie sheng- baoluo guoji shuangnianzhan dahui tezhan/Special Exhibition of the 23rd Biennial of São Paulo*, ed. Caroline Chiu and Josette Mazzella di Bosco Balsa (Hong Kong: Hanart TZ Gallery, 1996), p. 9.

16   Chang Tsong-zung, "The Sky in the Landscape," in *Qiu Shi-hua: Landscape Painting* (Prague: Galerie Rudolfinum, 2000), pp. 23–30.

17   Bernhard Fibicher, "Qiu Shihua," in *Mahjong: Contemporary Chinese Art from the Sigg Collection*, ed. Bernhard Fibicher and Matthias Frehner, exh. cat. (Ostfildern, Ger.: Hatje Cantz Verlag, 2005), p. 240.

18   According to Chang Tsong-zung, Qiu approximates the state of quietude in painting by reducing the picture's sensory agitation. All elements of contrast, such as light, color, and shape, are reduced to a minimum. Chang, "Sky in the Landscape," p. 25.

19   Quoted in Fibicher and Frehner, *Mahjong: Contemporary Chinese Art from the Sigg Collection*, p. 240.

20   Quoted in John Tancock, *Insight: Paintings by Qiu Shihua*, exh. cat. (New York: Chambers Fine Art, 2005), p. 5, quoting from Chiu and Mazzella di Bosco Balsa, *Qiu Shihua*.

21   For a discussion of the high, level, and deep distances first articulated by Guo Xi (ca. 1000– ca. 1090), see Wen C. Fong et al., *Images of the Mind: Selections from the Edward L. Elliott Family and John B. Elliott Collections of Chinese Calligraphy and Painting at the Art Museum, Princeton University* (Princeton: The Art Museum, Princeton University, 1984), p. 23.

22   The analogy comparing Qiu's work with that of Ni Zan was first remarked upon by Martina Köppel- Yang. See Martina Köppel-Yang and Max Wechsler, *Qiu Shi-hua*, exh. cat. (Basel: Kunsthalle Basel; Schwabe, 1999).

23   In Yang Jiechang, *No-shadow Kick*, ed. Hou Hanru and Wei Xing, exh. cat. (Shanghai: Shanghai Duolun Museum of Art; Beijing: Tang Contemporary Art, 2008), pp. 80–81, this work is described as a "set of six paintings," but it includes only five triptychs.

24   Transcript of interview with Yang Jiechang, October 25, 2007, Guangzhou, in Asia Art Archive, "Materials of the Future: Documenting Contemporary Chinese Art from 1980–1990," partial translation, www.china1980s.org/en/interview _detail.aspx?interview_id=66.

25   Biographical information on Yang is drawn from Martina Köppel-Yang, "Yang Jiechang: Painting Beyond the Visual," April 26, 2001, Paris, statement written for Yang's solo exhibition at the museum of Hong Kong University, available on the artist's website www .yangjiechang.com; Asia Art Archive, 2007 interview; Fritz Hansel and Yang Jiechang, "Republic of Fritz Hansel: A Dialogue," in *No-shadow*

Kick, p. 218; and Yang Jiechang, "Action & Participation Painting," in Jérôme Sans, *China Talks: Interviews with 32 Contemporary Artists by Jérôme Sans*, ed. Chen Yun and Michelle Woo; trans. Chen Yun and Philip Tinari (Hong Kong: Timezone 8, 2009), pp. 152–55.

26   Köppel-Yang, "Yang Jiechang: Painting Beyond the Visual," www .yangjiechang.com.

27   Yang, "Action & Participation Painting," p. 153.

28   According to his wife, Martina Köppel-Yang, "The artist looks for experiences that make the viewer feel insecure and tries to push the perception or the experience of his work to a point where the individual life and the life as *natura naturans* as well as mind and body get close to each other." Köppel-Yang, "Yang Jiechang: Painting beyond the Visual," www.yangjiechang.com.

29   Interview with Qiu Zhijie as quoted in Davide Quadrio, "Daring to Fail: Qiu Zhijie's Need for Experimentation," in *Qiu Zhijie: Twilight of the Idols*, ed. Valerie Smith (Berlin: Haus der Kulturen der Welt; Revolver, 2009), unpaginated.

30   Qiu Zhijie is one of a number of Chinese artists to be influenced by the theory of Gesamtkunstwerk (total art), a concept first propounded by the composer Richard Wagner (1813–1883); see Qiu Zhijie and Shen Qibin, "Huji yu guantong: Shen Qibin Qiu Zhijie duihua" [Collaboration and total art], Qiu Zhijie Official Artist Website, Blog, May 11, 2012, www.qiuzhijie.com /blog/article.asp?id=530, accessed November 29, 2012. According to Christina Yu, Qiu's approach to total art can also be traced to his experience as one of the organizers of the "Long March Project," which she views as a turning point in his career. See Christina Yu, "In the Shadows of History," *ArtAsiaPacific*, no. 69 (July–August 2010), p. 99.

31   Since the bridge's inauguration, more than 2,000 suicides have been reported, far exceeding the 1,300 suicides recorded since 1937 at San Francisco's Golden Gate Bridge. See Yu, "In the Shadows of History," pp. 96–101.

32   Qiu's inaugural installation on this theme, "Ataraxic of Zhuangzi–A Suicidology of the Nanjing Yangzi River Bridge," took place at the Zendai Museum of Modern Art in Shanghai from July 4 to August 24, 2008. For a detailed discussion of that display, see Meiling Cheng, "De/visualizing

Calligraphic Archaeology: Qiu Zhijie's Total Art," *TDR: The Drama Review* 53, no. 2 (2009), pp. 17–34.

33   Qiu has written in detail about his state of mind at this time: "On November 4, 2009, I received a phone call from the Ullens Center saying they wanted me to stage a solo exhibition and they needed a proposal as soon as possible. Fifteen minutes later my daughter was born. When she fell gravely ill . . . the pediatrician warned us to prepare for the worst. . . . So I decided to write her a letter to let her know that even if she turned out to be retarded, I would love her all the same. . . . In fact the child turned out to be very healthy, but this very personal matter loomed in the background as I was making plans for the exhibition. It was then that I realized that I could turn this negative experience into a positive motivation. I decided to make a group of paintings for my daughter but was not sure how many. When I noticed that there are nine pairs of columns in the exhibition space, and that the Nanjing Yangzi River Bridge happens to have nine piers, the idea of thirty paintings as a central component of this exhibition naturally evolved. My daughter stayed in the hospital for a full month, during which I completed the exhibition proposal. Many plans for the installation—the contrast between the strong and weak elements—may have been informed by this special experience. Of course I have long been contemplating similar issues, so I approached the project as if I were standing on the Yangzi River Bridge confronting people who intended to commit suicide. I would then think of my daughter, and there were things that I wanted to tell her. That was my state of mind." Qiu Zhijie, "Wo yong xiaohao ziyang ziji" [Nourishing myself with wasted energy], *Yishu shijie* [Art world], June 2011, www .yishushijie.com/magazines /content-902.aspx; translated by Xin Wang.

34   See Ruth Olson and Abraham Chanin, *Naum Gabo; Antoine Pevsner*, exh. cat. (New York: The Museum of Modern Art, 1948), p. 18. My thanks to Joseph Scheier-Dolberg for this reference.

35   For biographical information on Duan Jianyu, see Monica Dematté, "Had She Been a Writer . . . Duan Jianyu and Her Painted Stories," in Zeng Tingke et al., *Duan Jianyu: Cunzhuang de youhuo/The Seduction of Village*, organized by Vitamin Creative Space,

Guangzhou (Hong Kong: Blue Kingfisher, 2011), unpaginated.

36   Not all of Duan's ten ink images on cardboard are of Chinese subjects. Other images include a Dutch windmill and tulips and Mount Fuji. Zeng et al., *Duan Jianyu*, colorpl. 5.

37   See Josef Helfenstein's "Introduction," in Josef Helfenstein, Yve-Alain Bois, and Clare Elliott, *Robert Rauschenberg: Cardboards and Related Pieces*, exh. cat. (Houston: Menil Foundation; New Haven: Yale University Press, 2007), pp. 10–15.

38   Britta Erickson in Peter Fischer, ed., *Shanshui: Poetry without Sound? Landscape in Contemporary Chinese Art* (Ostfildern, Ger.: Hatje Cantz Verlag; Lucerne: Kunstmuseum Luzern, 2011), p. 113, quoting the artist's statement in "The History of Landscape," in *Huang Yan, 1990–2006*, exh. cat. (Beijing: Xin Dong Cheng Space for Contemporary Art, 2006), p. 38.

39   During the '85 New Wave, Huang was involved in the artist group the Northern Path, founded by Wang Changbai (b. 1957), who taught at Huang's middle school in the early 1980s.

40   Huang Yan, *2005–2010 Huang Yan: Wunian zuopin huiguzhan/ A Retrospective of the Past 5 Years*, exh. cat. (Shanghai: Leo Gallery; Hong Kong: Hong Kong Arts Centre, 2010), unpaginated.

41   For a discussion of this dichotomy and how it relates to contemporary Chinese photography, see Wu Hung, *Re-imagining the Real: Photography Show: Gao Lei, Shi Guorui, Yang Fudong, Zhuanghui*, 4 vols. (Jakarta: Yuz Foundation, 2010), *Shi Guorui* volume, pp. 17–19.

42   Jon Burris, *At Work: Twenty-five Contemporary Chinese Artists* (South San Francisco: Long River Press, 2011), p. 99.

43   For biographical information on Shi Guorui, see Meng Cai and Mei Li, "Shi Guorui Artron Interview," video, August 16, 2010, http://video.artron .net/show_news.php?newid=184526; "Shi Guorui," in Fischer, *Shanshui: Poetry without Sound?*, p. 175; and Wang Yin, "Shi Guorui: Zuozai zhaoxiangji li de sheyingjia" [Shi Guorui: The photographer who sits in the camera], *Nanfang zhoukan* [Southern weekly], September 26, 2007, www.infzm.com/content /6847.

44   Jori Finkel, "Standing in the Dark, Catching the Light," *New York Times*, October 22, 2006, p. A34. For Shi's image of the Great Wall, see

Luc Tuymans, Ai Weiwei, Fan Di'an, and Philippe Pirotte, eds., *The State of Things* (Brussels and Beijing: BOZAR Centre for Fine Arts; Tielt: Lannoo Books, 2009), pp. 156–57. For his image of Mount Everest, see Fischer, *Shanshui: Poetry without Sound?*, pp. 177–79. Shi's large-scale panoramas recall those of New York–based artist Vera Lutter (b. 1960), but unlike Lutter, who favors urban subjects, Shi has preferred landscapes, and he has disavowed any prior knowledge of Lutter's work (personal communication between the artist and Christopher Phillips, Curator, International Center of Photography, New York).

45   The first recorded description of the camera obscura was made by the Chinese philosopher Mozi (ca. 470–390 B.C.); see Joseph Needham, *Science and Civilisation in China*, vol. 4, part 1, *Physics* (Cambridge and New York: Cambridge University Press, 1962), p. 82.

46   "There's an element of performance in the way he puts this recording device in the landscape and places himself inside it. His body becomes part of the work, even though it is not visible in the resulting photograph." Finkel, "Standing in the Dark, Catching the Light," p. A34, quoting San Francisco art dealer Cheryl Haines.

47   For the history and influence of the panorama, see Stephen Oettermann, *The Panorama: History of a Mass Medium* (New York: Zone Books, 1997).

48   Finkel, "Standing in the Dark, Catching the Light," p. A34.

49   For another image of Shanghai from a different vantage point taken in 2007, see Wu, *Re-imagining the Real*, pp. 26–27.

50   Gan Xu, "China Spectacle," in Mark H. C. Bessire, *Stairway to Heaven: From Chinese Streets to Monuments and Skyscrapers* (Hanover, N.H., and Lewiston, Me.: University Press of New England for Bates College Museum of Art, 2009), p. 69.

51   See the website of the Shanghai Arts and Crafts College, http://116.236.134.229/jsp/search /searchItem.jsp?table=MeiXiao _PictureInfo&column=ID&mode= picDetailInfoBoard&order=sort&id= 58&key=179, accessed April 9, 2013. See also "Phantom Landscapes Series and Ancient Traditional Painting," the first of three essays for a lecture delivered at the Kansas City Art Institute, trans. Michelle Ni, August 2009, www.yangyongliang.com /article.html.

52   I am indebted to Joseph Scheier-Dolberg for this reference.

53   After the establishment of the PRC in 1949, power lines and smokestacks became an important motif in many "traditional" landscape paintings; see Fu Baoshi's *Ode to Yuhuatai* (1958), illustrated in Anita Chung, *Chinese Art in an Age of Revolution: Fu Baoshi (1904–1965)*, exh. cat. (Cleveland: Cleveland Museum of Art; New Haven: Yale University Press, 2011), p. 139.

54   In an interview with Mikala Tai, Yang professed, "After traveling abroad I have come to feel deeply sorry that [China] has done such a deficient job of preserving its past. A country with such an ancient civilization that is so full of the traces of its history is being replaced by a new, soulless state that is littered with concrete." See Mikala Tai, "In Conversation," in *Yang Yongliang*, ed. Mikala Tai (Melbourne, Vic.: Melbourne International Fine Art, 2010), p. 29 (retranslated by this author from the Chinese).

55   Quotation as translated by Thomas Bartz in "The Mirror of Time," in David Rosenberg, *Yang Yongliang: Landscapes* (Hong Kong: Thircuir Limited, 2011), p. 7.

56   Interview with Zhang Zhaohui, "Cong xuehuahua dao zuo yishujia" [From learning to paint to being an artist], October 30, 2003, www.xdsf .com/bbs/thread-1390-1-1.html.

57   For information about the founding of China Art Archive and Warehouse, see http://www.aaa.org .hk/FieldNotes/Details/1202?lang =eng. I am indebted to Jane DeBevoise for this reference.

58   At the same time, Ai has participated in major government-sponsored undertakings such as the 2008 Beijing Olympics, for which he collaborated with the architects Herzog & de Meuron on the design of the "Bird's Nest," the new National Stadium.

59   Ai Weiwei, "Here and Now," originally posted on his blog on May 10, 2006; published in *Ai Weiwei's Blog: Writings, Interviews, and Digital Rants, 2006–2009*, ed. and trans. Lee Ambrozy (Cambridge, Mass.: MIT Press, 2011), p. 50.

60   For an example of Xing's early work in the collection of the Metropolitan Museum, see *Born with the Cultural Revolution*, dated 1995 (2009.539.3a–c).

61   Rachel Duffell, "ID'entity Check," *Kee Magazine*, January 2010, p. 21.

62   Wu Hung and Christopher Phillips, *Between Past and Future: New Photography and Video from China*, exh. cat. (Chicago: David and Alfred Smart Museum of Art, University of Chicago; New York: International Center of Photography; Göttingen: Steidl Publishers, 2004), p. 214.

63   David Hockney's analysis of Chinese painting and its influence on his "Cubist" photomontages makes a similar point. See Philip Haas and David Hockney, *A Day on the Grand Canal with the Emperor of China; or, Surface Is Illusion But So Is Depth*, filmed in 1988 (New York: Milestone, 1991), 46 minutes.

64   Wu and Phillips, *Between Past and Future*, p. 214.

65   A similar aestheticization of subject matter occurs in Xing's eerily beautiful photographs of electronic trash; the artist's *disCONNEXION* series (2002–3) is discussed and illustrated in Lisa Botos, Joanne Ooi, and Rae Leung, eds., *Xing Danwen*, exh. cat. (Hong Kong: Ooi Botos Gallery, 2009), p. 56.

66   In an interview with Britta Erickson, Xing spoke of the adverse ramifications of modernization on Chinese society: "When people who live in old, very crowded courtyard houses suddenly have to move to high-rise buildings, they feel happy to have a toilet, a kitchen and all the basic conveniences. At the same time, they are no longer living as a big family with their neighbours. In the new, massive residential buildings, people might never even bump into their neighbours in the elevator. People might have a bigger space to themselves—and yet feel very isolated and lonely in their heavenly cubes." "Interview with Xing Danwen to Talk about *Urban Fiction*," conducted by Britta Erickson via email February 27–March 10, 2006, Digital Archive, Gallery TPW, Toronto, http://archive.gallerytpw.ca/index.php?c=essay&h=archive&id=119.

67   As Wu Hung has argued, "In theory, demolition and relocation were conditions for the capital's modernization. In actuality, these conditions brought about a growing alienation between the city and its residents: they no longer belonged to one another." Wu Hung, *Transience: Chinese Experimental Art at the End of the Twentieth Century* (Chicago: David and Alfred Smart Museum of Art, University of Chicago, 1999), p. 112, as quoted in Madeline Eschenburg, "Xing Danwen: Revealing the Masquerade of Modernity," *Yishu: Journal of Contemporary Chinese Art* 8, no. 4 (July–August 2009), p. 59.

68   The *Seven Intellectuals* films are inspired by a group of third-century scholars, known as the Seven Sages of the Bamboo Grove, who sought to insulate themselves from the turmoil accompanying dynastic transition by "losing themselves in pure thought and discussion" while advocating "freedom of individual expression and hedonistic escape from extremely corrupt politics." See Yang Fudong, "A Thousand Words: Yang Fudong Talks about The Seven Intellectuals," *Artforum* 42 (September 2003), pp. 182–83. For additional information about the Seven Sages, see James C. Y. Watt et al., *China: Dawn of a Golden Age, 200–750 AD*, exh. cat. (New York: The Metropolitan Museum of Art, 2004), pp. 8, 206–9.

69   Unlike many artists of his generation who were eager to reject tradition, Yang acknowledges that "tradition is inevitably part of the backdrop of my work." See Yang Fudong, "Commercial or Art, I Simply Wanted to Film Things That Interested Me," interviewed by Harada Yukiko, 2006, www.shanghartgallery.com/galleryarchive/texts/id/545, accessed March 25, 2013.

70   Ken Johnson, "From an Ancient Bamboo Grove to Modern China." *New York Times*, May 29, 2009, p. C30. Asked if he separates photographs and moving images in his mind, Yang has observed, "Psychologically they're one and the same to me. I take photos as films of a single frame. I've been influenced by the work of people like Sugimoto Hiroshi [b. 1948] and Jeff Wall [b. 1946], and pictures taken by photographers of their ilk truly are one-second movies." Yang, "Commercial or Art," interview, 2006.

71   The song lyrics were written by Yang Fudong, while Zhou Qing composed the music and performed it for the film. Email communication between Xin Wang and the artist, March 22, 2013.

72   The English is taken directly from the subtitles in the film. A more literal translation of the Chinese text might be rendered as "Silently, on the small boat sits the young girl Liu Lan."

73   The two films are *Song of the Fishermen* (*Yu guang qu*) of 1934, directed by Cai Chusheng (1906–1965), and *The Fisherwoman* (*Yujia nü*) of 1943, directed by Bu Wancang (1903–1974). The relationship of these two movies to *Liu Lan* is discussed in Lin Xiaoping, "The Video Works of Yang Fudong: An Ultimate Escape from a Global Nightmare," in Xiaoping Lin, *Children of Marx and Coca-Cola: Chinese Avant-garde Art and Independent Cinema* (Honolulu: University of Hawai'i Press, 2010), pp. 165–72. Xin Wang has pointed out that the woodblock-printed opening title of *Liu Lan* echoes a similar woodcut title used in *The Fisherwoman*. The opening sequence of *The Fisherwoman*, with its images of a sunlit lake and water reeds, also finds close parallels in *Liu Lan*.

74   Peter Fischer, "Qiu Anxiong," in Fischer, *Shanshui: Poetry without Sound?*, p. 155, quoting an email from the artist to Uli Sigg, December 2010. In the same email, Qiu stressed that a modern extension of that tradition must be "a continuation of a spiritual value . . . not just a preservation of a material, a technique, a form, like preserving a corpse, or as a seasoning spice on the production line of the consumption of contemporary art."

75   After graduating, Qiu worked for a year in a design firm in Shenzhen, Guangdong Province, before returning to Chengdu to paint full-time. He and some friends opened Bistro, a place for artists such as Zhou Chunya (b. 1955), Zhang Xiaogang (b. 1958), and Shen Xiaotong (b. 1968) to meet. See Meg Maggio, "Biennial Wonder Boy," Artzine China, www.artzinechina.com/display_print.php?a=198, accessed July 6, 2011, and Victoria Lu, "Qiu Anxiong," in *China Art Book*, ed. Uta Grosenick and Caspar H. Schübbe (Cologne: DuMont, 2007), p. 283.

76   Maggio, "Biennial Wonder Boy." Qiu reports that at the time, he was deeply influenced by the widespread revival of interest in the Chinese classics, particularly after he began to read the popular explications of Confucian and Buddhist texts by Nan Huaijin (1917–2012), an author who wrote such books as *Tao & Longevity: Mind-Body Transformation; an Original Discussion about Meditation and the Cultivation of Tao*, trans. Wen-kuang Chu; ed. Karen Allen (York Beach, Maine: S. Weiser, 1984); *The Story of Chinese Zen*, trans. Thomas Cleary (Boston: C. E. Tuttle, 1995); and *Lunyu biecai* [Prelection on the Analects of Confucius] (Shanghai: Fudan University Press, 2005).

Xin Wang interview with Qiu Anxiong in Shanghai, October 26, 2010.

77   For William Kentridge see Mark Rosenthal, ed., *William Kentridge: Five Themes*, exh. cat. (San Francisco: San Francisco Museum of Modern Art; West Palm Beach: Norton Museum of Art, 2009). For his entry in the Shanghai Biennale, see *Shanghai Biennale 2000* (Shanghai: Shanghai Painting and Calligraphy Press, 2000), pp. 106–9. In an email to Xin Wang (April 1, 2013), the artist confirmed that he was introduced to Kentridge's work while studying at Kassel via exhibitions and archival materials, which inspired him to begin experimenting with the medium of animation. The two artists did not meet in person until 2008.

78   Although Kentridge works most often in charcoal, he also uses erasures and modifications to a single drawing as a feature of his animations. See Rosalind Krauss, "'The Rock': William Kentridge's Drawings for Projection," *October* 92 (Spring 2000), pp. 3–35.

79   Fischer, "Qiu Anxiong," p. 155.

80   Chang Tsong-zung, "The World Seen from Afar," www.hanart.com/artist_detail.php?l=4&id=27&s=3.

81   I am indebted to Xin Wang for identifying the content of this broadcast.

82   In 2007–9 Qiu completed *New Classic of Mountains and Seas II*. See www.moma.org/collection/object.php?object_id=135052, accessed March 25, 2013.

83   Richard E. Strassberg, ed. and trans., *A Chinese Bestiary: Strange Creatures from the Guideways through Mountains and Seas* (Los Angeles: University of California Press, 2002), p. xiii. Strassberg notes that in 1597 this compendium acquired an accompanying set of illustrations. See also Anne Birrell, trans., *The Classic of Mountains and Seas* (London and New York: Penguin Books, 1999).

84   The island at the opening of the film recalls *Misty River, Layered Peaks* by Wang Shen (ca. 1048– after 1103), now in the collection of the Shanghai Museum. See Alfreda Murck, *Poetry and Painting in Song China: The Subtle Art of Dissent*, Harvard-Yenching Institute Monograph Series 50 (Cambridge, Mass.: Harvard University Asia Center for the Harvard-Yenching Institute, 2000), pp. 151–53, fig. 10. The pristine plain on which farmers

first till the soil resembles *Autumn Colors on the Que and Hua Mountains* by Zhao Mengfu (1254–1322), and a lone fisherman in a boat is modeled directly on *Fisherman on a Winter River* by Ma Yuan (ca. 1160/65–1225). For Zhao Mengfu's painting, in the National Palace Museum, Taipei, see Wen C. Fong and James C. Y. Watt, *Possessing the Past: Treasures from the National Palace Museum, Taipei*, exh. cat. (New York: The Metropolitan Museum of Art, 1996), pl. 140. For Ma Yuan's painting, in the Tokyo National Museum, see Richard Edwards, *The Heart of Ma Yuan: The Search for a Southern Song Aesthetic* (Hong Kong: Hong Kong University Press, 2011), pl. 5.

85   Qiu's animation pointedly recalls the destruction of the World Trade Center on September 11, 2001, and images associated with the 2003 invasion of Iraq, including the hooded torture victim from Abu Ghraib pictured on the cover of *The Economist* (May 8, 2004).

86   Quoted by Yuko Hasegowa, "Witness of an Enchanted Land—Qiu Anxiong" (2008), www.qiuanxiong .com/en/article2008.html, accessed July 6, 2011.

87   Quotations are from Qiu Anxiong, *New Classic of Mountains and Seas*, trans. Philip Tinari, 2005, www.qiuanxiong.com/en /article2006.html, accessed April 16, 2011.

88   Ou Ning, "Qiu Anxiong's Latest Work and Modern Weekly's 'China Dream' Special Issue," www .alternativearchive.com/ouning /article.asp?id=721, accessed March 25, 2013.

89   Joseph Scheier-Dolberg has commented that John Heartfield (Helmut Herzfeld, 1891–1968), a member of Berlin Dada and one of the pioneers of photomontage during the 1920s and 1930s in Germany, turned his back on the normal mechanisms for display and dissemination, choosing instead to publish his images in magazines, a vehicle he found better suited to his politically engaged artistic practice. See Andrés Mario Zervigón, *John Heartfield and the Agitated Image: Photography, Persuasion, and the Rise of Avant-garde Photomontage* (Chicago and London: University of Chicago Press, 2012).

90   A pivotal figure in the Southern Artists Salon, Chen co-organized the group's first "Experimental Show" in 1986–87. In 1990 he became a founding member of the Big Tail Elephant Group, a loosely structured experimental art collective, along with Lin Yilin (b. 1964), Xu Tan (b. 1957), and Liang Juhui (1959– 2006). See www.chenshaoxiong.net /?p=1195, accessed March 25, 2013. He also has participated in a number of international exhibitions, biennials, and triennials in Vienna, Guangzhou, Shanghai, Gwangju, and Venice.

91   See Xin Wang, "Seeing and Disbelieving: Exploring Chen Shaoxiong's Ink Animation Videos," in *Modern Art Asia: Papers on Modern and Contemporary Asian Art* (London: Enzo Arts and Publishing, 2012), pp. 213–24. Chen's videos can be viewed on his website, www .chenshaoxiong.net. For Chen's earlier photographic montages, see *Chen Shaoxiong* (Hong Kong: Timezone 8, 2009).

92   Pauline Yao, "Time after Time: A Dialogue between Chen Shaoxiong and Pauline J. Yao," March 2009, www.chenshaoxiong.net/?p=850, accessed March 25, 2013.

93   *Ink City, Ink Things, Ink Diary,* and *Ink History* are available for viewing on the artist's YouTube channel: www.youtube.com /watch?v=JuZmDPaI-P4&list =UUQP5mtDB4OYFi _Z8OPyKiWA&index=15.

94   See Wang, "Seeing and Disbelieving," pp. 220–21. Wang points out that Chen's preoccupation with objects recalls a similar preoccupation on the part of Wen Zhenheng (1585–1645) in his text *Superfluous Things* (1621), which was written to offer guidance in selecting personal possessions. See Craig Clunas, *Superfluous Things: Material Culture and Social Status in Early Modern China* (Honolulu: University of Hawaiʻi Press, 2004). See also Rosalind Krauss, "Perpetual Inventory," *October* 88 (Spring 1999), pp. 86–116.

95   Hou Hanru, "Chen Shaoxiong: From Portable Streets to Private Diplomacy" (2009), in *Chen Shaoxiong*, ed. Robin Peckham (Hong Kong: Timezone 8, 2009), unpaginated. Also available on the artist's website: http://chenshaoxiong.net/?p=844.

96   Ibid.

97   In 2009, Chen Shaoxiong moved to Beijing, a change of location that undoubtedly colored his view of China's political and historical identity.

98   The *New York Times* review of the new National Museum of China notes that the Cultural Revolution is treated with "a single photograph and three lines of text" as "the only reference to that era," tucked into a corner of the giant edifice. See Ian Johnson, "At China's New Museum, History Toes the Party Line." *New York Times*, April 3, 2011, p. A1, www .nytimes.com/2011/04/04/world /asia/04museum.html.

99   For a list of Sun's videos, see *Sun Xun*, a portfolio produced by ShangART (2011). For a recent installation, see *Hammer Projects, 1999–2009* (Los Angeles: Hammer Museum, 2009), pp. 367–71. Since 2009 Sun and his studio have been located in Beijing.

100   Karen Smith, "Moving Images; Moving Concepts: A Survey of the Moving Images 1988–2011," in *Moving Image in China: Video Art 1988–2011*, ed. He Juxing (n.p.: Shijie yishu chubanshe, 2011), p. 138.

101   See, for example, Kentridge's *Procession on Anatomy of Vertebrates* and *Portage*, both created in 2000, with drawing and collage against book pages. See Rosenthal, *William Kentridge: Five Themes*, pp. 148–49.

102   Kentridge has made prints as an integral part of his creative process for more than thirty years. He has observed that many of his projects, including animated films, had their origin as a piece of printmaking. See "William Kentridge Five Themes: Process," MoMA Multimedia, www.moma.org /explore/multimedia/videos/95/555, accessed March 25, 2013.

103   The term "cynical realism" was coined by Li Xianting in 1991. See Li Xianting, "Fang Lijun yu wanshi xianshi zhuyi" [Fang Lijun and cynical realism], in *Fang Lijun: Piping wenji* [Fang Lijun: Collection of essays] (Beijing: Culture and Art Publishing House, 2010), p. 81. See also Li Xianting, "Fang Lijun and Cynical Realism," in *Fang Lijun* (Changsha: Hunan Fine Arts Publishing House, 2001), p. 18 (English, p. 22), written in 1991, amended in 1996 and 2000, as cited in "Fang Lijun: Swim or Sink," in Karen Smith, *Nine Lives: The Birth of Avant-Garde Art in New China*, new ed. (Hong Kong: Timezone 8, 2008), p. 139.

104   For the fullest biographical account in English, see "Fang Lijun: Swim or Sink," in Smith, *Nine Lives*, pp. 128–77.

105   Commenting on the shaving of his head, Fang has stated, "I was going through a period of confusion about what I was being taught and couldn't find my own direction artistically. It must have been the heat of summer or something. Coincidentally, soon after I saw some photographs that a classmate had taken of the farmers from Taihang Mountain. I recognised the physique as being perfect for the paintings I wanted to create. Somehow I translated these farmers into bareheaded figures." Ibid., pp. 148–49.

106   From Fang Lijun, "A Primitive State of Humanity," in Sans, *China Talks*, p. 17.

107   I am paraphrasing Li Xianting as quoted in Andreas Schalhorn, "Fang's Heads," in *Fang Lijun: Life Is Now* (Jakarta: CP Foundation, 2006), p. 32.

108   Quoted in Cees Hendrikse, ed., *Writing on the Wall: Chinese New Realism and Avant-Garde in the Eighties and Nineties*, exh. cat. ([Groningen, Neth.]: Groninger Museum, 2008), p. 90.

109   Fang has acknowledged David Hockney's depictions of California swimming pools as one source of inspiration for his aquatic images, though he asserts that their imagery and intent make them quite distinct. See Fang Lijun and Luo Yi, *Xiang yegou yiyang shengcun* [Living like a wild dog] (Beijing: Culture and Art Publishing House, 2010), pp. 67–69.

110   Smith, *Nine Lives*, p. 171.

111   Fang, "Primitive State of Humanity," p. 18.

112   In June of 1956 Mao composed the poem "Swimming—To the Tune of Shui diao ge tou" expressing his wish to control and repurpose the river: "A bridge will fly to span the north and south, / turning a deep chasm into a thoroughfare; / Walls of stone will stand upstream to the west, / to hold back Wushan's clouds and rain, / til a smooth lake rises in the narrow gorges. / The mountain goddess if she is still there, / will marvel at a world so changed." See *Mao Zedong Poems* (n.p.: Open Source Socialist Publishing, 2008), p. 31, http://socialistpublishing .files.wordpress.com/2010/05 /maopoems-newsetting.pdf.

113   ArtDepot interview with Liu Wei, May 13, 2010, www.artcomb .com/thread-12113-1-1.html. See also Wei Wei, "Liu Wei: Xushu ziwo de youxi" [Liu Wei: The game of self-expressing], *Dongfang yishu* [Oriental art], no. 19 (2006), pp. 82–89.

114   For examples of Liu's early work, see Li Xianting, *Liu Wei & Ye Yongqing*, exh. cat. (Beijing: Gallery of the Central Academy of Fine Arts, 1997); Fibicher and Frehner, *Mahjong: Contemporary Chinese Art from the Sigg Collection*, pp. 314–17; and Hendrikse, *Writing on the Wall*, pp. 94–97.

115 Liu Wei has acknowledged that he intended the words "flower" and "painting" to be synonymous: "There is no mistake in using these two words at the same time: to me, painting and flowers are the same thing." See Nataline Colonnello, "Liu Wei 'The Floating Spirit of Flowers,'" 2004 essay formerly available on the website of Galerie Urs Meile, Lucerne.

116 Quoted in ibid. According to Ni Youyu, the albums were created after an eighteen-month hiatus in Liu's work brought on by the end of an eleven-year romantic relationship. Recovering his equilibrium after a period of dissolute behavior and self-examination in which the artist confronted the unruly physical realities of human existence, he was able to complete the entire series with relative ease. See Ni Youyu's essay in *Luohua liushui: Liu Wei/ Blossom Fall, Stream Flow: Liu Wei*, exh. cat. (Shanghai: Hongqiao hualang/Red Bridge Gallery, 2006).

117 See Nataline Colonnello, "Liu Wei," in Fibicher and Frehner, *Mahjong: Contemporary Chinese Art from the Sigg Collection*, p. 314. Liu also has observed, "Confusion makes totality. I think that to use different media and styles is a way to pick up the gauntlet. Oil painting, water color, ink, Chinese landscape painting, calligraphy. . . . If you want to mix them together it is very difficult, but to me it is very obvious that they are one and the same thing—painting." Quoted in Colonnello, "Liu Wei 'The Floating Spirit of Flowers.'"

118 The identification of this figure is confirmed by Colonnello, who notes that Liu Wei has referred to Qi Baishi as the "grandpa of China." See Colonnello, "Liu Wei 'The Floating Spirit of Flowers.'"

ABSTRACTION

1 Shūjirō Shimada, "Concerning the I-P'in Style of Painting," part 1, trans. James Cahill, *Oriental Art*, n.s., 7, no. 2 (Summer 1961), p. 68. Shimada's quotation is from Zhu Jingxuan's *Tangchao minghua lu*, as translated in Alexander Soper, "The Famous Painters of the T'ang Dynasty," *Archives of the Chinese Art Society of America* 4 (1950), p. 20.

2 It was Su Shi (1037–1101) who declared, "My calligraphy follows my own hand, without bothering with details," as cited in Wen C. Fong et al., *Images of the Mind: Selections from the Edward L. Elliott Family and John B. Elliott Collections of Chinese Calligraphy and Painting at the Art Museum, Princeton University* (Princeton: The Art Museum, Princeton University, 1984), p. 76.

3 For Kline's debt to East Asian calligraphy, see Alexandra Munroe, ed., *The Third Mind: American Artists Contemplate Asia, 1860–1969*, exh. cat. (New York: Solomon R. Guggenheim Museum, 2009), p. 410; for Motherwell, see ibid., p. 415; for Marden, see Jonathan Hay, "Marden's Choice" and "Interview with Brice Marden," in *Brice Marden: Chinese Work*, exh. cat. (New York: Matthew Marks Gallery, 1999), pp. 7–11 and 19–31.

4 Gordon S. Barrass, *The Art of Calligraphy in Modern China*, exh. cat. (London: British Museum Press, 2002), p. 163.

5 Ibid., p. 164.

6 At the academy Wang advanced his command of classical techniques of character structure under the tutelage of Sha Menghai (1900–1992) while being exposed to the radical combinations of script types practiced by Lu Weizhao (1899–1980). He also studied with Zhu Lesan (1902–1984). See Wang Dongling, "Wo de xueshu daolu yu tihui" [Some thoughts on my path to calligraphy], in *Wang Dongling chuangzuo shouji* [Wang Dongling's notes on making art], Wang Dongling shufa luncong [Wang Dongling on calligraphy series] (Beijing: China Renmin University Press, 2011), p. 45.

7 Xu Jiang, ed., *Wang Dongling shufa yishu* [Wang Dongling's work] (Beijing: Rong Bao Zhai Press, 2007), p. 290.

8 Email correspondence between the artist and Xin Wang, August 2, 2012.

9 For *Being Open and Empty*, see Xu, *Wang Dongling shufa yishu* [Wang Dongling's work], p. 363. For *Dark (Heaven) and Yellow (Earth)*, see ibid., pp. 356, 357; and Wang, *Wang Dongling chuangzuo shouji* [Wang Dongling's notes on making art], p. 132.

10 Zhang Yu, "Ink and Wash Is a Kind of Spirit," in *Zhang Yu: Yiwei dangdai yishujia de ge'an yanjiu/A Case Study on a Contemporary Artist: 1984–2008*, ed. Yin Shuangxi (Changsha: Hunan Fine Arts Publishing House, 2008), p. 35, electronic ed., http://artist.artron.net /show_news.php?newid=245358.

11 Ibid. This is the author's translation from the Chinese: "以虚无的态度专心试验虚无。"

12 For a detailed discussion of the first five decades of Li's life and art, see Jerome Silbergeld and Gong Jisui, *Contradictions: Artistic Life, the Socialist State, and the Chinese Painter Li Huasheng* (Seattle: University of Washington Press, 1993).

13 Ibid., p. 57.

14 Ibid., p. 162.

15 Ibid., pp. 204–10.

16 See, for example, Li Xianting, *Nianzhu yu bichu/Prayer Beads and Brush Strokes*, exh. cat. (Beijing: Beijing Tokyo Art Projects, 2003), p. 27.

17 From "Curator's Notes on Prayer Beads and Brush Strokes," in ibid., p. 10.

18 Li Huasheng, Interview by Ling Xiao, March 17, 2003, www.hanart .com/artist_detail.php?l=1&id =73&s=2, accessed January 20, 2013.

19 For examples of Ding Yi's work, see *Ding Yi: Gaikuo de, chouxiang de/ Specific, Abstracted* (Beijing: Gold Wall Press; Xiyuan Publishing House, 2011). For Lu Qing, see Li, *Nianzhu yu bichu/Prayer Beads and Brush Strokes*, pp. 37–40, 72. For Chen Guangwu, see Chen Guangwu, "Zhishi shufa/Just Calligraphy," in ibid., pp. 32–35.

20 Gao Minglu has sought to distinguish the abstractions of Li Huasheng and other contemporary Chinese artists from Western "minimalism" by labeling their works "maximalism." See Gao Minglu, *Zhongguo jiduo zhuyi/Chinese Maximalism*, exh. cat. (Chongqing: Chongqing Publishing House, 2003).

21 Martina Köppel-Yang, "Yang Jiechang: Painting beyond the Visual," in Alice King and Martina Köppel-Yang, *Enlightened Blackness: Ink Paintings by Yang Jiechang* (Hong Kong: Alisan Fine Arts, 2001).

22 Fritz Hansel and Yang Jiechang, "Republic of Fritz Hansel: A Dialogue," in Yang Jiechang, *No-shadow Kick*, ed. Hou Hanru and Wei Xing, exh. cat. (Shanghai: Shanghai Duolun Museum of Art; Beijing: Tang Contemporary Art, 2008), p. 218.

23 Ibid.

24 Martina Köppel-Yang makes this connection. See Köppel-Yang, "Yang Jiechang: Painting beyond the Visual," unpaginated.

25 According to Köppel-Yang, "In his series *100 Layers of Ink* [Yang Jiechang] subverts the technique as well as the aesthetic appearance of Chinese painting by obsessively putting layers on layers of ink, thus creating a black object that does neither show skill, nor imagery, nor personality. In fact, one can consider this a deconstruction of Chinese painting and its tradition into its basic elements: paper, water, ink, as well as the action of applying it to the paper." Ibid.

26 See Hou Hanru, "Towards a World of Poets — Yang Jiechang's Work," in Yang, *No-shadow Kick*, p. 2.

27 For other artists involved in the experimental ink movement, see Dong Xiaoming, ed., *Shiyan shuimo huigu, 1985–2000* [A retrospective of experimental ink and wash, 1985–2000], exh. cat., Shenzhen Fine Art Institute (Changsha: Hunan meishu chubanshe, 2005), and Pi Daojian and Wang Huangsheng, eds., *Zhongguo shuimo shiyan ershi nian* [China: 20 years of ink experiment] (Harbin: Heilongjiang meishu chubanshe, 2001).

28 For additional examples of Zhang Yu's activities ulterior to art making, see Wu Hung's essay in the present volume, especially pp. 23–24, nn. 22–23 and 26.

29 Biographical information about Zhang Yu is drawn from the "Chronology" published in Yin, *Zhang Yu: Yiwei dangdai yishujia de ge'an yanjiu/Case Study on a Contemporary Artist*, pp. 430–37, and Lu Peng, "Zhang Yu: A Personal History of Experiments in Ink and Wash," in ibid., pp. 416–21.

30 For examples of traditional Yangliuqing prints, see Clarissa von Spee, ed., *The Printed Image in China from the 8th to the 21st Centuries* (London: British Museum Press, 2010), nos. 34, 36, 40, 41.

31 Publications include *Ershi shijimo Zhongguo xiandai shuimo yishu zoushi* [Tendencies of Chinese modern ink art at the end of the twentieth century], ed. Zhang Yu, 5 vols. (Tianjin: Tianjin yangliuqing huashe, 1993, 1994, 1995, 1997; Heilongjiang: Heilongjiang meishu chubanshe, 2000); Zhang Yu, *Kaifang de Zhongguo shiyan shuimo* [Chinese open and experimental ink and wash] (Hong Kong: Yinhe chubanshe, 2002); Zhang Yu, *Zhongguo shiyan shuimo 1993–2003* [Chinese experimental ink and wash 1993–2003] (Heilong-jiang: Heilongjiang meishu chubanshe, 2004).

32 Zhang, "Ink and Wash Is a Kind of Spirit," p. 33.

33 This observation, made in 1996, is quoted in Lu, "Zhang Yu: Personal History of Experiments in Ink and Wash," p. 420. See also Zhang, "Ink and Wash Is a Kind of Spirit," p. 33.

34 Britta Erickson, "On Zhang Yu's Ink and Wash," in Yin, *Zhang Yu: Yi wei dangdai yishujia de ge'an yanjiu/Case Study on a Contemporary Artist*, p. 408.

35   The work was first published in Yin, *Zhang Yu: Yi wei dangdai yishujia de ge'an yanjiu/ Case Study on a Contemporary Artist*, p. 17.

BEYOND THE BRUSH

1   For Huang Yongping, see Philippe Vergne and Doryun Chong, eds., *House of Oracles: A Huang Yong Ping Retrospective*, 2 vols. in 1, exh. cat. (Minneapolis: Walker Art Center, 2005). For Cai Guo-Qiang, see Thomas Krens and Alexandra Munroe, *Cai Guo-Qiang: I Want to Believe*, exh. cat. (New York: Solomon R. Guggenheim Museum, 2008). In 2006 the Metropolitan Museum hosted a smaller installation, "Cai Guo-Qiang on the Roof: Transparent Monument"; see *Cai Guo-Qiang: Transparent Monument* (Milan: Charta, 2006).

2   The artist Zhang Yu has also categorized Cai as an experimental ink painter. To support this contention, Zhang cites an article about the Japanese photographer Nobuyoshi Araki in which Nobuyoshi offered the following: "The appearance of Cai Guo-Qiang's mode of art is basically due to the existence of the Chinese thought of ink and wash." He continued: "The new century is a demarcation line. It will be an era in which the ink and wash spirit dominates. I envy you your character of 'being soaked in ink and wash.'" See Zhang Yu, "Ink and Wash Is a Kind of Spirit," in *Zhang Yu: A Case Study on a Contemporary Artist: 1984–2008*, ed. Yin Shuangxi (Changsha: Hunan Fine Arts Publishing House, 2008), p. 37, electronic ed., http://artist.artron.net/show_news.php?newid=245358.

3   The exhibition was held at the Culture Palace of Xiamen, September 28–October 5, 1986.

4   Huang Yongping, "Xiamen Dada: Postmodern?" (1986), trans. Yu Hsiao-hwei, in Vergne and Chong, *House of Oracles*, pp. 76–77 (text vol.).

5   Ibid., p. 76. The original text is excerpted in the Chinese translation of *House of Oracles*; see Philippe Vergne and Doryun Chong, *Zhanbuzhe zhi wu: Huang Yongping hui gu zhan* (Shanghai: Shanghai renmin chubanshe, 2008), p. 79. Huang here summarizes a famous conversation recorded in the "Knowledge Wandered East" chapter of the *Zhuangzi*. For a full translation of this passage, see Burton Watson, *The Complete Works of Chuang Tzu* (New York: Columbia University Press, 1968), pp. 240–41. In 1985 the exhibition "Rauschenberg Overseas Cultural Interchange," sponsored by Rauschenberg, opened at the National Art Museum of China in Beijing. Huang did not see the exhibition but recognized the importance of the event. See Huang Yongping and Jane DeBevoise, "Conversation with Huang Yongping," Museum of Modern Art, October 15, 2010, www.aaa-a.org/2011/03/03/conversation-with-huang-yongping/, accessed March 28, 2013.

6   Huang, "Xiamen Dada: Postmodern?," p. 76 (text vol.).

7   Ibid., p. 77.

8   "Announcement of Burning" (1986), in "Xiamen Dada," in *U-turn: 30 Years of Contemporary Art in China (1983–1987)*, ed. Philip Tinari (New York: AW Asia and Office for Discourse Engineering, 2007), vol. 2.1. The burning took place on November 23, 1986.

9   Fei Dawei, "Two-Minute Wash Cycle: Huang Yong Ping's Chinese Period," trans. Tzu-Wen Cheng, in Vergne and Chong, *House of Oracles*, p. 9 (text vol.). Huang later described the sequence of events as follows: "In 1986, we submitted a proposal to the Fujian Art Museum to present an exhibition—we wrote a proposal which we knew would have a high chance of being accepted but did not provide details about the real project we had in mind. On the day of the exhibition, we abandoned our fake submitted proposal and instead curated an exhibition of found [mostly random construction] materials, primarily found in the museum's surroundings. When the museum officials realized this was not what we had proposed to do, they shut down the exhibition. It was up for about two hours." Huang and DeBevoise, "Conversation," www.aaa-a.org/2011/03/03/conversation-with-huang-yongping/.

10   Huang produced a similar scroll in 2003 titled *Long Drawing of the Bat Project*. See Vergne and Chong, *House of Oracles*, no. 38 (plates vol.).

11   See, for example, *Four Paintings Created According to Random Instructions and Wheel* (1985), illustrated in ibid., p. 10, nos. 1, 2 (plates vol.). In his 1985 essay "Paintings Made Following a Procedure (Determined by Me) and Yet Unrelated to Me (Nonexpressive)," the artist explicated that "using this random method to solve the problem of choosing colors, developing the composition, and determining the final look of a work of art allowed me to deal exclusively with numbers, which are nonvisual and nonaesthetic, and thus enabled me to get away from the deliberate (or nondeliberate) control of the laws of form. In other words, it was possible to get away from personal preferences for certain colors and compositions, to regard all pigments as being one and the same—regardless of the different colors, warm or cold, oil or water-based—and to consider all compositions as good, that is, to make no distinction between good and bad compositions. Both color and composition thus lost their meaning." Vergne and Chong, *House of Oracles*, p. 65 (text vol.). Also see "Non-Expressive Painting, the Overcoming of Aesthetic Taste and the Constraints of Expression," in Martina Köppel-Yang, *Semiotic Warfare: The Chinese Avant-Garde, 1979–1989; a Semiotic Analysis* (Hong Kong: Timezone 8, 2003), pp. 134–36.

12   This 1985 photograph was appended in "The Artist's Statement on His Activities from 1980 to 1986," p. 3, one of the artist's personal notes selectively reproduced and translated in Vergne and Chong, *House of Oracles*, p. 35 (text vol.). This image documented the making of *The Four Paintings Created According to Random Instructions* (1985), "which consisted in making a roulette wheel and choosing and numbering the pigments myself, then documenting the results of spinning the roulette wheel and throwing the dice during the painting process, organizing the data (numbers as to the composition pattern and pigment) into a table, and finally, applying these random choices." The artist went on to remark, "This is one of my important series." Ibid., p. 36. Note that the translation provided in the catalogue, "The Four Paintings Created According to Random Instructions," does not correspond literally to the artist's original text, in which he labels the series "非表达绘画—转盘系列," literally, "Non-Expressive Paintings—Roulette-Wheel Series." See ibid., p. 35, for the original Chinese text.

13   For Huang's *Bat Project*, see Fei Dawei, ed., *Bat Project: Bat Project II* (Orsières: Guy and Myriam Ullens Foundation, 2003), and Vergne and Chong, *House of Oracles*, pp. 60–79 (plates vol.).

14   Wang Bomin, *Zhongguo huihua shi* [History of Chinese painting] (Shanghai: Shanghai renmin meishu chubanshe, 1982); Herbert Read, *Xiandai huihua jianshi* [A Concise History of Modern Painting (originally published in 1959)] (Shanghai: Shanghai renmin meishu chubanshe, 1979).

15   Fei Dawei has commented on this work: "Cultural history has continually been 'sullied,' it must therefore continually be washed and dried. The purpose of washing and drying is not to make this concept purer, however, but rather to make it 'dirtier.' Only when there is no pure culture can 'dirty' culture become more vivacious and wide-ranging." Fei, "Two-Minute Wash Cycle," in Vergne and Chong, *House of Oracles*, p. 8 (text vol.). As Huang Yongping has stated: "Book washing is somewhat similar to Wittgenstein's view of language. He once said, 'Now and then, some wordings should be removed from language and be sent to be washed—and after that, they can be brought back into communication.' What I do can be summed up as the following: 'washing' is both the method and the goal, because I don't believe that language can be brought back into communication after having been washed. In other words, communication is in reality a 'dirty form.' In addition, 'book washing' is not about making culture cleaner; rather, it tries to make its dirtiness more evident to the eye." From "To Beat the West with the East and to Beat the East with the West," Huang Yongping interviewed by Hou Hanru, August 1992, excerpted in Vergne and Chong, *House of Oracles*, p. 14 (text vol.).

16   *Magiciens de la terre*, exh. cat. (Paris: Éditions du Centre Pompidou, 1989), p. 153.

17   Huang re-created a multistory version of this work, with one thousand prongs holding objects of varying degrees of cultural significance, for the 2012 Shanghai Biennale. See the artist's page on the official exhibition website, www.shanghaibiennale.org/exhibitor/ and Chen Xhingyu, "In Shanghai, a Burst of Masterworks," *New York Times*, October 10, 2012, Arts sec., www.nytimes.com/2012/10/11/arts/11iht-rartshanghai11.html.

18   I am indebted to Xin Wang for pointing out essays by Qiu Zhijie and Yin Jinan that have commented on the fact that Huang, as well as other diasporic contemporary Chinese artists, explored Western postmodernist ideas while living in China but strategically mined their cultural heritage after resettling abroad. See Qiu Zhijie, "'Zhongguo pai' zhi wo jian" [My take on the "China card,"], in *Gei wo yige mianju* [Give

me a mask] (Beijing: China Renmin University Press, 2003), pp. 1–62, and Yin Jinan, "Xin guocui: 'chuantong' de dangdai xiaoyong" [New national essence: The effectiveness of "tradition" in contemporaneity], *Wenyi yanjiu/ Literature and Art Studies*, no. 5 (2002), pp. 123–35. Huang has summarized his strategy of mutual engagement with the East and the West as "To Beat the West with the East and to Beat the East with the West" in an interview with Hou Hanru, August 1992, in Vergne and Chong, *House of Oracles*, p. 17 (text vol.).

19   Vergne and Chong, *House of Oracles*, p. 40 (plates vol.).

20   See Krens and Munroe, *Cai Guo-Qiang: I Want to Believe*.

21   Cai's father, an amateur calligrapher, opened up the family home to traditional painters as a sort of gathering place. See *Wu Hung on Contemporary Chinese Artists* (Hong Kong: Timezone 8, 2009), p. 10.

22   *Magiciens de la terre*, pp. 162–63.

23   Wu Hung, "Once Again, Painting as Model: Reflections on Cai Guo-Qiang's Gunpowder Painting" (2005), in *Wu Hung on Contemporary Chinese Artists*, pp. 13–14.

24   "Chronology," in Krens and Munroe, *Cai Guo-Qiang: I Want to Believe*, p. 289. Writing about his *Project to Extend the Great Wall*, Cai noted, "I have mainly used gunpowder to express my ideas because I would like the movement caused by the explosion of my work to join and harmonize with the cosmic movement which has continued ever since the big bang." Cai Guo-Qiang, "The Project to Add 10,000 Meters to the Great Wall of China and Its Evolving Significance" (1993), trans. Naoko Aoki, in *Project for Extraterrestrials No. 10—Project to Add 10,000 Meters to the Great Wall of China*, ed. Yuichi Konno (Tokyo: Atelier Peyotl, 1994), p. 98.

25   Cai, "Project to Add 10,000 Meters to the Great Wall," p. 98.

26   Jeffrey Deitch and Rebecca Morse, eds., *Cai Guo-Qiang: Ladder to the Sky*, exh. cat. (Los Angeles: Museum of Contemporary Art, 2012), p. 124.

27   Commissioned by P3 Art and Environment, Tokyo, Cai enlisted a Japanese tourist agency not only to help defray the costs of the project but to recruit volunteers to help with its execution. Jiayuguan marks the end of the Ming-era wall, but the Han dynasty wall actually extends farther west. See Mary S. Lawton, "Great Wall of China," *Grove Art Online*, *Oxford Art Online*, Oxford University

Press, www.oxfordartonline.com /subscriber/article/grove/art /T034175, accessed February 26, 2013.

28   As Cai described it, "At dusk, the fuse was detonated and a wall of fire and smoke slithered across the plain like a night-crawling dragon." Deitch and Morse, *Cai Guo-Qiang: Ladder to the Sky*, p. 124.

29   Serizawa Takashi notes that in 1990, Cai "brought with him many of his tall, thin, Chinese sutra-style notebooks, in which he had freely drawn his various plans in Chinese black ink and gunpowder." See Serizawa Takashi, "Focus," in Dana Friis-Hansen, Octavio Zaya, and Serizawa Takashi, *Cai Guo-Qiang*, Contemporary Artists (London: Phaidon, 2002), p. 102. Two such "sketchbook" albums dating, respectively, to 1990 and 1993 have been published. See Krens and Munroe, *Cai Guo-Qiang: I Want to Believe*, figs. 55, 56. Another series was displayed in conjunction with large-scale, multipanel screens depicting proposed projects, not all of which have been realized. See ibid., nos. 8–12. Wu Hung has observed that "a majority of his gunpowder paintings are actually 'think pieces,' as their major role has been to help him articulate ideas through visual images." See *Wu Hung on Contemporary Chinese Artists*, p. 10.

30   Cai Guo-Qiang and Fei Dawei, "To Dare to Accomplish Nothing," in Dorothée Charles, *Cai Guo-Qiang*, exh. cat. (New York: Thames & Hudson, 2000), p. 132.

31   "Silvery serpent" is a reference to a famous poem by Mao Zedong: "Snow on the Pattern of Qin Yuanchun" (沁园春: 雪 1936), particularly "The mountains dance like silver snake." See a full translation of the poem in Mao Zedong, Zhao Hengyuan, and Paul Woods, *Mao Zedong shici/ Mao's Poems* (Tianjin: Tianjin renmin chubanshe, 1993), pp. 66–69.

32   This phrase was associated originally with Yue Fei (1103–1142), a fiercely patriotic military general who led the defense of the Southern Song dynasty against invaders from northern China.

33   I am indebted to Jane DeBevoise in a private communication for this interpretation of Cai Guo-Qiang's *Project to Extend the Great Wall*.

34   Hong Hao created a prototype for this series in July 1988; see Hong Hao, *Cang jing/Selected Scriptures, 1992–2000* ([China, ca. 2006]), p. 46. For Hong's comments on this work,

see Joris Escher and Martijn Kielstra, eds., *The Selected Scriptures of Hong Hao*, exh. cat. (Amsterdam: Canvas Foundation, 1999), p. 14.

35   Escher and Kielstra, *Selected Scriptures of Hong Hao*, p. 14.

36   Ibid., p. 16.

37   For a diagram illustrating the standard format of Chinese woodblock-printed books, see Sören Edgren, *Chinese Rare Books in American Collections*, exh. cat. (New York: China Institute in America, 1984), p. 15.

38   A catalogue was published at the end of the six-year international tour; see *Rauschenberg Overseas Culture Interchange*, exh. cat. (Washington, D.C.: National Gallery of Art, 1991). Hong Hao speaks about the influence of this exhibition in the October 30, 2003, interview by Zhang Zhaohui, "Cong xue huahua daozuo yishujia" [From learning to paint to being an artist], www.xdsf .com/bbs/thread-1390-1-1.html.

39   Escher and Kielstra, *Selected Scriptures of Hong Hao*, p. 24.

40   Ibid., p. 28.

41   See ibid., p. 22, where this print is dated 1995. The print illustrated here, however, is dated 1999.

42   See Maxwell K. Hearn, "Pictorial Maps, Panoramic Landscapes, and Topographic Paintings: Three Modes of Depicting Space during the Early Qing Dynasty," in *Bridges to Heaven: Essays on East Asian Art in Honor of Professor Wen C. Fong*, ed. Jerome Silbergeld, Dora C. Y. Ching, Judith G. Smith, and Alfreda Murck (Princeton: Princeton University Press, 2011), vol. 1, pp. 93–114.

43   Ai has created more than one *Map of China*. The earliest, now in the Sigg Collection, is dated 2003. See Bernhard Fibicher and Matthias Frehner, eds., *Mahjong: Contemporary Chinese Art from the Sigg Collection*, exh. cat. (Ostfildern, Ger.: Hatje Cantz Verlag, 2005), p. 221.

44   Ai may have intended a similar message in his *Fairy Tale*, which brought together 1,001 individuals from all over China for Documenta 12 in 2007. See the chapter on the *Fairy Tale* project in Urs Meile, ed., *Ai Weiwei: Works 2004–2007* (Lucerne: Galerie Urs Meile, 2007), pp. 153–69.

45   China's building boom has uncovered vast numbers of Neolithic and Han dynasty vessels, which have flooded the market, becoming commercial objects. Perhaps as a protest against the market forces that have commodified such objects or to emphasize that these pots were

once regarded as everyday wares of no special value, Ai has dropped them, plunged them into vats of bright colors, or "branded" them with overpainted logos for Coca-Cola. See Philip Tinari, "Postures in Clay: The Vessels of Ai Weiwei," in *Ai Weiwei: Dropping the Urn; Ceramic Works, 5000 BCE–2010 CE*, ed. Joseph N. Newland, exh. cat. (Glenside, Pa.: Arcadia University Art Gallery, 2010), pp. 30–47.

46   See Nataline Colonnello, "Ai Weiwei," in *Shanshui: Poetry without Sound? Landscape in Contemporary Chinese Art*, ed. Peter Fischer (Ostfildern, Ger.: Hatje Cantz Verlag; Lucerne: Kunstmuseum Luzern, 2011), p. 63.

47   Dick van Broekhuizen and Jan Teeuwisse, eds., *Xiānfēng!: Beeldhouwkunst van de Chinese avant-garde/Chinese Avant-garde Sculpture*, exh. cat. (Zwolle: Waanders; The Hague: Museum Beelden aan Zee, 2005), p. 28. For other examples from Wang Jin's *Dream of China* series, see Aric Chen and Meg Maggio, *Wang Jin*, exh. cat. (New York: Friedman Benda, 2007).

48   For information about Wang's biography and earlier work, see Wu Hung, *Transience: Chinese Experimental Art at the End of the Twentieth Century* (Chicago: David and Alfred Smart Museum of Art, University of Chicago, 1999), pp. 157–59, 189.

49   Wu Hung, "A Chinese Dream by Wang Jin," (2000), in *Wu Hung on Contemporary Chinese Artists*, p. 41.

50   See Asian Contemporary Art Week (ACAW), "Open Portfolios Online: Interview with Jian-Jun Zhang," April 21, 2009, www.acaw.info/?p=114, accessed March 2, 2013.

51   For *Ink Garden of Re-Creation* (2002), see Robert C. Morgan, "Memory and the Process of Historical Time," in *Zhang Jian-Jun* (Singapore: iPreciation, 2007), pp. 58–60.

52   ACAW, "Open Portfolios Online: Interview with Jian-Jun Zhang." For additional biographical information, see Britta Erickson, "Visual Experience of Time and Cultural Form: Installations by Zhang Jian-Jun," *CHINESE-ART .COM*, December 1, 2002, http:// artasiamerica.org/documents/5308 /127, accessed March 4, 2013, and Robert C. Morgan, "Zhang Jian-Jun: Memory and the Process of Historical Time," *Yishu: Journal of Contemporary Chinese Art* 6 (September 2007), pp. 56–57.

53   Britta Erickson, "Zhang Jianjun," in Fischer, *Shanshui: Poetry without*

Sound?, p. 217. Zhang first mentioned the idea for using silicone in a diary entry for December 3, 2003: "I had seen silicone rubber in high tech magazines like *Domus* and *Abitare*, and found it beautiful. I wanted my next sculptures to be really of this age. I feel I am borrowing the energy of these materials, of these colors and textures." Quoted in Margaret Sheffield, "Jian Jun Zhang," in *Art Projects International: Ten Years* (New York: Art Projects International, 2003), p. 77.

54   Quoted in Wu, *Transience: Chinese Experimental Art*, p. 133.

55   For a discussion of Chinese scholars' rocks, see "Chinese Scholars' Rocks: An Overview," in Robert D. Mowry, *Worlds within Worlds: The Richard Rosenblum Collection of Chinese Scholars' Rocks*, exh. cat. (Cambridge, Mass.: Harvard University Art Museums, 1997), pp. 19–36. For the artist's comments on this work, see Zhan Wang, *The New Suyuan Stone Catalogue*, ed. Philip Tinari and Angie Baecker; trans. Philip Bloom, Michael Hatch, and Alan Yeung (Milan: Charta, 2011), p. 39.

56   *Artificial Rock #10* is relatively modest in scale, but Zhan has also produced monumental examples equivalent to the largest specimens in Suzhou gardens. He has imitated other forms, as well, including meteorites. See the *New Patching Sky Project* (2000–2002) in Zhang Qunsheng, ed., *Zhan Wang*, Jinri Zhongguo yishujia/Chinese Artists of Today (Lanzhou: Gansu People's Fine Arts Publishing House, 2008), pp. 236–49.

57   Daniel Szehin Ho, trans., "Of Mammoths and Pietas: Conversation with Zeng Fanzhi," September 9, 2010, www.randian-online.com /np_feature/a-conversation-with -zeng-fanzhi/, accessed March 5, 2013.

58   Li Xianting, "Zeng Fanzhi: Mask," February 1998, www.shanghartgallery .com/galleryarchive/texts/id/157, accessed March 5, 2013. Commenting on this shift, Zeng has stated, "In 1989 I felt the need to give up imitating and to start from within and from my daily life." See Ho, "Of Mammoths and Pietas."

59   Zeng Fanzhi, "Human Nature," interview, August 13, 2008, in Jérôme Sans, *China Talks: Interviews with 32 Contemporary Artists by Jérôme Sans*, ed. Chen Yun and Michelle Woo; trans. Chen Yun and Philip Tinari (Hong Kong: Timezone 8, 2009), p. 175.

60   Zeng's interest in sculpture developed slowly. In 1993 he moved to Beijing and about seven years later began to collect ancient sculptures and objects and to study them in museums: "Looking at sculptures suddenly made me want to create sculpture. I'd absorbed a lot from various angles; I was prepared, ready to sculpt. . . . But to create these sculptures, I wanted something connected with the past." Quoted in Ho, "Of Mammoths and Pietas."

61   In commenting on his paintings of twisted and broken tree branches, Zeng recalled being inspired by a wisteria vine: "I was stimulated by the sensation I got from this snapped thing . . . that's the feeling you get from wisteria branches, the sudden sharp twists of a wintry tree branch; it's breaking off, suddenly breaking off." Wu Hung, *2010 Zeng Fanzhi*, exh. cat. (Shanghai: Rockbund Art Museum, 2010), p. 76, translation of a quotation from Pi Li and He Lijun, *Wo, women—Zeng Fanzhi de huihua, 1991–2003* [I, we—The painting of Zeng Fanzhi, 1991–2003] (Wuhan: Hubei Fine Arts Publishing House, 2003), p. 163.

62   See Wu, *2010 Zeng Fanzhi*.

63   I am indebted to Xin Wang for helping to define how artists have made use of their "multiple pasts" in much the same, unsystematic way that they embraced "Western" influences in the 1980s, "devouring whatever was available through translation and jumbling nineteenth- and early twentieth-century philosophical canons, Western modernist traditions, and postmodern developments without caring much about historiography" (private communication).

SELECTED BIBLIOGRAPHY

GENERAL WORKS

Ai Weiwei, ed. *Young Chinese Artists, Text and Interviews: Chinese Contemporary Art Awards, 1998–2002*. Hong Kong: Timezone 8, 2002.

Andrews, Julia F., and Gao Minglu. *Fragmented Memory: The Chinese Avant-Garde in Exile*. Columbus, Ohio: Wexner Center for the Arts, Ohio State University, 1993.

Asia Art Archive (AAA). Vast digital collection of primary and secondary source material about contemporary art in Asia. www.aaa.org.hk.

Barrass, Gordon S. *The Art of Calligraphy in Modern China*. Exh. cat. London: British Museum Press, 2002.

Berghuis, Thomas J. *Performance Art in China*. Hong Kong: Timezone 8, 2006.

Bessire, Mark. *Stairway to Heaven: From Chinese Streets to Monuments and Skyscrapers*. Exh. cat., Bates College Museum of Art, Lewiston, Me. Hanover, N.H.: University Press of New England, 2009.

Bowles, Frances, ed. *China Onward: The Estella Collection. Chinese Contemporary Art, 1966–2006*. Humlebæk, Denmark: Louisiana Museum of Modern Art, 2007.

Broekhuizen, Dick van, and Jan Teeuwisse, eds. *Xiānfēng!: Beeldhouwkunst van de Chinese avant-garde/Chinese Avant-garde Sculpture*. Exh. cat. The Hague: Museum Beelden aan Zee; Zwolle: Waanders, 2005.

Chang Tsong-zung and Robert Lord. *Power of the Word*. Exh. cat. New York: Independent Curators International, 2001.

Chen Long, ed. *Shanghai Biennale 2000*. Shanghai: Shanghai shuhua chubanshe, 2000.

Chiu, Melissa. *Breakout: Chinese Art outside China*. Milan: Charta, 2006.

Dong Xiaoming, ed. *Shiyan shuimo huigu, 1985–2000* [A retrospective of experimental ink and wash, 1985–2000]. Exh. cat., Shenzhen Fine Art Institute. Changsha: Hunan Fine Arts Publishing House, 2005.

Doran, Valerie C., ed. *China's New Art, Post-1989/Hou 89 zhongguo xin yishu*. Exh. cat. Hong Kong: Hanart TZ Gallery, 1993.

Erickson, Britta. *On the Edge: Contemporary Chinese Artists Encounter the West*. Stanford, Calif.: Iris & B. Gerald Cantor Center for Visual Arts at Stanford University, 2004.

Fei Dawei, ed. *'85 Xinchao Dangan* [Archives of the '85 New Wave]. Shanghai: Shanghai renmin chubanshe, 2007.

Fibicher, Bernhard, and Matthias Frehner, eds. *Mahjong: Contemporary Chinese Art from the Sigg Collection*. Ostfildern, Germany: Hatje Cantz Verlag, 2005.

Fischer, Peter, ed. *Shanshui: Poetry without Sound? Landscape in Contemporary Chinese Art*. Ostfildern, Germany: Hatje Cantz Verlag; Lucerne: Kunstmuseum Luzern, 2011.

Gao Minglu. *Zhongguo dangdai meishu shi 1985–1986* [A history of contemporary Chinese art]. Shanghai: Shanghai People's Press, 1991.

——, ed. *Inside Out: New Chinese Art*. Exh. cat. San Francisco: San Francisco Museum of Modern Art; New York: Asia Society Galleries, 1998.

——. *Zhongguo jiduo zhuyi/Chinese Maximalism*. Exh. cat. Chongqing: Chongqing Publishing House, 2003.

——, ed. *'85 Meishu yundong/ The '85 Movement*. 2 vols. Guilin: Guangxi Normal University Press, 2008.

——. *Total Modernity and the Avant-Garde in Twentieth-Century Chinese Art*. Cambridge, Mass.: MIT Press, 2011.

Gao Minglu and Li Xianting. *Zhongguo xiandai yishu zhan* [China avant-garde]. Nanning: Guangxi renmin chubanshe, 1989.

Grosenick, Uta, and Caspar H. Schübbe, eds. *China Art Book*. Cologne, Germany: DuMont, 2007.

Hay, Jonathan. "Ambivalent Icons: Five Chinese Painters in the United States." *Orientations* 23, no. 7 (July 1992), pp. 37–43.

He Juxing, ed. *Zhongguo yingxiang yishu/Moving Image in China: 1988–2011*. Beijing: Culture and Art Publishing House/Shijie yishu chubanshe, 2011.

——. *Moving Image in China, 1988–2011: La più completa retrospettiva sulla videoarte cinese/The Most Complete Retrospective on Chinese Video Art*. Exh. cat., Centro per l'Arte Contemporanea Luigi Pecci, Prato, Italy. Cinisello Balsamo, Milan: Silvana, 2012.

Hendrikse, Cees, ed. *Writing on the Wall: Chinese New Realism and Avant-Garde in the Eighties and Nineties*. Exh. cat. [Groningen, Netherlands]: Groninger Museum, 2008.

Hou Hanru. *On the Mid-Ground*. Hong Kong: Timezone 8, 2002.

Hu Yung-fen. *Hou jieyan yu hou bajiu: Liang'an dangdai meishu duizhao* [Post-martial laws vs. post-'89: The contemporary art in Taiwan and China]. Taichung: National Taiwan Museum of Fine Arts; Artist Publishing, 2007.

Hua Tianxue, Ai Weiwei, and Feng Boyi, eds. *Bu hezuo fangshi/Fuck Off*. [China, 2000.]

Huang Zhuan, ed. *Qiyun: Chouxiang shi zhong guanyu ziyou de biaoda/ An Expression Concerning Liberty*. Exh. cat. Guangzhou: Lingnan Art Publishing House, 2007.

Kuo, Jason C. *Chinese Ink Painting Now*. Seattle: Marquand Books, 2010.

Leng Lin. *Shi wo* [It's me]. Beijing: Zhongguo wenlian chubanshe, 2000.

Li Xianting. *Zhongyao de bunshi yishu* [Study of contemporary Chinese art: The significance does not lie in art]. Nanjing: Jiangsu Fine Arts Publishing House, 2000.

——. *Nianzhu yu bichu/Prayer Beads and Brush Strokes*. Exh. cat. Beijing: Beijing Tokyo Art Projects, 2003.

Lü Peng. *A History of Art in 20th Century China*. Milan: Charta, 2010.

——, ed. *Thirty Years of Adventures: Art and Artists from 1979*. Hong Kong: Timezone 8; Blue Kingfisher Limited, 2011.

Lü Peng, Zhu Zhu, and Gao Qianhui, eds. *Zhongguo xin yishu sanshi nian/ Thirty Years of Adventures*. Beijing: Timezone 8, 2010.

Martin, Jean Hubert, et al. *Magiciens de la terre.* Exh. cat., Musée National d'Art Moderne–Centre Georges Pompidou; La Grande Halle de la Villette, Paris. Paris: Editions du Centre Pompidou, 1989.

Obrist, Hans-Ulrich. *Hans Ulrich Obrist: The China Interviews.* Edited by Philip Tinari and Angie Baecker. Hong Kong: Office for Discourse Engineering, 2009.

Pi Daojian and Huangsheng Wang, eds. *Zhongguo shuimo shiyan ershi nian* [China: 20 years of ink experiment]. Exh. cat., Guangdong Museum of Art. Harbin: Heilongjiang meishu chubanshe, 2001.

Sans, Jérôme. *China Talks: Interviews with 32 Contemporary Artists by Jérôme Sans/Duihua Zhongguo: Jieluomu Sangsi yu 32 wei dangdai yishujia fangtan.* Edited by Chen Yun and Michelle Woo; translated by Chen Yun and Philip Tinari. Hong Kong: Timezone 8, 2009.

Shen, Kuiyi, and Julia F. Andrews. *Blooming in the Shadows: Unofficial Chinese Art, 1974–1985.* Exh. cat. New York: China Institute Gallery, 2011.

Sheng Hao; essays by Joseph Scheier-Dolberg and Yan Yang. *Fresh Ink: Ten Takes on Chinese Tradition.* Exh. cat. Boston: MFA Publications, 2010.

Silbergeld, Jerome, and Dora C. Y. Ching, eds. *ARTiculations: Undefining Chinese Contemporary Art.* Princeton: P. Y. and Kinmay W. Tang Center for East Asian Art, Princeton University, 2010.

Silbergeld, Jerome, with Cory Y. Liu and Dora C. Y. Ching. *Outside In: Chinese x American x Contemporary Art.* Exh. cat. Princeton: Princeton University Art Museum; P. Y. and Kinmay W. Tang Center for East Asian Art, Princeton University, 2009.

Smith, Karen, ed. *Nine Lives: The Birth of Avant-Garde Art in New China.* Hong Kong: Timezone 8, 2008.

Tinari, Philip, ed. *U-turn: 30 Years of Contemporary Art in China.* 2 vols. New York: AW Asia and Office for Discourse Engineering, 2007.

Tuymans, Luc, Ai Weiwei, and Fan Di'an. *The State of Things.* Exh. cat. Brussels and Beijing: BOZAR Center for Fine Arts; Tielt: Lanoo Books, 2009.

Wang, Sabine. *Writing on the Wall: Chinese New Realism and Avant-Garde in the Eighties and Nineties.* Edited by Cees Hendrikse. [Groningen, Netherlands]: Groninger Museum, 2008.

Wilson, Mark, and Sue-An van der Zijpp, eds. *New World Order: Contemporary Installation Art and Photography from China.* [Groningen, Netherlands]: Groninger Museum, 2008.

Wu Hung. *Transience: Chinese Experimental Art at the End of the Twentieth Century.* Chicago: David and Alfred Smart Museum of Art, University of Chicago, 1999.

——. *Exhibiting Experimental Art in China.* Chicago: David and Alfred Smart Museum of Art, University of Chicago, 2000.

——, ed. *Chinese Art at the Crossroads: Between Past and Future, Between East and West.* London: Institute of International Visual Arts; Hong Kong: New Art Media, 2001.

——. *The First Guangzhou Triennial. Reinterpretation: A Decade of Experimental Chinese Art (1990–2000).* Exh. cat. Guangzhou: Guangdong Museum of Art, 2002.

——. *Variations of Ink: A Dialogue with Zhang Yanyuan.* New York: Chambers Fine Art, 2002.

——. *Making History: Wu Hung on Contemporary Art.* Hong Kong: Timezone 8, 2008.

——. *Internalizing Changes: Contemporary Chinese Art and Urban Transformation.* The Geske Lectures 2008. Lincoln: The University of Nebraska, 2009.

——, ed. *Wu Hung on Contemporary Chinese Artists.* Hong Kong: Timezone 8, 2009.

——. *Contemporary Chinese Art: Primary Documents.* New York: Museum of Modern Art, 2010.

Wu Hung and Christopher Phillips. *Between Past and Future: New Photography and Video from China.* Chicago: David and Alfred Smart Museum of Art, University of Chicago; New York: International Center of Photography in collaboration with Asia Society; Göttingen, Germany: Steidl Publishers, 2004.

Wu Hung, Wang Huangsheng, and Feng Boyi. *Reinterpretation: A Decade of Experimental Chinese Art: 1990–2000.* Guangzhou: Guangdong Museum of Art, 2002.

Wu Hung, Peggy Wang, and J. May Lee Barrett. *Shu: Reinventing Books in Contemporary Chinese Art.* Exh. cat. New York: China Institute Gallery, China Institute, 2006.

Yang, Alice. "Beyond Nation and Tradition: Art in Post-Mao China." In *Why Asia? Contemporary Asian and Asian American Artists,* pp. 107–18. New York: New York University Press, 1998.

Zhang Yiguo. *Brushed Voices: Calligraphy in Contemporary China.* Exh. cat. New York: Miriam & Ira D. Wallach Art Gallery, 1998.

Zhang Yu. *Zhongguo shiyan shuimo, 1993–2003* [Chinese experimental ink and wash, 1993–2003]. Heilongjiang: Heilongjiang meishu chubanshe, 2004.

INDIVIDUAL ARTISTS

Ai Weiwei

Ai Weiwei. *Ai Weiwei.* Art Salon. Videodisc, 41 mins. New York: China Institute in America, 2009.

——. "Fake-Fuck." In *China Talks: Interviews with 32 Contemporary Artists by Jérôme Sans,* pp. 8–15. Hong Kong: Timezone 8, 2009.

——. *Ai Weiwei. Dropping the Urn: Ceramic Works, 5000 BCE–2010 CE.* Edited by Joseph N. Newland. Exh. cat. Glenside, Pa.: Arcadia University Art Gallery, 2010.

——. *Cishi cidi/Time and Place.* Guilin: Guangxi Normal University Press, 2010.

——. *Ai Weiwei's Blog: Writings, Interviews, and Digital Rants, 2006–2009.* Translated by Lee Ambrozy. Cambridge, Mass.: MIT Press, 2011.

Ai Weiwei and Mark Siemons. *Ai Weiwei: So Sorry.* Exh. cat., Haus der Kunst München. Munich and London: Prestel, 2009.

Buergel, Roger M. *Ai Weiwei: Barely Something.* Edited by Dirk Krämer and Klaus Maas. Exh. cat. Duisburg, Germany: Museum DKM/Stiftung DKM, 2010.

Dziewior, Yilmaz, ed. *Ai Weiwei: Art/Architecture.* Translated by Sabine Bürger, Tim Beeby, and Volker Ellerbeck. Exh. cat. Bregenz, Austria: Kunsthaus Bregenz, 2011.

Hua Tianxue, Ai Weiwei, and Feng Boyi, eds. *Bu hezuo fangshi/Fuck Off.* [China, 2000.]

Kataoka, Mami, Kerry Brougher, and Charles Merewether. *Ai Weiwei: According to What?* Exh. cat., organized by the Mori Art Museum, Tokyo, and the Hirshhorn Museum and Sculpture Garden, Smithsonian Institution, Washington, D.C. Munich and New York: Prestel, 2012.

Meile, Urs, ed. *Ai Weiwei: Works 2004–2007.* Lucerne: Galerie Urs Meile, 2007.

Merewether, Charles, ed. *Ai Weiwei: Works, Beijing 1993–2003.* Hong Kong: Timezone 8, 2003.

——. *Ai Weiwei: Under Construction.* Exh. cat., Sherman Contemporary Art Foundation and Campbelltown Arts Centre, Sydney. Sydney: University of New South Wales Press, 2008.

Smith, Karen. *Ai Weiwei: Illumination.* Exh. cat. New York: Mary Boone Gallery, 2008.

Smith, Karen, Hans-Ulrich Obrist, and Bernard Fibicher. *Ai Weiwei.* London: Phaidon, 2009.

Stahel, Urs, and Daniela Janser, eds. *Ai Weiwei: Interlacing.* Göttingen, Germany: Steidl, 2011.

Tinari, Philip. "A Kind of True Living." *Artforum* 45 (Summer 2007), pp. 453–59.

Wilson, Mark, and Sue-an van der Zijpp, eds. *Ai Weiwei.* Exh. cat. Groningen, Netherlands: Groninger Museum, 2008.

Cai Guo-Qiang

Brewinska, Maria. *Cai Guo-Qiang.* Exh. cat. Warsaw: Zacheta Narodowa Galeria Sztuki, 2005.

Cai Guo-Qiang. "The Project to Add 10,000 Meters to the Great Wall of China and Its Evolving Significance," translated by Naoko Aoki, August 10, 1993. In *Project for Extraterrestrials No. 10—Project to Add 10,000 Meters to the Great Wall of China,* edited by Yuichi Konno, p. 98. Tokyo: Atelier Peyotl, 1994.

——. *Sai Kokkyo, kan Taiheiyo yori/Cai Guo Qiang "From the Pan-Pacific."* Exh. cat., Iwaki City Art Museum. [Iwaki-shi]: Iwaki Shiritsu Bijutsukan, 1994.

——. *Husi luanxiang/Day Dreaming: Cai Guo-Qiang.* Exh. cat. Taibei: Cherng Piin Gallery, 1998.

——. *Cai Guo-Qiang.* New York: Thames & Hudson, 2000.

———. *Cai Guo-Qiang*. Exh. cat., Shanghai Meishu Guan. Shanghai: Shanghai Painting and Calligraphy Press, 2002.

———. *Cai Guo-Qiang: Head On*. Exh cat., Deutsche Guggenheim Berlin. Ostfildern, Germany: Hatje Cantz Verlag, 2006.

———. *Cai Guo-Qiang: Transparent Monument*. Exh. cat., The Metropolitan Museum of Art, New York. Milan: Charta, 2006.

———. "Cai Guo-Qiang dashiji" [Cai Guo-Qiang chronicle]. In *Cai Guo-Qiang: Woshi zheyang xiangde* [Cai Guo-Qiang: Here's what I think], pp. 214–35. Guilin: Guangxi Normal University Press, 2010.

———. Artist's website: www .caiguoqiang.com.

Cai Guo-Qiang and Gerald Matt. *Cai Guo-Qiang: I Am the Y2K Bug*. Exh. cat., Kunsthalle Wien. Cologne, Germany: Verlag der Buchhandlung Walther König, 1999.

Cai Guo-Qiang and David Rodríguez Caballero. *Cai Guo-Qiang: Fuegos artificiales negros (On Black Fireworks)*. Exh. cat. Valencià: IVAM Institut Valencià d'Art Modern, 2005.

Cai Guo-Qiang, Zhao Yang, and Weijing Li. *Cai Guo-Qiang: Woshi zheyang xiangde* [Cai Guo-Qiang: Here's what I think]. Guilin: Guangxi Normal University Press, 2010.

Cavallucci, Fabio, ed. *Cai Guo-Qiang*. Exh. cat., Galleria Civica di Arte Contemporanea, Trento. Cinisello Balsamo, Milan: Silvana, 2002.

Chang, Wan-jen. Essay on Cai Guo-Qiang's *Project to Extend the Great Wall of China by 10,000 Meters*. In *The Wall*, pp. 258–67. Taipei: National Museum of History, 2000.

Deitch, Jeffrey, and Rebecca Morse, eds. *Cai Guo-Qiang: Ladder to the Sky*. Exh. cat. Los Angeles: Museum of Contemporary Art, 2012.

Friis-Hansen, Dana, Octavio Zaya, and Serizawa Takashi. *Cai Guo-Qiang*. Contemporary Artists. London and New York: Phaidon, 2002.

Heartney, Eleanor. "Cai Guo-Qiang: Illuminating the New China." *Art in America* 90, no. 5 (May 2002), pp. 92–97.

Heon, Laura Steward, and Robert Pogue Harrison. *Cai Guo-Qiang: Inopportune*. Exh. cat. North Adams, Mass.: MASS MoCA, 2004.

Krens, Thomas, and Alexandra Munroe. *Cai Guo-Qiang: I Want to Believe*. Exh. cat., Solomon R. Guggenheim Museum, New York; National Art Museum of China, Beijing; Guggenheim Museum Bilbao. New York: Guggenheim Museum, 2008.

Schwabsky, Barry. "Tao and Physics: The Art of Cai Guo-Qiang." *Artforum* 35, no. 10 (Summer 1997), pp. 118–21, 155.

Chen Shaoxiong

Chen Shaoxiong. *Chen Shaoxiong: Multi-Landscape*. Vitamin Creative Space Publication Project 1. Guangzhou: Vitamin Creative Space, 2004.

———. Interview by Huang Xiaoyan, May 28, 2007, for the Asia Art Archive. www.china1980s.org/files /interview/csxftfinalised _201102081613356873.pdf.

———. Artist's website, which includes links to view his video works in full: www.chenshaoxiong.net.

Chen Shaoxiong and Meg Maggio. *Ink History: Video Animation by Chen Shaoxiong*. Beijing: Pekin Fine Arts, 2012.

Hou Hanru. "Chen Shaoxiong: From Portable Streets to Private Diplomacy." In *Chen Shaoxiong*, edited by Robin Peckham, unpaginated. Hong Kong: Timezone 8, 2009.

Wang Xin. "Seeing and Disbelieving: Exploring Chen Shaoxiong's Ink Animation Videos." In *Modern Art Asia: Papers on Modern and Contemporary Asian Art*, pp. 213–24. London: Enzo Arts and Publishing, 2012.

Yao, Pauline J. "Time after Time: A Dialogue between Chen Shaoxiong and Pauline J. Yao," March 2009. www.chenshaoxiong.net/?p=850.

Duan Jianyu

Dematté, Monica. "Apotheosis of the Imagination: Duan Jianyu's Approach to Painting," June 4, 2011. www.duanjianyu.cn/article_view _en.asp?displaypage=1&sort _id=30&id=180&url=index _en.asp?id1=30@sort1=2.

Duan Jianyu. "Duan Jianyu: Wenben yu huihua" [Duan Jianyu: Text and painting]. Artist talk. Ullens Center for Contemporary Art, September 17, 2008. http://cul.sohu.com/20081128 /n260913416.shtml.

———. *Niuyue Bali Zhumadian/New York Paris Zhumadian*. Guangzhou: Vitamin Creative Space, 2008.

———. Artist's website: www .duanjianyu.cn.

Duan Jianyu and Hu Fang. *Daizhe xigua qu lüxing/How to Travel with a Watermelon*. Exh. cat. Guangzhou: Vitamin Creative Space, 2006.

Hu Fang. "Duan Jianyu: How to Travel with a Watermelon." Translated by Philip Tinari, April 26, 2006. www .vitamincreativespace.com/en /project/viewProject.do?id=20008.

Pu Hong. "Duan Jianyu: The Seduction of Village." *Leap: The International Art Magazine of Contemporary China*, no. 7 (February 2011). http://leapleapleap.com /2011/03/duan-jianyu-the-seduction-of-village/.

Smith, Karen. *A Potent Force: Duan Jianyu and Hu Xiaoyuan*. Shanghai: Rockbund Art Museum, 2013.

Zeng Tingke, Hu Fang, and Vitamin Creative Space, eds. *Duan jianyu: Cunzhuang de youhuo/ The Seduction of Village*. Hong Kong: Blue Kingfisher, 2011.

Fang Lijun

Fang Lijun. *Fang Lijun*. Exh. cat. Amsterdam: Stedelijk Museum, 1998.

———. *Fang Lijun*. Changsha: Hunan Fine Arts Publishing House, 2001.

———. "A Primitive State of Humanity." In *China Talks: Interviews with 32 Contemporary Artists by Jérôme Sans*, pp. 16–21. Hong Kong: Timezone 8, 2009.

Fang Lijun and Luo Yi. *Xiang yegou yiyang shengcun* [Living like a wild dog]. Beijing: Culture and Art Publishing House, 2010.

Leng Lin. *Shi wo* [It's me]. Beijing: Zhongguo wenlian chubanshe, 2000.

Lu, Carol Yinghua. *Xiang yegou yiyang shenghuo: 1963–2008 Fang Lijun wenxian dang'an zhan* [Living like a wild dog: 1963–2008 archive exhibition of Fang Lijun]. Taipei: Shijie yishu chubanshe, 2009.

Lü Peng and Chun Liu, eds. *Fang Lijun*. Vol. 1, *Biannian jishi/Chronicles*. Beijing: Culture and Art Publishing House, 2010.

———. *Fang Lijun*. Vol. 2, *Piping wenji/ Collection of Essays*. Beijing: Culture and Art Publishing House, 2010.

Ochs, Alexander, Jim Supangkat, Andreas Schalhorn, and Yi Ying. *Fang Lijun: Life Is Now*. Exh. cat., Galeri Nasional Indonesia, Jakarta. Jakarta: CP Foundation, 2006.

Smith, Karen. "Fang Lijun: Swim or Sink." In Karen Smith, *Nine Lives: The Birth of Avant-Garde Art in New China*, pp. 128–77. New ed. Hong Kong: Timezone 8, 2008.

Zhang Zikang, ed. *Fang Lijun*. Beijing: Today Art Museum, 2006.

Fung Mingchip

Doran, Valerie C. "Scripting Time." *Asian Art News*, May–June 2011, pp. 52–57.

———. "Freeing Time: The Calligraphy of Fung Ming Chip." *Orientations* 42, no. 8 (December 2011), pp. 116–19.

Fung Mingchip. *Fung Ming-chip*. Hong Kong: Hanart TZ Gallery, 1999.

———. *Fung Ming Chip Solo Exhibition*. Taipei: Taipei Fine Art Museum, 1999.

———. *The Paintings of Fung Ming Chip*. Exh. cat. London: Goedhuis Contemporary, 2000.

———. *Recent Paintings by Fung Ming Chip*. Exh. cat. New York: Goedhuis Contemporary, 2005.

———. *Recent Work, Fung Ming Chip*. Exh. cat. Hong Kong: Alisan Fine Arts, 2006.

———. *Fung Ming Chip Solo Exhibition*. Hong Kong: Sin Sin Fine Art, 2010.

Gu Wenda

Bessire, Mark H. C., ed. *Wenda Gu: Art from Middle Kingdom to Biological Millennium*. Exh. cat., University of North Texas Art Gallery, Denton; Kansas City Art Institute; Institute of Contemporary Art at Maine College of Art, Portland. Cambridge, Mass.: MIT Press, 2003.

Gu Wenda. Interview by Jane DeBevoise, November 4, 2009, for the Asia Art Archive. www .china1980s.org/en/interview_detail .aspx?interview_id=39.

———. *Shuimo lianjinshu: Gu Wenda de shiyan shuimo/Ink Alchemy: The Experimental Ink of Gu Wenda*. Edited by Huang Zhuan. Exh. cat. Guangzhou: Lingnan Art Publishing House, 2010.

———. Artist's website. www
.wendagu.com/noflash.html.

Shi Jian. "Gu Wenda fangtan"
[An interview with Gu Wenda]. In
'85 Xinchao Dang'an, I [Archives of
the '85 New Wave, I], edited by Fei
Dawei. Shanghai: Shanghai renmin
chubanshe, 2007.

Hong Hao

Escher, Joris, and Martijn Kielstra,
eds. The Selected Scriptures of Hong
Hao/Hong Hao Cang jing. Exh. cat.
[Amsterdam]: Canvas Foundation,
1999.

Feng Boyi. "Hong Hao de 'Shu'"
[Hong Hao's 'Books']. Oriental Art
Classics, no. 5 (2006), pp. 104–7.

Hong Hao. "A Dispensable
Supplement." In New Anecdotes
of Social Talk, pp. 29–31. Beijing:
Beijing guoji yiyuan meishuguan,
1995.

———. "Cong xue huahua dao zuo
yishujia" [From learning to paint to
being an artist]. Interview by Zhang
Zhaohui, October 30, 2003. www
.xdsf.com/bbs/thread-1390-1-1.html.

———. Hong Hao. Exh. cat. Tokyo:
Base Gallery, 2004.

———. Cang jing/Selected Scriptures,
1992–2000. [China, ca. 2006].

Li Xianting and Di'an Fan. "Hong Hao
de banhua zhi lu" [Hong Hao's
prints]. Dongfang yishu [Oriental art],
no. 17 (2009), pp. 74–75.

Pi Li and Katherine Don, eds. Twelve:
Chinese Contemporary Art Awards
2006. Exh. cat., Shanghai Zendai
Museum of Modern Art. Shanghai:
Chinese Contemporary Art Awards,
2006.

Tancock, John, and Hong Hao, eds.
Elegant Gathering: Hong Hao's
Opening. Exh. cat. New York:
Chambers Fine Art, 2007.

Huang Yan

Chang Tsong-zung and Petr Nedoma.
A Strange Heaven: Contemporary
Chinese Photography/Huanying
tiantang: Zhonghua dangdai sheying
ji. Edited by Susan Acret. Exh. cat.,
Galerie Rudolfinum, Prague. Hong
Kong: Asia Art Archive, 2003.

Erickson, Britta. "Huang Yan." In
Shanshui: Poetry without Sound?
Landscape in Contemporary Chinese
Art, edited by Peter Fischer, p. 113.
Ostfildern, Germany: Hatje Cantz
Verlag; Lucerne: Kunstmuseum
Luzern, 2011.

Huang Yan. 2005–2010 Huang Yan:
Wunian zuopin huiguzhan/A
Retrospective of the Past 5 Years.
Shanghai: Leo Gallery; Hong Kong:
Hong Kong Arts Centre, 2010.

Prearo, Giampaolo, ed. Huang Yan.
Milan: G. Prearo, 2007.

Huang Yongping

Fei Dawei, ed. Bat Project: Bat Project II.
Exh. cat., Venice Biennale. Orsières,
Switzerland: Guy & Myriam Ullens
Foundation, 2003.

Huang Yongping. Interview by
Anthony Yung, March 3, 2008, for the
Asia Art Archive. www.china1980s
.org/files/interview/hypft
_201111221207372253.pdf.

———. "Art as a War of Imagining."
In China Talks: Interviews with 32
Contemporary Artists by Jérôme Sans,
pp. 22–27. Hong Kong: Timezone 8,
2009.

Huang Yongping and Jane DeBevoise.
"Conversation." October 15, 2010.
www.aaa-a.org/2011/03/03
/conversation-with-huang-yongping/.

Huang Yongping and Ya-Ling Chen.
"Dada Is Dead, Beware of the Fire:
An Interview with Huang Yong Ping."
Tout-Fait: The Marcel Duchamp
Studies Online Journal 2, no. 5
(April 2004). www.toutfait.com
/issues/volume2/issue_5/interviews
/ping/ping.html.

Loisy, Jean de, Richard Leydier, and
Gilles A. Tiberghien. Huang Yong
Ping: Myths. Exh. cat. Paris: Galerie
Kamel Mennour, 2009.

Tinari, Philip, ed. "Xiamen Dada."
In U-turn: 30 Years of Contemporary
Art in China (1983–1987), vol. 2.1.
New York: AW Asia and Office
for Discourse Engineering, 2007.

Vergne, Philippe, and Doryun Chong,
eds. House of Oracles: A Huang
Yong Ping Retrospective. Exh. cat.
Minneapolis: Walker Art Center, 2005.

Wang Minan. "Huang Yongping de
yiyi" [The significance of Huang
Yongping]. Dushu, no. 8 (February
2008), pp. 104–13.

Wu Meichun, ed. Huang Yongping.
Fuzhou: Fujian Meishu Press, 2002.

Li Huasheng

Li Bing, ed. Shuimo bu dengyu
shuimohua/Ink Is Not Equivocal to
Ink Painting: Li Huasheng, Zhang Yu,
Liang Quan Art Exhibition. Beijing:
Hejingyuan Art Gallery, 2008.

Li Huasheng. Li Huasheng huaji/Li
Huasheng: An Individualistic Artist.
Exh. cat., Chinese Culture Center
of San Francisco, Alisan Fine Arts,
Hong Kong. [Hong Kong, 1998.]

———. Interview by Ling Xiao, March
17, 2003. www.hanart.com
/artist_detail.php?l=1&id=73&s=2.

Li Xianting. Nianzhu yu bichu/Prayer
Beads and Brush Strokes. Exh. cat.
Beijing: Beijing Tokyo Art Projects,
2003.

Silbergeld, Jerome, and Gong Jisui.
Contradictions: Artistic Life, the
Socialist State, and the Chinese
Painter Li Huasheng. Seattle:
University of Washington Press,
1993.

Liu Dan

Erickson, Britta. "Liu Dan: To Paint
the Unmeasurable." Orientations 43,
no. 2 (March 2012), pp. 137–41.

Liu Dan. "Liu Dan in Conversation
with Jane DeBevoise and Colleagues,"
March 25, 2010. www.aaa-a.org/2010
/06/04/conversation-with-liu-dan/.

Moss, Hugh. Ink: The Art of Liu Dan.
Hong Kong: Umbrella, 1993.

Mowry, Robert D. "Rocks, Trees and
the Ink Paintings of Liu Dan and Zeng
Xiaojun." In Trees and Rocks: Paintings
by Liu Dan and Zeng Xiaojun, pp. 6–7.
Exh. cat. New York: The Chinese
Porcelain Company, 2008.

Munroe, Alexandra. "Why Ink?
The Art of Liu Dan." In Liu Dan:
Alternative Visions, pp. 7–17. Exh. cat.
[Japan]: Takashimaya, 1993.

Sheng Hao. "Liu Dan." Orientations
41, no. 7 (October 2010), pp. 62–65.

Liu Wei

Erickson, Britta. "Architecture, Sex,
Rotting, Dissolving: Paint!" In Liu
Wei & Zhao Gang, 2001. Exh. cat.
Surry Hills NSW, Aust.: Ray Hughes
Gallery, 2001.

He Juju. "Liu Wei: Huabi hua xianshi
wei 'fuxiu'" [Liu Wei: Transforming
reality into "decay"]. August 31,
2012. http://collection.chinaluxus
.com/Ars/20120831/217689.html.

Li Xianting. "Gifted Painter: On
Liu Wei & Ye Yong-Qing's Exhibition
and After." In Liu Wei & Ye Yongqing.
Exh. cat. Beijing: Gallery of the
Central Academy of Fine Arts, 1997.

Liu Wei. Luohua liushui: Liu Wei/
Blossom Fall, Stream Flow: Liu Wei.
Exh. cat. Shanghai: Hongqiao
hualang/Red Bridge Gallery, 2006.

———. "ArtDepot Interview with
Liu Wei." Interview by H4, May 13,
2010. www.artcomb.com/thread
-12113-1-1.html.

Sun Xin. "A Conversation between
Liu Wei and Lv Shun." Dongfang
yishu: Dajia [Oriental art: Master],
no. 3 (2006), pp. 14–25.

Wei Wei. "Liu Wei: Xushu ziwo
de youxi" [Liu Wei: The game of
self-expressing]. Dongfang yishu
[Oriental art], no. 19 (2006),
pp. 82–89.

Zhang Li. Liu Wei: 2005 zhishang
zuopin zhan/Works on Paper, Liu Wei
2005. Exh. cat. Shanghai: Shanghai
Gallery of Art Three on the Bund,
2005.

Qiu Anxiong

Chang Tsong-zung. "The World
Seen from Afar." www.hanart.com
/artist_detail.php?l=4&id=27&s=3.

Fischer, Peter. "Qiu Anxiong." In
Shanshui: Poetry without Sound?
Landscape in Contemporary Chinese
Art, edited by Peter Fischer, p. 155.
Ostfildern, Germany: Hatje Cantz
Verlag; Lucerne: Kunstmuseum
Luzern, 2011.

Hasegowa, Yuko. "Witness of an
Enchanted Land—Qiu Anxiong"
(2008). www.qiuanxiong.com/en
/article2008.html.

Lu, Victoria. "Qiu Anxiong." In China
Art Book, edited by Uta Grosenick
and Caspar H. Schübbe, p. 283.
Cologne, Germany: DuMont, 2007.

Maggio, Meg. "Biennial Wonder Boy."
Artzine China. www.artzinechina
.com/display_print.php?a=198.

Ou Ning. "Qiu Anxiong's Latest Work
and Modern Weekly's 'China Dream'
Special Issue." www.alternativearchive
.com/ouning/article.asp?id=721.

Qiu Anxiong. New Classic of
Mountains and Seas. Translated by
Philip Tinari, 2005. www.qiuanxiong
.com/en/article2006.html.
Clips available on youtube.com.

Qiu Shihua

Buhlmann, Britta, and Udo Kittelmann, eds. *Qiu Shihua*. Exh. cat., Nationalgalerie im Hamburger Bahnhof, Hamburg; Museum für Gegenwart, Berlin; Museum Pfalzgalerie Kaiserslautern. Düsseldorf: Richter & Fey, 2012.

Chang Tsong-zung, Yan Shanchun, and Chitim Lai. *Qiu Shi-hua: Landscape Painting*. Exh. cat. Prague: Galerie Rudolfinum, 2000.

Chiu, Caroline, and Josette Mazzella di Bosco Balsa, eds. *Qiu Shihua: Niansan jie shengbaoluo guoji shuangnianzhan dahui tezhan/ Special exhibition of the 23rd São Paulo Biennial: Qiu Shi-hua*. Hong Kong: Hanart TZ Gallery, 1996.

Köppel-Yang, Martina, and Max Wechsler. *Qiu Shi-hua*. Exh. cat. Basel: Kunsthalle Basel; Schwabe, 1999.

Tancock, Jonathan. *Insight: Paintings by Qiu Shihua*. Exh. cat. New York: Chambers Fine Art, 2005.

Wechsler, Max. "Qiu Shihua—The Image as an Epiphany." Galerie Urs Meile, 2009. www.galerieursmeile .com/fileadmin/images/Artists /QIU_SHIHUA/QIU_SHIHUA_TEXTS /Qiu-Shihua_The-Image-As -Epiphany_Max-Wechsler_E.pdf.

Qiu Zhijie

Cheng, Meiling. "De/visualizing Calligraphic Archaeology: Qiu Zhijie's Total Art." *TDR: The Drama Review* 53, no. 2 (2009), pp. 17–34.

Li Yumin, ed. *Qiu Zhijie*. Fuzhou: Fujian Meishu Press, 2004.

Qiu Zhijie. *Gei wo yige mianju* [Give me a mask]. Beijing: Renmin University of China Press, 2003.

——. *Zhongyao de shi xianchang/ The Scene Is Most Important*. Beijing: China Renmin University Press, 2003.

——. *Ziyou de youxianxing/The Boundary of Freedom*. Beijing: China Renmin University Press, 2003.

——. *The Shape of Time: Light Calli-photography by Qiu Zhijie*. New York: Chambers Fine Art, 2006.

——. "All We Can See Can Only Disappear." In *China Talks: Interviews with 32 Contemporary Artists by Jérôme Sans*, pp. 54–59. Hong Kong: Timezone 8, 2009.

——. *Qiu Zhijie*. Art Salon. Videodisc, 55 mins. New York: China Institute in America, 2009.

——. "The Boundary of Freedom: A Personal Statement on Assignment No. 1 (*Zuoye Yihao*) (1994/2003)," translated by Kristen Loring. In Wu Hung, *Contemporary Chinese Art: Primary Documents*, pp. 188–89. New York: Museum of Modern Art, 2010.

——. "Wo yong xiaohao ziyang ziji" [Nourishing myself with wasted energy]. *Yishu shijie* [Art world], June 2011. www.yishushijie.com /magazines/content-902.aspx.

——. Artist's website: www .qiuzhijie.com.

Sans, Jérôme, and Guo Xiaoyan, eds. *Qiu Zhijie: Wuzhi zhe de pobing shi/ Breaking the Ice; a History*. Hong Kong: Timezone 8, 2009.

Smith, Valérie, ed. *Qiu Zhijie: Twilight of the Idols*. Exh. cat., Haus der Kulturen der Welt, Berlin. Berlin: Revolver, 2009.

Yu, Christina. "Qiu Zhijie: In the Shadows of History." *ArtAsiaPacific*, no. 69 (July–August 2010), pp. 96–101.

Ren Jian

Ren Jian. "Ren Jian: Zhongguo dangdai yishu zhuwenti de duihua" [Ren Jian: Conversations on the many problems pertinent to Chinese art at the moment]. *Meishu* [Fine arts], no. 5 (May 1988), p. 11.

——. "Ren Jian: Zai yangchun baixue yu xiali baren zhijian" [Ren Jian: Between elite and ordinary art], interview by Zhou Xuesong. *Dongfang yishu: Dajia* [Oriental art: Master], no. 241 (November 2011), pp. 62–65.

Tang, Stephanie H. "Northern Art Group." In *U-turn: 30 Years of Contemporary Art in China*, edited by Philip Tinari, vol. 2.4. New York: AW Asia and Office for Discourse Engineering, 2007.

Wang Huangsheng, Guo Xiaoyan, and Dong Bingfeng, eds. *Cong "jidi" dao "tiexiqu": Dongbei dangdai yishu zhan, 1985–2006/From "Polar Region" to "West of the Tracks": Contemporary Art of Northeast China (1985–2006)*. Guangzhou: Lingnan Art Publishing House, 2006.

Zhou Yan. "Beifang yishu qunti" [Northern Art Group]. In *'85 Meishu yundong/The '85 Movement*, vol. 2, pp. 158–73. Guilin: Guangxi Normal University Press, 2008.

Shao Fan

Fan Di'an and Ai Weiwei. *Shao Fan*. Beijing: Gallery of Central Academy of Fine Arts, 1996.

Feng Boyi. "Marginalization and Insulation: On Shao Fan's Painting and Art," translated by Benedict Armour. Galerie Urs Meile, Beijing and Lucerne, 2012. www.galerieursmeile.com /fileadmin/images/Artists/SHAO _FAN/Shao_Fan_Texts/FengBoyi _MarginalizationAndInsulation _E_2012.pdf.

Fischer, Volker. "Shao Fan: The Ming Deconstructivist." In Volker Fischer and Stephan von der Schulenburg, *Sit in China: An Excursion through 500 Years of the Culture of Sitting*, pp. 32–39. Fellbach, Germany: Edition Axel Menges, 2009.

Moss, Chris. "Shao Fan at Chelsea: Fertile Ground." *Telegraph.co.uk*, April 26, 2008. www.telegraph.co.uk /gardening/3347809/Shao-Fan-at -Chelsea-fertile-ground.html.

Pan Zhen. "Shao Fan: 'Bawan' Zhongguo gudian yuansu" [Shao Fan: "Play with" China's traditional elements]. *Da Meishu* [All], no. 9 (2005), pp. 26–27, 135.

Paparoni, Demetrio. *Shao Fan: An Incurable Classicist*. Shanghai: Contrasts Gallery, 2010.

Shao Fan. "Appreciation of Oldness." Galerie Urs Meile, Beijing and Lucerne, 2012. www.galerieursmeile .com/fileadmin/images/Artists /SHAO_FAN/Shao_Fan_Texts /ShaoFan_ShenLao_E_2012.pdf.

Victoria and Albert Museum. "Chairs by Designer Shao Fan," July 2, 2012. www.vam.ac.uk/content/articles/c /chairs-by-designer-shao-fan/.

Wang Min'an. "Jubilancy from Graft: Emptiness, History and Competition." Galerie Urs Meile, Beijing and Lucerne, 2009. www.galerieursmeile .com/fileadmin/images/Artists /SHAO_FAN/Shao_Fan_Texts /WangMinan_ShaoFan_2009_E.pdf.

Shi Guorui

Finkel, Jori. "Standing in the Dark, Catching the Light." *New York Times*, October 22, 2006, p. A34.

Hamlin, Jesse. "With Just a Tiny Beam of Light, Shi Guorui Captures Panoramic Images of Famed Sites." *SFGate*, December 2, 2006, entertainment section. www.sfgate .com/entertainment/article /With-just-a-tiny-beam-of-light -Shi-Guorui-2483894.php#src=fb.

Li Tao. "Yong zuigulao de sheying shoufa jilu shijian" [Capturing time with the oldest photographic method]. *Vie-mode*, no. 7 (2005), pp. 60–61.

Meng Cai and Mei Li. "Shi Guorui Artron Interview." Video, August 16, 2010. http://video.artron.net /show_news.php?newid=184526.

Shi Guorui. *Rebirth: Camera Obscura Work by Shi Guorui*. Exh. cat. Hong Kong: Asia One Books; Los Angeles: L & M Arts, 2011.

Wang Yin. "Shi Guorui: zuozai zhaoxiangji li de sheyingjia" [Shi Guorui: The photographer who sits in the camera]. *Nanfang zhoukan* [Southern weekly], September 26, 2007. www. www.infzm.com /content/6847.

Wilson, Mark, and Sue-An van der Zijpp, eds. *New World Order: Contemporary Installation Art and Photography from China*. [Groningen, Netherlands]: Groninger Museum, 2008.

Wu Hung. *Re-imagining the Real: Photography Show: Gao Lei, Shi Guorui, Yang Fudong, Zhuanghui*. Jakarta, Indonesia: Yuz Foundation, 2010.

Song Dong

Shen Qibin, ed. *Song Dong*. Exh. cat. Shanghai: Shanghai Zendai Museum of Modern Art, 2008.

Song Dong. Interview by Huangfu Binghui. *Yishu: Journal of Contemporary Chinese Art* 1, no. 1 (May 2002), pp. 83–90.

——. "Zai qianwei yishu de langchao zhong jishui" [Striking water in the waves of avant-garde art]. Interview by David Clark, October 10, 2003. www.artlinkart .com/cn/artist/txt_ab/911brz /92chrtt.

——. "Living Many Lives." In *China Talks: Interviews with 32 Contemporary Artists by Jérôme Sans*, pp. 64–71. Hong Kong: Timezone 8, 2009.

——. *Song Dong*. Art Salon. New York: China Institute in America, 2009. Videodisc, 39 mins.

Song Dong, Christophe W. Mao, and Yin Xiuzhen, eds. *Song Dong: Kuaizi/Chopsticks*. Exh. cat. New York: Chambers Fine Art, 2002.

Sun Xun

Borysevicz, Mathieu. "Sun Xun." In *Hammer Projects, 1999–2009*, pp. 367–71. Los Angeles: Hammer Museum, 2009.

Smith, Karen. "Uncertain Endings: The Animated Short Films of Sun Xun." Platform China. www.platformchina.org/en/article_show.asp?id=68.

Sun Xun. *Sun Xun*. Art Salon. New York: China Institute in America, 2009. Videodisc, 50 mins.

——. *Sun Xun*. Portfolio produced by ShanghART, 2011. www.shanghartgallery.com/galleryarchive/handout.htm?id=2826.

——. *Sun Xun: 2010 Zhongguo dangdai yishu jiang: Zuijia nianqing yishujia/2010 Chinese Contemporary Art Awards: Best Young Artist*. Hong Kong: Blue Kingfisher Limited, 2011.

Wang Dongling

Wang Dongling. *The Paintings of Wang Dongling*. Exh. cat. New York: Goedhuis Contemporary, 2002.

——. *Wang Dongling chuangzuo shouji* [Wang Dongling's notes on making art]. Wang Dongling shufa luncong [Wang Dongling on calligraphy series]. Beijing: China Renmin University Press, 2011.

——. *Wang Dongling tan xiandai shufa* [Wang Dongling on modern calligraphy]. Beijing: China Renmin University Press, 2011.

Xu Jiang, ed. *Wang Dongling shufa yishu* [Wang Dongling's works]. Beijing: Rong Bao Zhai Press, 2007.

——, ed. *Wang Dongling shufa yishu/The Way of Calligraphy: Wang Dongling's Work*. Shanghai: Shanghai Painting and Calligraphy Press, 2011.

Wang Jin

Chen, Aric, and Meg Maggio. *Wang Jin*. Exh. cat. New York: Friedman Benda, 2007.

Leng Lin. *Shi wo* [It's me]. Beijing: Zhongguo wenlian chubanshe, 2000.

Mihalca, Matei. "Passionate Statement: Avant-garde Artist Concocts Social Commentary from Art." *Far Eastern Economic Review*, January 29, 1994.

Wang Tiande

Goodman, Jonathan. "Wang Tiande at Chambers Fine Art." *Art in America*, April 2005. Electronic ed. in the digital archive of www.chambersfineart.com.

Ink Painting Biennial of Shenzhen. *Diyi jie Shenzhen guoji shuimohua shuangnianzhan wenji/The First International Ink Painting Biennial of Shenzhen: Essays*. Nanning: Guangxi Fine Arts Publishing House, 1998.

——. *Disan jie Shenzhen guoji shuimohua shuangnianzhan wenji/The Third International Ink Painting Biennial of Shenzhen: Essays*. Shenzhen: Shenzhen Municipal People's Government, 2003.

Wang Tiande. *Made by Tiande*. Exh. cat. New York: Chambers Fine Art, 2004.

——. *Made by Tiande II*. Exh. cat. New York: Chambers Fine Art, 2007.

——. *Wang Tiande: Tuibian zhong de shanshui/Landscape Transformations*. Exh. cat. Hong Kong: Alisan Fine Arts, 2007.

Wu Hung. *Variations of Ink: A Dialogue with Zhang Yanyuan*. Exh. cat. New York: Chambers Fine Art, 2002.

Wu Shanzhuan

Chang Tsong-zung and Yin Shuangxi. "Wu Shanzhuan in Conversation with Chang Tsong-zung and Yin Shuangxi during the 1st CAFA Museum Biennial: Super Organism." December 26, 2011. www.artspy.cn/html/video/0/883.shtml.

Huang Zhuan. "Comments on Wu Shanzhuan's Works." *Gallery Magazine*, no. 2 (1999).

Li Xianting. "Xinchao Meishujia 3: Wu Shanzhuan" [New Wave artist 3: Wu Shanzhuan]. *Zhongguo meishu bao* [Fine arts in China], no. 40 (October 5, 1987).

Wang Xiaojian. "The 75% red 20% black 5% white exhibition." *Zhongguo meishu bao* [Fine arts in China], no. 38 (September 22, 1986).

Wu Shanzhuan. "Guanyu zhongwen" [On Chinese]. *Meishu* [Fine arts], no. 8 (1985), p. 61.

——. *Wu Shanzhuan: Guoji hongse youmo/Red Humour International*. Hong Kong: Asia Art Archive, 2005.

——. Interview by Anthony Yung, September 9, 2009, for the Asia Art Archive. www.china1980s.org/files/interview/wszftfinal_201105061441138867.pdf.

——. "Red Humor." In *China Talks: Interviews with 32 Contemporary Artists by Jérôme Sans*, pp. 112–17. Hong Kong: Timezone 8, 2009.

Xing Danwen

Botos, Lisa, Joanne Ooi, and Rae Leung, eds. *Xing Danwen*. Exh. cat. Hong Kong: Ooi Botos Gallery, 2009.

Duffell, Rachell. "'ID'entity Check." *Kee Magazine*, January 2010, pp. 20–23.

Erickson, Britta. "Interview with Xing Danwen to Talk about *Urban Fiction*," conducted via email February 27–March 10, 2006. Digital Archive, Gallery TPW, Toronto. http://archive.gallerytpw.ca/index.php?c=essay&h=archive&id=119.

Eschenburg, Madeline. "Xing Danwen: Revealing the Masquerade of Modernity." *Yishu: Journal of Contemporary Chinese Art* 8, no. 4 (July–August 2009), pp. 51–66.

Flynn, Paul. "Xing Danwen." *Artist Profile*, no. 7 (April 2009), pp. 60–64.

Gu Zheng. "Projecting the Reality of China through the Lens: On the Artistic Practice of Xing Danwen." *Yishu: Journal of Contemporary Chinese Art* 5, no. 1 (March 2006), pp. 91–96.

Koon Yee-wan. "Seeing Things Her Way." *Muse*, December 2010, pp. 97–99.

Maerkle, Andrew. "Xing Danwen's Chinese Fantasy." *ArtAsiaPacific*, no. 49 (Summer 2006), pp. 22–23.

Smith, Karen. "Xing Danwen" In *The Chinese: Photography and Video from China*, edited by Susanne Kohler, Annelie Lütgens, and Anja Westermann, pp. 118–19. Wolfsburg, Germany: Kunstmuseum Wolfsburg, 2004.

Vine, Richard. "Beijing Confidential." *Art in America*, February 2009, pp. 84–93.

Xing Danwen. Interview by Mark Rainey, October 2006. http://urbismanchester.files.wordpress.com/2010/01/xingdanwen-interview.pdf.

——. Interview by Li Zhenhua, October 2007. www.artlinkart.com/cn/artist/txt_ab/264axzl.

——. "When Art Happened," translated by Caly Moss. *Leap: The International Art Magazine of Contemporary China*, no. 15 (June 2012). http://leapleapleap.com/2012/07/when-art-happened/.

Xing Danwen and Thomas Chen. "Trash Talk with Photographer Danwen Xing." *Petite Mort*, no. 3 (2005). www.petitemort.org/issue03/25_danwen-xing/.

Xu Bing

Abe, Stanley K. "No Questions, No Answers: China and *A Book from the Sky*." *Boundary 2* 25, no. 3 (Fall 1998), pp. 169–92.

Cameron, Dan. *Xu Bing: Introduction to New English Calligraphy*. Exh. brochure. New York: New Museum of Contemporary Art, 1998.

Cayley, John. *Description of "A Book from the Sky."* London: Hanshan Tang Books, 1997.

——. "Writing (Under-) Sky: On Xu Bing's *Tianshu*." In *A Book of the Book: Some Works and Projections about the Book and Writing*, edited by Jerome Rothenberg and Steven Clay, pp. 497–503. New York: Granary Books, 2000.

Cotter, Holland. "Art in Review: Metalanguage of Chinese and English." *New York Times*, August 26, 1994, p. C26.

——. "Calligraphy, Cavorting Pigs and Other Body-Mind Happenings." *New York Times*, Friday January 25, 2002, p. E45.

Doran, Valerie. "Xu Bing: A Logos for the Genuine Experience." *Orientations* 32, no. 8 (October 2001), pp. 80–87.

Erickson, Britta. "Process and Meaning in the Art of Xu Bing." In *Three Installations by Xu Bing*, pp. 2–32. Exh. cat. Madison: Elvehjem Museum of Art, University of Wisconsin-Madison, 1991.

——. "Evolving Meanings in Xu Bing's Art: A Case Study of Transference." In *Chinese Art at the End of the Millennium*, edited by John Clark, pp. 224–32. Hong Kong: New Art Media, 2000.

——. *The Art of Xu Bing: Words without Meaning, Meaning without Words.* Exh. cat. Washington, D.C.: Arthur M. Sackler Gallery, Smithsonian Institution, 2001.

Fan Di'an. "The Pursuit of Eternity: Seeking Xu Bing's Route to Creativity." *Meishu yanjiu* [Fine arts research] 53, no. 1 (February 1989), pp. 37–40.

Fang Zhen-ning. "A Thoughtful Absurdity: On Xu Bing's Art." *Yishujia* [Artists], no. 319 (December 2001), pp. 428–35.

Gao Minglu. "Meaninglessness and Confrontation in Xu Bing's Art." In Julia F. Andrews and Gao Minglu, *Fragmented Memory: The Chinese Avant-Garde in Exile*, pp. 28–31. Exh. cat. Columbus, Ohio: Wexner Center for the Arts, Ohio State University, 1993.

Goodman, Jonathan. "Bing Xu: 4,000 Characters in Search of a Meaning." *Art News* 93, no. 7 (September 1994), pp. 99–101.

——. "Xu Bing: The Cage of Words." *ArtAsiaPacific*, no. 26 (Spring 2000), pp. 46–49.

Hamlish, Tamara. "Prestidigitation: A Reply to Charles Stone." *Public Culture* 6, no. 2 (1994), pp. 419–42.

Hay, Jonathan. "Ambivalent Icons: Works by Five Chinese Artists Based in the United States." *Orientations* 23, no. 7 (July 1992), pp. 37–43.

Hou Hanru. "Xu Bing: Atop the Point of a Frozen Peak." *Xiongshi meishu* [Lion fine art], no. 235 (September 1990), pp. 133–35.

Hu Heqing. "Xu Bing's 'Book from the Sky' with New Wave Calligraphy." *Beijing shufa yanjiu* [Beijing calligraphy research] 55, no. 5 (1993).

Kaldis, Nick. "Trans-boundary Experiences: A Conversation between Xu Bing and Nick Kaldis." *Yishu: Journal of Contemporary Chinese Art* 6, no. 2 (June 2007), pp. 76–93.

Kao Chien Hui. "Analyzing a Decade of Contemporary Chinese Art through a Study of Xu Bing's Work from Three Periods." *Yishujia* [Artists], no. 293 (1999), pp. 281–87.

Karatani, Koujin. "Xu Bing." In *Xu Bing: A Book from the Sky*. Exh. cat. Tokyo: Tokyo Gallery, 1991.

Karetzky, Patricia Eichenbaum. "A Modern Literati: The Art of Xu Bing." *Oriental Art* 47, no. 4 (2001), pp. 47–52.

Kesner, Ladislav. *Sü Ping: Kniha z nebe a kaligrafická triad/Xu Bing: A Book from the Sky and Classroom Calligraphy*. Exh. cat. Prague: National Gallery, 2000.

Rawanchaikul, Toshiko. "Xu Bing." In *The 1st Fukuoka Asian Art Triennale 1999*. Exh. cat. Fukuoka: Fukuoka Asian Art Museum, 1999.

Reuter, Laurel. "Into the Dark Sings the Nightingale: The Work of Xu Bing." In *Xu Bing*, pp. 1–3. Exh. brochure. Grand Forks: North Dakota Museum of Art, 1992.

——. "Musing into Winter." *Art Journal* 53, no. 3 (1994), pp. 46–59.

Silbergeld, Jerome, and Dora C. Y. Ching, eds. *Persistence-Transformation: Text as Image in the Art of Xu Bing*. Princeton: P. Y. and Kinmay W. Tang Center for East Asian Art, Department of Art and Archaeology, Princeton University, 2006.

Spears, Katherine, ed. *Tianshu: Passages in the Making of a Book*. London: Bernard Quaritch Ltd., 2009.

Stone, Charles. "Xu Bing and the Printed Word." *Public Culture* 6, no. 2 (1994), pp. 407–10.

Sturman, Peter C. "Measuring the Weight of the Written Word: Reflections on the Character-Paintings of Chu Ko and the Role of Writing in Contemporary Chinese Art." *Orientations* 23, no. 7 (1992), pp. 44–52.

Tomii, Reiko, David Elliott, Robert E. Harrist Jr., and Andrew Solomon. *Xu Bing*. London: Albion Books, 2011.

Tsao Hsingyuan and Roger T. Ames, eds. *Xu Bing and Contemporary Chinese Art: Cultural and Philosophical Reflections*. Albany: State University of New York Press, 2011.

Wang, Eugene Yuejin, and Ann Wilson Lloyd. *Xu Bing: Language Lost*. Exh. cat. Boston: Massachusetts College of Art, 1995.

Wu Hung. "A Ghost Rebellion: Notes on Xu Bing's 'Nonsense Writing' and Other Works." *Public Culture* 6, no. 2 (1994), pp. 411–18.

Xu Bing. Interview by Jane DeBevoise and Anthony Yung, July 18, 2009, for the Asia Art Archive. www.china1980s.org/files/interview/xbftfinal_201105091341595898.pdf.

——. "Playing with Words." In *China Talks: Interviews with 32 Contemporary Artists by Jérôme Sans*, pp. 118–25. Hong Kong: Timezone 8, 2009.

——. *Xu Bing banhua/Xu Bing Prints*. Beijing: Culture and Art Publishing House, 2009.

Yang Fudong

Beccaria, Marcella, ed. *Yang Fudong*. Exh. cat., Castello di Rivoli, Museo d'Arte Contemporanea. Milan: Skira, 2006.

Cervera Fernández, Isabel. *Yang Fudong*. Exh. cat. Segovia: Museo de Arte Contemporáneo Esteban Vicente, 2008.

Fonnesbech, Pernille Damsted, and Anne Hagen Kielgast, eds. *China in Transition: Yang Fudong*. Exh. cat. Copenhagen: GL Strand, 2007.

Johnson, Ken. "From an Ancient Bamboo Grove to Modern China." *New York Times*, May 29, 2009, p. C30.

Lin Xiaoping. "The Video Works of Yang Fudong: An Ultimate Escape from a Global Nightmare." In Lin Xiaoping, *Children of Marx and Coca-Cola: Chinese Avant-garde Art and Independent Cinema*, pp. 165–72. Honolulu: University of Hawai'i Press, 2010.

Tinari, Philip, and Angie Baecker, eds. *Yang Fudong: Seven Intellectuals in Bamboo Forest*. Exh. cat. Stockholm: Jarla Partilager; Beijing: Office for Discourse Engineering, 2008.

Wu Hung. *Re-imagining the Real: Photography Show: Gao Lei, Shi Guorui, Yang Fudong, Zhuanghui*. Jakarta, Indonesia: Yuz Foundation, 2010.

Yang Fudong. "A Thousand Words: Yang Fudong Talks about *The Seven Intellectuals*." *Artforum* 42 (September 2003), pp. 182–83.

——. "Commercial or Art, I Simply Wanted to Film Things That Interested Me." Interview by Harada Yukiko, 2006. www.shanghartgallery.com/galleryarchive/texts/id/545.

——. "The Conundrums of Idealism and Ideology." In *China Talks: Interviews with 32 Contemporary Artists by Jérôme Sans*, pp. 146–51. Hong Kong: Timezone 8, 2009.

Yang Jiechang

King, Alice, and Martina Köppel-Yang. *Enlightened Blackness: Ink Paintings by Yang Jiechang*. Exh. cat. Hong Kong: Alisan Fine Arts, 2001.

Yang Jiechang. "One Hundred Layers of Ink." In *Diyi jie Shenzhen guoji shuimohua shuangnianzhan wenji/ The First International Ink Painting Biennial of Shenzhen: Essays*, pp. 273–75. Nanning: Guangxi Fine Arts Publishing House, 1998.

——. Interview by Huang Xiaoyan and Anthony Yung, October 25, 2007, for the Asia Art Archive. www.china1980s.org/files/interview/yjcftfinal_201105231217369546.pdf.

——. *Wu ying jiao/No-shadow Kick*. Edited by Hou Hanru and Wei Xing. Exh. cat. Shanghai: Shanghai Duolun Museum of Art; Beijing: Tang Contemporary Art, 2008.

——. "Action & Participation Painting." In *China Talks: Interviews with 32 Contemporary Artists by Jérôme Sans*, pp. 152–55. Hong Kong: Timezone 8, 2009.

——. "Eros, Global, Chaos." Interview by Larys Frogier, June 2011. www.artlinkart.com/en/article/overview/035cxyli/latestupload.

Yen, Julia. "Nam June Paik's Belt: A Dialogue between Julia Yen and Yang Jiechang." *Shijue shengchan/Visual Production* 3 (2007), pp. 46–57.

Yung, Anthony. "Yang Jiechang: The Beauty of Impurity." *Leap: The International Art Magazine of Contemporary China*, no. 17 (October 2012), pp. 128–37.

Yang Yongliang

Gu Zheng. "If You Dare Look Closely—Yang Yongliang's Experiment of Shanshui Photo Image." *Chip Foto-Video Digital*, February 2008, pp. 34–35.

Rosenberg, David. "The Mirror of Time." In *Yang Yongliang: Landscapes*, pp. 5–11. [Hong Kong]: Thircuir, 2011.

Stone-Banks, Blake. "Digital Dreams." *Artnet Magazine*, March 3, 2010. www.artnet.com/magazineus/reviews/banks/digital-generation3-3-10.asp.

Suri, R. A. "The Surreal Landscape of Yang Yongliang." *Kunst-Blog.com*, November 3, 2009. http://kunst-blog.com/2009/03/the_surreal_lan.php.

Yang Yongliang. *Zhi shui zhi shang/ On the Quiet Water*. Exh. cat. Beijing: OFOTO Gallery, 2008.

———. "Phantom Landscapes series and the Art of Traditional Painting: Three Essays for a Lecture Delivered at Kansas City Art Institute." August 2009. www.yangyongliang.com.

———. *Yang Yongliang*. Edited by Mikala Tai. Exh. cat. Melbourne, Australia: Melbourne International Fine Art, 2010.

———. "Yang Yongliang." Interview by Emma Chi, June 2010. www.shift.jp.org/en/archives/2010/06/yang_yongliang.html.

Zeng Fanzhi

Hegyi, Lóránd, and Lü Peng. *Zeng Fanzhi*. Exh. cat. Saint-Etienne: Musée d'Art Moderne, 2007.

Li Xianting. "Zeng Fanzhi: Mask," February 1998. www.shanghartgallery.com/galleryarchive/texts/id/157.

Wu Hung. *2010 Zeng Fanzhi*. Exh. cat. Wuhan: Hubei Fine Arts Publishing House, 2010.

Zeng Fanzhi. "A Relentless Soul—Dialogues between Li Xianting and Zeng Fanzhi," February 5, 2003. www.shanghartgallery.com/galleryarchive/texts/id/163.

———. "Human Nature." In *China Talks: Interviews with 32 Contemporary Artists by Jérôme Sans*, pp. 174–79. Hong Kong: Timezone 8, 2009.

———. *Zeng Fanzhi: Every Mark Its Mask*. Essay by Richard Shiff. Ostfildern, Germany: Hatje Cantz Verlag, 2010.

Zeng Fanzhi and Daniel Szehin Ho. "Of Mammoths and Pietas: Conversation with Zeng Fanzhi." September 9, 2010. www.randian-online.com/np_feature/a-conversation-with-zeng-fanzhi/.

Zhan Wang

Erickson, Britta. "Material Illusion: Adrift with the Conceptual Sculptor Zhan Wang." *Art Journal* 60, no. 2 (Summer 2001), pp. 73–81.

Zhan Wang. *Zhan Wang: Garden Utopia*. Edited by Fan Di'an and Lu Jie. Beijing: National Art Museum of China; Long March Space, 2008.

———. *The New Suyuan Stone Catalogue*. Edited by Philip Tinari and Angie Baecker; translated by Philip Bloom, Michael Hatch, and Alan Yeung. Milan: Charta, 2011.

Zhang Qunsheng, ed. *Zhan Wang*. Jinri Zhongguo yishujia/Chinese Artists of Today. Lanzhou: Gansu People's Fine Arts Publishing House, 2008.

Zhang Huan

Chiu, Melissa, ed. *Zhang Huan: Altered States*. Exh. cat. New York: Asia Society; Milan: Charta, 2007.

Dziewior, Yilmaz, ed. *Zhang Huan*. Exh. cat., Kunstverein Hamburg; Museum Bochum. Ostfildern, Germany: Hatje Cantz Verlag; Hamburg: Kunstverein Hamburg, 2003.

Dziewior, Yilmaz, RoseLee Goldberg, and Robert Storr. *Zhang Huan*. Contemporary Artists. London and New York: Phaidon, 2009.

Leng Lin. "Yong shenti qu ganshou he biaoxian" [To feel and express with the body]. In Leng Lin, *Shi wo* [It's me], pp. 143–45. Beijing: Zhonggou wenlian chubanshe, 2000.

Wei, Lilly. *Zhang Huan: Selected Works, 1995–2006*. Exh. cat. New York: Max Lang Gallery, 2006.

Wu Hung. *Zhang Huan Gongzuoshi: Yishu yu laodong/Zhang Huan Studio: Art and Labor*. Guilin: Guangxi Normal University Press, 2009.

Zhang Huan. "Communicating with Disappeared Spirits." In *China Talks: Interviews with 32 Contemporary Artists by Jérôme Sans*, pp. 180–85. Hong Kong: Timezone 8, 2009.

———. *Chuang shiji/Dawn of Time*. Shanghai: Shanghai wenyi chubanshe, 2010.

Zhang Jianjun

Cohen, Joan Lebold. "Zhang Jianjun and Barbara Edelstein: A Studio Visit." *Artzine*, 2007. www.artzinechina.com/display_print.php?a=486.

Erickson, Britta. "The Contemporary Artistic Deconstruction—and Reconstruction—of Brush and Ink Painting." *Yishu: Journal of Contemporary Chinese Art* 2, no. 2 (June 2003), pp. 82–89.

Morgan, Robert C. *Zhang Jian-Jun*. Singapore: iPreciation, 2007.

———. "Zhang Jian-Jun: Memory and the Process of Historical Time." *Yishu: Journal of Contemporary Chinese Art* 6, no. 3 (September 2007), pp. 54–60.

Sheffield, Magaret. "Jian Jun Zhang." In *Art Projects International: Ten Years*, pp. 70–80. New York: Art Projects International, 2003.

Zhang Jianjun. Interview by Anthony Yung, March 3, 2009, for the Asia Art Archive. www.china1980s.org/files/interview/zjjftfinalised_201102021633402121.pdf.

———. "Open Portfolios Online: Interview with Jian-Jun Zhang," April 21, 2009. Asian Contemporary Art Week. www.acaw.info/?p=114.

Zhang Yu

Li Bing, ed. *Ink Is Not Equivocal to Ink Painting: Li Huasheng, Zhang Yu, Liang Quan Art Exhibition*. Beijing: Hejingyuan Art Gallery, 2008.

Qu Deyi and Jingxin Zhong, eds. *Zhiyin: Zhang Yu xiuxing de henji/ Fingerprints: Traces of Zhang Yu's Self-Cultivation*. Exh. cat. Taipei: Kuandu Museum of Fine Arts, 2009.

Yin Shuangxi, ed. *Zhang Yu: A Case Study on a Contemporary Artist: 1984–2008*. Changsha: Hunan Fine Arts Publishing House, 2008.

Zhang Yu, ed. *Guohua shijie* [World of traditional Chinese painting]. 4 vols. Tianjin: Tianjin yangliuqing huashe, 1986–91.

———, ed. *Ershi shijimo Zhongguo xiandai shuimo yishu zoushi* [Tendencies of Chinese modern ink art at the end of the twentieth century]. 5 vols. Tianjin: Tianjin yangliuqing huashe, 1993 (vol. 1), 1994 (vol. 2), 1995 (special vol.), 1997 (vol. 3); Heilongjiang: Heilongjiang meishu chubanshe, 2000 (vol. 4).

———. *Kaifang de Zhongguo shiyan shuimo* [Chinese open and experimental ink and wash]. Hong Kong: Yinhe chubanshe, 2002.

———. *Zhongguo shiyan shuimo, 1993–2003* [Chinese experimental ink and wash, 1993–2003]. Heilongjiang: Heilongjiang meishu chubanshe, 2004.

Page numbers in *italics* refer to illustrations. Figure numbers in **bold** refer to works in the exhibition.